W9-BBY-874

More Praise for **Building the Brand-Driven Business**

"Scott Davis and Michael Dunn have created a step-by-step guide to igniting a brand revolution within your company. They present a practical approach for executives at all levels of a company to develop a passion for branding in a personal and directed way."
—Gary E. Knell, president and CEO of Sesame Workshop

"The golden thread that ties together every corporate activity—the idea in the engineer's mind, the focus of the press operator on the factory floor, the promotional material from the marketing department, the attitude of the sales-force and the attentiveness of customer service agents—is a pure and undying devotion to the hundreds of nuances of the one word captured within the spine of this book, BRAND."
—Michael Moritz, partner, Sequoia Capital

"In *Building the Brand-Driven Business,* Scott Davis and Michael Dunn give us a powerful new conceptual framework on the understanding of branding: 'Operationalizing the Brand.' For the first time, we are shown a road map on how to deliver the brand promise in every customer contact and with each employee. This redefines brand marketing as we know it."
—Peter Sealey, Ph.D., former head of global marketing, Coca-Cola Company, and adjunct professor of marketing, Haas School of Business, University of California, Berkeley

"Davis and Dunn help business leaders understand how to build a platform for sustainable competitive advantage through effective and sophisticated global brand management. Given the increased globalization and consolidation in the financial services sector, it could not be more timely."
—Hans-Ueli Goetz, Head Group Branding, UBS AG

"A must for future success in a consolidating retail environment. Takes you to another stage in building elevated levels of brand equity."
—Tom Ward, CEO, Maidenform

"*Building the Brand-Driven Business* is a soon-to-be classic 'how to' textbook on truly taking control of your brand and bringing it to life across, as Davis and Dunn call it, every brand touchpoint."
—Dipak Jain, associate dean for academic affairs, Kellogg School of Management

Also by Scott M. Davis

Brand Asset Management: Driving Profitable Growth
Through Your Brands

Building the Brand-Driven Business

Scott M. Davis, Michael Dunn

Foreword by David A. Aaker

Building the Brand-Driven Business

Operationalize Your Brand to Drive Profitable Growth

JOSSEY-BASS
A Wiley Imprint
www.josseybass.com

Copyright © 2002 by John Wiley & Sons, Inc. All rights reserved.

Published by Jossey-Bass
A Wiley Imprint
989 Market Street, San Francisco, CA 94103-1741   www.josseybass.com

No part of this publication may be reproduced, stored in a retrieval system, or transmitted in any form or by any means, electronic, mechanical, photocopying, recording, scanning, or otherwise, except as permitted under Section 107 or 108 of the 1976 United States Copyright Act, without either the prior written permission of the Publisher, or authorization through payment of the appropriate per-copy fee to the Copyright Clearance Center, Inc., 222 Rosewood Drive, Danvers, MA 01923, 978-750-8400, fax 978-750-4470, or on the web at www.copyright.com. Requests to the Publisher for permission should be addressed to the Permissions Department, John Wiley & Sons, Inc., 111 River Street, Hoboken, NJ 07030, (201) 748-6011, fax (201) 748-6008, e-mail: permcoordinator@wiley.com.

Jossey-Bass books and products are available through most bookstores. To contact Jossey-Bass directly call our Customer Care Department within the U.S. at 800-956-7739, outside the U.S. at 317-572-3986 or fax 317-572-4002.

Jossey-Bass also publishes its books in a variety of electronic formats. Some content that appears in print may not be available in electronic books.

Library of Congress Cataloging-in-Publication Data

Davis, Scott M., 1964-
    Building the brand-driven business : operationalize your brand to drive profitable growth / Scott M. Davis, Michael Dunn ; foreword by David A. Aaker.-1st ed.
        p. cm.- (Jossey-Bass business & management series)
        ISBN 0-7879-6255-4
    1. Brand name products. 2. Product management. I. Dunn, Michael. II. Title. III. Series.
        HD69.B7 D384 2002
        658.8'27-dc21

                                                2002008567

Printed in the United States of America

FIRST EDITION
HB Printing   10 9 8 7 6 5 4 3 2 1

The Jossey-Bass
Business & Management Series

Debbie, Ethan, Benjamin, and Emma, every day you make me a better husband, father, and man because of the unconditional love you shower upon me. You continue to stretch my heart in ways I could never have imagined.

Vic, to new beginnings and the next phase of this wonderful journey. With love.

‑‑ Contents

⎯ᴧᴧᴧ⎯ Foreword

In today's tumultuous corporate environment, brand builders face pressure to deliver short-term profits and to enhance shareholder value. Shareholders often have a difficult time understanding that the brand is an asset that requires as much nurturing and investment as any other asset if its value is expected to grow over time. Thus, they tend to focus on near-term financial results that seem accurate, timely, and reliable, rather than measures of brand strength, which seem ambiguous and are often unavailable. Pressure to perform in the short term is accentuated by the misconception that current earnings predict future earnings. As a result, managers are strongly incentivized to deliver on current earnings, and since brand-building investment often involves a short-term net expense, there is a tendency to reduce support of it.

In addition, most companies today are operating in a business environment characterized by overcapacity and severe price and margin pressure. Achieving differentiation is more and more difficult, especially tied to product attributes or functional benefits, which can be easily copied by competitors. The result is more emphasis on price and erosion of the brand, and less effort expended on innovation and driving a consistent brand experience. Product proliferation seems to add confusion rather than vitality and differentiation.

What can be done to continue to build brand assets in the face of this short-term mind-set, as well as a hostile business environment? In my view, there are two imperatives, both addressed by this book.

The first imperative is to develop brand-building programs that are cost-efficient as well as effective and credible. Firms no longer have the luxury of funding ineffective or marginal brand-building programs. You need to move the needle while husbanding resources. A focus on brand touchpoints can help in part because the impact of any brand-building program is determined at the specific touchpoint that the customer experiences. A touchpoint-driven program can lead to effective brand building, often without spending extraordinary amounts of money, because it can involve enhancing what the organization is currently doing, as opposed to continuously inventing new-to-the-world programs.

The second imperative is to create a brand-driven culture, so that pressures to reduce brand building will be countered and so that the responsibility of building brands becomes everyone's job, rather than solely the domain of marketing. Brand assimilation does just that, by creating a host of "champions" for the brand-building effort. The key is to get everyone on board and to make sure that all who touch the brand know how they can help enhance the brand experience within their job.

This book will help any brand strategist to better understand the basics of harnessing the organization to build brands by providing a much-needed emphasis on energizing employees in the organization to understand and live the brand. When the employees in the organization can be energized to live the brand, a strengthened brand usually results; when organizational commitment is lacking, any brand-building effort is unfulfilled or, worse, sets expectations that can never be met, internally or externally.

In addition to providing new perspectives, concepts, and tools to help brand builders engage their organization, Scott Davis and Michael Dunn share their brand touchpoint perspective, which is a new way to look at the creation of the brand-customer relationship.

The authors, both colleagues of mine whom I have worked with in many contexts, are seasoned and gifted brand strategists. Their insight and experience help make this book a significant contribution that will influence the way brands are created and managed.

San Francisco, California   DAVID A. AAKER
July 2002   VICE CHAIRMAN OF PROPHET

⟶⟋⟍⟍⟋⟍⟋⟍⟋⟍⟋⟍⟋⟍ Acknowledgments

This book was definitely written by more people than the two authors listed on the front cover. If ever there has been a collaborative effort supported by an incredible team spirit, *Building the Brand-Driven Business* is one.

This book is the culmination of many client projects, practitioner interviews, best practice studies, and countless hours of developing intellectual capital. So many thanks are owed.

First, a special thanks goes to the relentless internal team that supported this book from the get-go. At the forefront is Cindy Levine, who gave us the guidance, support, and thought leadership that usually takes an entire team to provide.

Tina Longoria, Caity Meaney, and Beth Palmer provided us with the content and editing support that was absolutely required for this book to reach the stage at which you are seeing it now.

The "kitchen cabinet team members" provided us with the fodder and intellectual capital that drove much of the content of this book. That team included Stephen Berman, Ben Bidlack, Ethan Drogin, Andrew Flynn, Cathy Halligan, Kathryn Hohenrieder, Judy Hopelain, Suzy Jacoby, Scott Jampol, Liza Lanier, Kim Larson, Michael Million, Laura Moran, Dan Morrison, Michael Petromilli, Tessie Popoff, Jeff Smith, and Jason Stavers. Also, Dave Aaker's insights and "blessing" of this book were important factors in making sure we were additive to the already incredible rich body of brand work that exists today.

An additional thanks goes out to Jill Steele and Karen Woon, who put in some long hours on the final edit and to Tammy Hicks, whose work on graphics and the "small" details helped to bring this book to a close.

Second, an important thank-you goes to Carl Bochmann, whose mentoring web has now been cast over more brand zealots than he will ever know. Carl's insightful, challenging, and always "on-brand" perspectives throughout the writing of this project have absolutely made it a better book.

Third, a big thank-you goes out to the many clients, new friends, and old friends who have lent their wisdom to this book, including Bob Lachky at Anheuser-Busch, Tom O'Toole at Hyatt, Karl Ploeger at H&R Block, David May at Goldman Sachs, Jill Weaver at Allstate, Bob Greenberg at Panasonic, Sara Lipson at AT&T, Teresa Poggenpohl at Accenture, Denise Yohn at Sony, William Pate at Bell South, Len Tacconi at Merck, Jeff Herbert at Beverage Partners Worldwide, Jim McDowell at BMW, Nancy J. Wiese at XEROX, Becky Saeger at Visa, John Saunders at T. Rowe Price, Alan Brown at Nuveen, Andreas Eggert at Wyeth, Susan Atteridge at TXU, Ed Faruolo at CIGNA, James McDonald at BMW, Anne Greer at 3M, Ruth Fornell at Teradata, Randi Nelson at Itron, Bill Stoessel at Medtronics, Anna Catalano at BP, Bernhard Eggli at UBS and Kirk Stewart, and Nelson Farris from Nike.

Two final thank-you's. First to Michael Palmer at the Association of National Advertisers, who is such a big supporter of this book, as well as one of the finest people we have ever run across. Second, to Kathe Sweeney and the gang at Jossey-Bass, who truly made the development of this book a pleasure and continue to represent the epitome of professional publishing.

From Scott M. Davis: a special heartfelt thank-you to my parents, Ron and Beverly, who are always there for me and continue to help me find my way. All my love and thanks to my wife, Debbie, who is the love of my life and once again shouldered the burden of writing another book. By all accounts, she should really be listed as an additional coauthor to this book. And, to my twin six-year-old boys, Ethan and Benjamin, and my three-year-old daughter, Emma, whom I love more than they could ever possibly understand or imagine. By the way, the answer to your question "Are you done writing your book, Daddy?" is, finally, yes.

From Michael Dunn: I am deeply indebted to my assistant, Megan Bigelow, for actually keeping everyone at bay long enough for me to free up some mornings to get a little writing done, and to my colleagues on Prophet's leadership team, who worked just as hard to the same end. My next set of thanks goes to my mother, Mary, brother Sean, sister Chrissy, and the whole Daley clan, for loving me, supporting me, and sticking by me from the beginning. Lastly I want to thank my life partner, Victor, and our dog, Lucky, who bore the brunt of my absence and occasional ill temper throughout the course of the "book project" with grace, humor, lots of doggy licks, and unwavering encouragement.

Glencoe, Illinois   SCOTT M. DAVIS
San Francisco, California   MICHAEL DUNN
July 2002

The black T-shirt on the front cover, which is 100 percent cotton and of the highest quality, can be either a $3 T-shirt or a $30 T-shirt. It can be sold in either a deep-discount retail store or a high-end, prestigious retail store. That black T-shirt's ultimate value is directly linked to the brand name found on the T-shirt's inside collar, the company behind it, and the employees who support it.

Taking Control of Your Brand's Destiny

*F*ortune magazine's 2002 ranking of "Best Companies to Work For" had some familiar names on the list: Southwest Airlines, Intel, Microsoft, Wal-Mart, FedEx, Charles Schwab, American Express, Goldman Sachs, and Harley-Davidson.[1] One month later, *Fortune's* annual "Most Admired Companies" issue was released, and those exact same companies were at the top of that list too.[2] From a brand perspective, these cross-over companies and brands tell a wonderful story. Think about the employees working for each of these well-known brands. They embody what the brand stands for. They are walking billboards for everything that great branded companies hope to achieve, and they live the brand on a daily basis, within a culture that revolves around the customer's relationship with the brand.

This high level of pride and customer focus, coupled with great performance and strong brand leadership, has helped them become ranked among the most admired companies (brands) in the world. Importantly, these companies are not being rated on just a few variables; the "most admired" ranking is a function of eight key attributes that are directly tied to the way they conduct business internally and the overall performance of their business externally:

1. Admired as a leader in innovation

2. Admired for their financial soundness

3. Admired for having strong employee talent

4. Admired for their use of corporate assets

5. Admired for the long-term investment value they provide

6. Admired for the level of social responsibility they embrace

7. Admired for the quality of management they have

8. Admired for the level of quality their products and services provide

To make both lists means only one thing: these companies understand the power of their brands, both internally and externally. Within great branded companies, all employees clearly understand what their brand's promise is and what role they need to play in bringing that promise to life. This understanding allows each employee to know what decisions or actions will reinforce the brand or denigrate the brand relative to their day-to-day responsibilities—for example:

- A call comes in, and customer service or the call center knows exactly how to handle it in a way that is consistent with the brand.

- Research and Development works on innovations that help perpetuate the promise of the brand and build brand loyalty.

- The sales force is commissioned to deliver on the promise made by the brand, not on quotas.

- An opportunity comes up to extend the brand or co-brand with another company, and senior management knows exactly whether it is in line with its brand objectives.

- Human Resources knows exactly how a job description should read and which candidates are consistent with what the brand stands for and which candidates should not be considered.

Whether it is CIGNA having Mondrian-style murals in all service and sales offices that display customer testimonials, Medtronic (also on both *Fortune* lists) completely redesigning its headquarters to be consistent with its brand, or Wal-Mart having most employees owning stock in the company, brand-driven companies have all found the right formula for helping their employees bring their brand to life on a daily basis, resulting in scores of brand zealots within the company and tremendous levels of external success.

THE SINGLE GREATEST ISSUE BRAND BUILDERS FACE

Still, the reality is that for every Intel and FedEx, there are hundreds of companies that are struggling with how to start building a brand-driven business. We believe that senior executives are more in line than ever before with the idea that the brand is one of the greatest untapped assets they have at their disposal to drive long-term growth. The challenge is that most do not even know where to begin. Here are a few common challenges voiced by C-level executives (that is, direct reports to the CEO):

> "I conceptually get that a brand is an asset, but I just can't see how that translates into longer-term strategy."

> "I conceptually get that a brand is an asset, but I just can't see how that helps me with the day-to day-pressures that I face in running this business."

> "I do not know anything about building a brand."

> "I have too many other things to worry about in building this company."

> "I do not have any control over my brand [or the final touch], as our distributors really have the ultimate responsibility for selling our brand."

> "I just increased our advertising budget by 25 percent this year. Isn't that enough?"

> "That is why I hired our new vice president of marketing."

> "You want me to train all twenty thousand of our employees?"

> "Where would I even start?"

This last question sets the stage for this book.

OPERATIONALIZING YOUR BRAND

Building the Brand-Driven Business was written to show companies how to go beyond jump-starting the brand-building process by figuring out the most effective way to deliver their brand across every interaction with customers and other stakeholders and through every employee within the company. We call this holistic brand concept *operationalizing the brand*. It means that all employees will work in a cohesive and consistent way in support of the brand and its promise to guarantee that customers and other stakeholders are always satisfied and even delighted with their brand experience.

Whether it is making sure that your in-store, catalogue, and online efforts are all aligned with your brand, or that your customer service representatives are talking about the brand in the same way as your sales force, or that all external messaging efforts are totally consistent with one another, a brand-driven business developed through operationalizing your brand is the desired end state.

The term *operationalizing the brand* may sound awkward, much like the term *reengineering* first did in the late 1980s, but we believe it is effective in connoting the sense of urgency that companies require in order to figure out how to bring their brand to life more effectively and efficiently, across every dimension of their business. By embracing the concept of operationalizing the brand, companies are embracing the fact that they control the outcome of addressing the most important opportunity area they have in front of them: bringing their brand to life internally, which in turn allows them to deliver on the brand externally in the most consistent, cohesive, and effective manner possible. Said another way, operationalizing the brand will help a company ultimately take total control of its brand's destiny.

Success in operationalizing the brand really depends on achieving success within five specific brand-driven areas:

1. Achieving total alignment between the business and brand strategy

2. Demonstrating a clear and consistent level of commitment to brand building by top executives within the organization

3. Controlling critical interactions your customers and stakeholders have with your brand, based on what your brand stands for

4. Transforming your company into a brand-driven organization and culture, which includes having all employees understand the brand's promises, the role they need to play in bringing the brand to life within their functional area, and the critical importance of permanently changing their behaviors in accordance with what the business and brand strategies are trying to accomplish

5. Implementing a consistent measurement and reward system that allows companies to monitor, benchmark, and upgrade their brand performance

By achieving success in each of these areas, you are maximizing your chances for leveraging your greatest untapped asset—your brand—and also achieving your longer-term financial and strategic objectives, with the brand as the primary enabler.

THE REST OF THE BOOK

This book is designed to provide a road map of how best to accomplish these five key operationalizing objectives.

The chapters in Part One explain why holistically managing your brand is more critical than ever and set up the premise that business and brand strategy are one and the same thing.

Chapter One, "Understanding the Brand's Powerful New Role," discusses how brand is increasingly playing a more important role within all types of companies and shows why it is important to further this thinking and ensure that the brand plays a driving role within your organization. The chapter discusses the specific benefits of doing this and highlights key organizations that are following this strategy today.

Chapter Two, "Connecting Business Strategy to Brand Strategy," talks specifically about integrating a company's brand and business strategy. It provides both the approach to start to link these two together and the rationale for why this is the only way to think about strategy going forward. The chapter addresses three specific questions:

- How do I best align my business and brand strategy together?
- What role does the brand need to play for our company to achieve its longer-term strategic and financial goals?
- How do I get senior management to agree that the brand is our most critical asset?

The chapters in Part Two discuss operationalizing your brand in terms of all the different brand touchpoints, or interactions that a customer or stakeholder has with your brand, and details strategies for identifying and prioritizing these brand touchpoints along the purchase cycle.

Chapter Three, "Understanding and Prioritizing High-Impact Brand Touchpoints," introduces a framework for identifying and assessing all brand touchpoints. This chapter will help you to identify each of these brand touchpoints and then set up a mechanism for prioritizing each touchpoint relative to its degree of influence on your customer and stakeholder as well as to your ability to control it as you go forward. The chapter addresses the following specific questions:

- What are all the touchpoints that exist between my brand and a current or potential customer or stakeholder?
- How am I performing against each of those brand touchpoints?
- What strategy do I need to embrace to leverage the numerous brand touchpoints at my disposal most successfully?
- How do I start to gain some consistency and more effectively manage all of my brand's touchpoints?

Chapters Four through Six then organize all of the brand touchpoints identified in Chapter Three into the three distinct stages that a customer goes through in the course of developing a relationship with your brand.

Chapter Four, "The Pre-Purchase Experience: Making the Brand-Prospect Connection," explores the strategies and brand touchpoints leveraged in what we are calling the pre-purchase experience. In particular, this chapter takes you through the various stages potential customers go through as they move from initial brand awareness to trying to determine which brands they will consider for purchase.

Chapter Five, "The Purchase Experience: The First Step in Delivering on the Promise," addresses the issue of trying to take more control over the purchase process through the various brand touchpoints a company can employ to maximize the sale.

Chapter Six, "The Post-Purchase Experience: Solidifying the Brand-Customer Relationship," examines how to maximize the actual experience a customer has with a brand during and after use of the product or service. It explains all of the tactics a company has at its disposal to keep a customer satisfied after the sale and, most important, to keep the relationship alive over time so that when that customer is looking to purchase again or try another branded product or wants to make a recommendation to someone else, your brand will come to mind first.

The brand touchpoint wheel in Figure 1 illustrates the sequence of topics discussed in Chapters Four through Six, which address the following questions:

- How do I control all of the brand touchpoints that constitute the experience a customer may have with my brand?
- How do I most effectively get my brand into a prospect's purchase consideration set, start to distinguish my brand's proposition from key competitor propositions, and make sure I keep true to my brand's promise?
- How do I ensure that a customer's experience with my product or service is consistent with the promise that the brand has made?
- How do I keep my customer engaged with the brand after the sale to make sure this person is having a good experience, in line with the brand's promise, and will keep the brand in mind when looking to repurchase again in my category?

Figure 1.   Brand Touchpoint Wheel.

Part Three is dedicated to helping companies understand how to bring the brand to life internally, so that current and potential customers experience the brand externally in a consistent way. The focus here is on those most responsible for delivering the brand promise on a daily basis: the entire employee base.

Chapter Seven, "Developing a Brand Metrics System: Driving Brand Building by What You Measure," discusses the importance of introducing metrics and measures that are meaningful and action oriented to make sure that all brand-building activities (that is, the brand touchpoints) are helping to achieve the goals and objectives initially established for the brand (as discussed in Chapter Two). In addition, the information provided by these metrics will help companies become smarter about future brand-building activities.

Chapter Eight, "Building a Brand-Based Culture: Focusing on the Brand-Employee Relationship Through Brand Assimilation," describes how to start to assimilate the brand within your organization, which becomes especially important for companies that are just starting to adopt a brand-driven philosophy for the first time. This chapter illuminates the concept of getting the brand to exist not just in your employees' hands and heads but also in their hearts. Brand-based incentives and career pathing are two of the methods discussed.

Chapter Nine, "Establishing a Brand-Based Organization: Focusing on the Structure and Roles to Support Brand-Driven Change," discusses how to start to implement a brand-based culture in which every employee truly lives the brand on a daily basis. It focuses on the structure and roles needed to support brand-driven change and contains several real-life examples from companies that have successfully implemented them.

The chapters in Part Three address the following specific questions:

- How do I reward brand-driven performance, and how do I measure and track the performance of brand-driven efforts?

- How do I get my twenty-five thousand employees to hear the same brand message at the same time?

- How do I get all of the employees to not only understand the brand but also actually believe in it and live it?

- How do I set up a sustainable brand-based organization over time?

By the time you reach the end of this book, you should have a clear picture of what you need to do to make a serious statement about the importance your brand plays in helping your company achieve its longer-term strategic and financial objectives. You will also know how to control and manage the brand at high-priority touchpoints, with various customers, and through all employees.

FROM CONCEPT TO REALITY

Throughout the book, we offer practical frameworks, case studies, lessons learned, and specific tactics that you can employ immediately. We draw on dozens of client cases, as well as interviews with twenty-five leading marketing and brand executives. Among the companies cited in this book are AT&T, Accenture, Allstate, Anheuser-Busch, BMW, Bell South, Coca-Cola, Eastman Kodak, General Electric, Goldman Sachs, H&R Block, Hyatt, Itron, Merck, Nike, Nuveen, Panasonic, Sony, T. Rowe Price, Teradata, 3M, TXU, Wyeth, Visa, and Xerox.

In addition, findings from Prophet's 2002 Best Practices study are sprinkled throughout the book. The study highlights what eighty companies are doing—and not doing—relative to building their brand.[3]

All of the principles presented in this book will work for both product and service companies, privately held and publicly held companies, for-profit and nonprofit companies, and big and small companies. We know this is the case because the frameworks presented have been successfully used in projects we conducted with many different types of organizations in a variety of industries, from retail to high tech to consumer durables to professional services.

We believe that by learning about operationalizing your brand, you have made a commitment to building a brand-driven business. By building a brand-driven business, you have made a commitment to ensuring the future success of your company. To work at its highest level, though, this book needs to be passed around. The more employees (from the top to the bottom) within your organization who both read and buy into *Building the Brand-Driven Business,* the more likely it is that these concepts will move from words on a page to reality within your company.

PART ONE

Making "Operationalizing the Brand" Your New Mantra

CHAPTER ONE

Understanding the Brand's Powerful New Role

T en years ago, most companies thought that focusing on the brand really meant focusing on the latest and greatest advertising campaign. In addition, they believed that for the most part, the brand was owned by the advertising agency, along with a freshly minted M.B.A., who was interested in making his or her mark on the brand before moving on to another assignment in eighteen months or so. There was the perception that building the brand was about money going out and not much coming back, and thus the view that a brand was an expense or a discretionary line item that could be either dialed up or down.

When the brand was talked about, it was always discussed as a series of tactics and never as strategy. Think about an advertising icon (like the Maytag repairman or the Marlboro cowboy) or a logo (like Nike's Swoosh) or a tag line (like "Where's the beef?") or a shape (such as the Absolut bottle) or a jingle (like the famous Alka Seltzer theme of "plop, plop, fizz, fizz . . .") or a sound (like the Intel five notes at the end of each commercial) or even a spokesperson (such as Colonel Sanders from Kentucky Fried Chicken). This is how most companies thought about brand.

This mind-set led to the fact that the biggest brand challenge in the early 1990s was senior management's misunderstanding of what brand building was all about, and thus building a case for maintaining a constant (or increasing) level of brand spending was almost unheard of. In fact, in a branding best-practices study conducted in 1995, two-thirds of senior executives interviewed stated that the single greatest threat to the future health of their brand was senior management's lack of understanding of what their brand stood for.[1]

BRANDS ARE MORE STRATEGIC THAN EVER

Fortunately, the challenges that brand builders face today have progressed to a much more strategic level. The importance of brand is better understood, as the implications are much more tightly linked to the bottom line. For this reason, most discussions about building the brand are much more strategically driven, as well as emotionally and politically charged (see Figure 1.1).

Patrick Marketing Group's recent brand effectiveness study shows that 96 percent of senior executives rated the importance of brand building as either vital or important to the company's future success. Mercer's recent study of brand-building investments shows that 84 percent of respondents said that their emphasis on brand building has increased over the past two to three years. The top two reasons for this increase, according to Mercer, are product commoditization and increased competition.

In addition, Prophet's 2002 Best Practices study shows that the top three goals for brand strategy today are increasing customer loyalty, differentiating oneself from the competition, and establishing market leadership—all strategic. Furthermore, our study shows that while 45 percent of respondents still consider senior management's lack of understanding of brand to be a threat, this represents a major improvement since the 1995 study.

Brands Are the Reason Companies Exist

For most companies today, the recognition that the brand is indeed the reason they exist is more the norm than the exception. There is now a widespread belief that the brand incorporates a combination of:

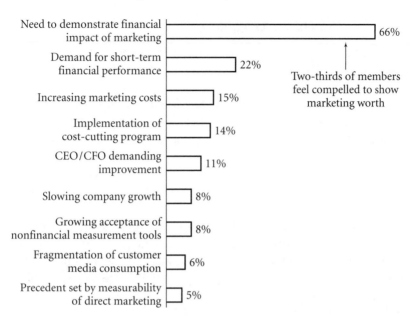

Figure 1.1. **Drivers of Interest in Marketing Performance Measurement.**
Source: 2001 Marketing Leadership Council Survey.

Promises made to customers . . .
based on multiple experiences over time . . .
delivered with a consistently high level of quality
and value . . .
that are perceived to be unparalleled relative to the
competition, . . .
ultimately resulting in deep, trust-based relationships . . .
which, in turn, garners great amounts of loyalty and
profits over time

In fact, more and more companies today are thinking about their brands in quantifiable terms. For many companies, the brand is seen as having a measurable value and a direct correlation to the bottom line. There is growing support for viewing and managing the brand as an asset and thus having the brand drive every strategic and investment decision.

Brands Are Valuable Assets

One way to think about the brand in more quantifiable terms was defined in *Brand Asset Management:*

> Brand Asset Management is the approach management should adopt to manage the brand as an asset, with every strategic and investment decision an organization makes either impacting or being impacted by the brand. A brand is a measurable, income-producing asset. The income contribution of brand can and should be measured and managed over time.[2]

We contend that the brand is the most powerful asset a company owns, followed closely by its people. In Hong Kong, Britain, Australia, and other major capitalistic countries, placing a value on the brand on the balance sheet is standard practice. In the United States, brand is still generally buried so deeply in goodwill that it can hardly be found in financial statements.

There are strong advocates for companies trying to place tangible values on intangible assets. For example, New York University Stern School of Business accounting and finance professor Baruch Lev recently recommended to the U.S. Securities and Exchange Commission that permanent changes be made in U.S. accounting practices to force companies to "institute an asset mentality and recognize that intangibles are assets just like inventory and machines."[3]

Jack Welch, the former CEO of General Electric, helped make the shift to an asset mentality at GE a permanent one when he stated, "Our most valuable assets are our intangible assets." Implied within his statement were both the GE brand and the GE employee base.

In recent discussions, we heard other top executives at major corporations talk about the brand in a similar manner. Denise Yohn, vice president of segment marketing and brand planning at Sony, defines brand as "a bundle of attributes, emotional and rational, intangible and tangible, that create value for all of a company's stakeholders (from employees to consumers)." Bob Lachky, vice president of brand management at Anheuser-Busch, defines brand as "a unique or differentiated product or service that has an identifiable image or personality, brought to life through a powerful relationship with a customer." And Karl Ploeger, vice president of creative service and brand management at H&R Block, defines brand as "your number one asset. It's your reputation. It's what people think of you and what you bring to the consumer."

In effect, the brand, if managed effectively and consistently, tells customers and other stakeholders exactly what you do and why you do it. It also tells management what they can and cannot do with the brand. Whether they choose to align their decisions with what the brand does or does not stand for is a different story (imagine Bausch and Lomb Mouthwash or Harley-Davidson Wine Coolers).

THE BENEFITS OF BRAND BUILDING ARE MORE EXPLICIT THAN EVER BEFORE

While it is nice to talk about getting the chief executive officer (CEO) and executive team on board with a consistent funding approach and mind-set to building the brand, the reality is that most companies today are so bottom line and short term focused that they cannot afford a more consistent and longer-term approach to building and investing in the brand.

Marketers are the primary brand evangelists within companies today and will gladly tell you something along these lines: "The challenge I face daily is pretty straightforward. My CEO is constantly pushing me to effectively show the link between brand building, shareholder value, and the bottom line." While we are not quite there yet, significant advances have been made in trying to make the financial impact and strategic benefits of building the brand more tangible.

Brand Asset Management identified ten key benefits tied to leveraging the brand more effectively:

1. Strong brands allow for *premium pricing* versus competitive products.

2. Strong brands give you *protection* against price wars.

3. Strong brands allow for *greater new product success* because of the implied endorsement.

4. Strong brands provide better *leverage when negotiating* with channel partners.

5. Strong brands make you more *attractive to potential co-branding partners.*

6. Strong brands make you a more *attractive licensing candidate.*

7. Strong brands help you *mitigate a brand crisis* more effectively, as customers are more forgiving.

8. Strong brands are a *magnet for recruiting* the best employees and retaining them over time. Similarly, strong brands usually drive *high levels of employee pride.*

9. Strong brands more readily *garner loyalty,* which in turn drives profitability.

10. Strong brands mandate *clarity in internal focus and brand execution.*[4]

These internal benefits make a strong argument for consistently focusing on brand building, day in and day out. The external benefits of what loyal customers can provide back to the company further strengthens the case for building the brand:

1. When customers are highly loyal to a brand, there is *minimal consideration of similar brands* in the purchase process.

2. When customers are highly loyal, they *request your brand by name.*

3. When customers are highly loyal, they *recommend your brand* to their friends and colleagues.

4. When customers are highly loyal to a brand, they *are more accepting of new products or services* offered by that brand.

5. When customers are highly loyal to a brand, they *refuse substitutes* and will wait longer or travel farther to get their brand of choice.

6. When customers are highly loyal to a brand, they will *continue to pay a price premium* for that brand.

Translating these sixteen benefits into the actual bottom-line impact (revenue increases and cost decreases) is a compelling demonstration of the brand's influence on the performance and bottom line of the company (see Figure 1.2).

The margin impact resulting from effective brand building should be obvious. The top-line revenue growth comes from a number of sources, from licensing to premium pricing. The bottom-line savings also come from a number of sources, from stronger negotiating power through lowering your marketing and selling costs. This bottom-line impact is supported by the following statistics, which even more explicitly show the financial impact of brand building:

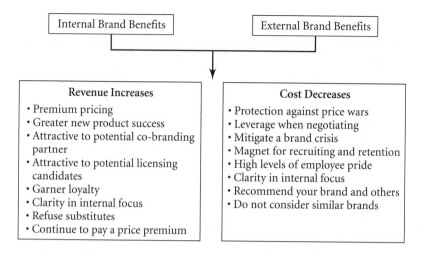

Figure 1.2.   Internal and External Brand Benefits.

- In some sectors, an increase of customer loyalty of just 2 percent is equivalent to a 10 percent cost-reduction program.[5]

- An increase of 5 percent in loyal customers (in some categories) can deliver 95 percent greater profitability over the lifetime of that customer.[6]

- Over 50 percent of customers would be willing to pay a 20 to 25 percent price premium to the brand that they are most loyal to before they would switch to a competitive brand.[7]

- Fifty percent of customers are willing to try a new product from a preferred brand because of the implied endorsement, credibility, and trust.[8]

- It takes seven to ten times the cost and effort to gain a new customer as it does to keep an existing customer.[9]

Probably the most profound proof that brand building pays off is EquiTrend's study of the impact of a company's brand equity, over time, on its return on investment (ROI). Brand equity is defined as the combination of consumers' awareness of the brand, the brand's perceived quality, consumers' associations with the brand, and consumers; loyalty to the brand. The study showed that firms experiencing the largest gains in brand equity saw their ROI average 30 percent, while those with the largest losses in brand equity saw their ROI average a negative 10 percent.

There are also several proof points in the marketplace of companies that have realized a true dollar impact from their brands:

- In 1997, Rolls Royce was sold to BMW and Volkswagen. Volkswagen bought all the plants and hard capital for over $1 billion; BMW bought the rights to the Rolls Royce brand for $66 million.
- Licensing for the Caterpillar brand has risen to over $800 million in the past decade, which alone makes it a Fortune 2000 company.
- Licensing for Ford and Harley-Davidson merchandise each totaled $1 billion in revenues. For Harley-Davidson, the $1 billion in licensed merchandise represented 15 percent of total revenues.

BRAND-BUILDING LESSONS HAVE NEVER BEEN RICHER

The revenue growth and cost savings associated with strong brands are only part of the story. Another reason that the climate for building the brand-driven business has never been better is that there are so many other powerful lessons to be learned from both successful and unsuccessful brands.

The Great Ones

The great brands continue to thrive years after they were introduced. GE, Hallmark, Goodyear, 3M, Sony, Nestlé, and Allstate have stayed true to their promise, as well as retained a high level of quality, innovation, and, most important, consistency. These companies have hit bumps in the road and have gone through trying times—none more trying than operating in a zero-growth economic climate, with cost pressures mounting and the stock market spiraling downward—but they have all stayed relevant and have endeared many of us to stick with them through thick and thin.

We have also seen newer brands enter our lexicon over the past twenty years, many of them strong, formidable brands that leveraged the same principles their stalwart predecessors did years before. Saturn, Home Depot, Starbucks, Amazon.com, and countless other newer brands have built trust-based relationships with us quickly that will most likely remain intact for years to come.

Every one of those companies mentioned represents the newer generation of brand stars and faces incredible brand and strategic challenges. Whether it is the fear of Starbucks becoming ubiquitous through its aggressive expansion plans, or Saturn trying to upscale its affordable cars to the mid-$20,000 range, or Hallmark dealing with electronic greeting cards, great brands generally come out of turbulent times stronger than they were before, continuing to find ways to stay relevant and remain true to their brand's promise.

How did these newer brands do it so quickly? Quite simply, they were the first to fill an unmet or unsatisfied need best, at the right time, with the right brand. US Robotics Palm Pilot's excellent timing and ability to meet the needs of its consumers helped it become a powerful brand. Apple's Newton, in contrast, which came almost three years earlier (almost a decade in technology years) and was developed from the same concept as the Palm Pilot, was created without the needs of its consumers in mind. The poor handwriting recognition, inadequate memory, and inability to communicate without a lot of costly additional gear made for a time-consuming and pricey unit. It did not meet the needs of mobile professionals the way the Palm Pilot did with a simpler, smaller personal digital assistant.

One reason the great businesses leverage the power of their brands so successfully is that they understand, as Peter Sealey eloquently summarized in *Simplicity Marketing* when he referenced a study conducted by Monitor, that "in the context of too much choice, brand becomes the shortest, most efficient path to potential satisfaction and tension release. Brands are playing a bigger role as the exasperated consumer's simplified shortcut to a purchase decision."[10]

Taking that one step further, the great businesses can generally summarize what their brand stands for in just a few words, which helps those companies communicate more effectively, internally and externally, relative to how and why they exist. Here are a few examples:

BRAND	BRAND'S POSITIONING
Dell	Customized
Intel	Speed
Volvo	Safety
Amazon.com	Convenience

FedEx	Guaranteed
Virgin	Irreverence
Continental	Service
Southwest	Fun

If you are an employee in one of the great businesses, those positioning words explicitly state what your company's ultimate purpose is and your role in bringing that purpose to life. If you are a potential or current customer, you have a straightforward statement of what you can and cannot expect to get as a result of associating with each of those brands. If you are a senior executive, it is crystal clear what will and will not work according to the brand and its promise.

Doesn't it make perfect sense that Virgin Insurance failed? Its positioning statement, "irreverent insurance," is a blatant oxymoron.

The Fallen Ones

Although there are countless brands that meet these challenges head-on and actually strengthen their competitive positioning, countless others lose their way, their relevance, and their esprit de corps and struggle to find their way back again.

At the time this book was written, several historically powerful brands were trying to stage a comeback. Think about Hewlett-Packard trying to define what business it is in, Gap's need to return to its heritage in the basics, or General Motors' attempt to figure out what to do with all of its brands.

Sadly, other great and familiar brands, such as Woolworth, Plymouth, Prelude, Oldsmobile, and *Mademoiselle,* were recently "put to sleep." And just recently, Ford announced it was discontinuing its Mercury Cougar and Lincoln Continental brands.

The Comeback Kids

Besides the lessons learned from the stalwart, confused, or recently deceased brands, there is a rich source of learning from the countless brands that were on their last legs and not only came back but came back stronger and with a vengeance. Each provides a powerful example of how to drive profitability by getting back to brand basics, or what we call *brand authenticity.* The ultimate testament to many of these comeback brands is that many dominate their categories again, after a prolonged absence from category relevancy.

Think adidas and IBM. Think Continental Airlines and Apple. Think Target and Banana Republic. Think Absolut and Schwinn. Think UPS and Volkswagen. Every one of these brands had been written off by the press, Wall Street, and their customers and either were facing Chapter 11 bankruptcy or were close to it. In fact, IBM's $8 billion loss in 1993 was thought to be the final nail in the slow-moving mainframe behemoth's coffin. Today, IBM is at the top of its game; it practically owns e-business and solutions and dominates technology services, which now account for almost half of its revenues and more than half of its profits. Most incredible is the fact that many customers, employees, stakeholders, and Wall Street now describe IBM as nimble.

The secrets to these comebacks are simple. They had the right leader, the right plan, and the right brand strategy. Importantly, each realized too that the right employees were critical to achieving comeback success. Once employees were on-board and knew explicitly what their role was, success was waiting right around the corner.

In effect, each of these comeback companies figured out a simple but powerful formula for resurrecting their brands and leveraging them in a way they never had before.

SO WHERE DO WE GO FROM HERE?

Although the value of the brand is better understood and the benefits are more explicit than ever before, the common approach to building the brand still remains somewhat nebulous and narrowly focused. As hard as companies try, more often than not, the brand still resides in marketing and continues to be viewed as a discretionary line item. In Prophet's 2002 Best Practices study, we learned that while executives understood that actual product and service use and experience were the most important tools in brand building, they still felt that their brand strength was most heavily reliant on the marketing budget (as opposed to human resources, training, research and development, or customer service). This perception has to change for any company that is serious about realizing the incredible listing of top-line and bottom-line benefits mentioned above.

We believe that three significant changes are necessary. First, senior management has to embrace brand building for it to be a success and for others in the organization to see that the company is serious about it. If management commitment is not sincere and appears to be nothing more than lip service, the branding efforts will fail. If senior management is able to look at brand building as an investment and not an expense and see that the brand needs to be nurtured and built over time, then the company will most likely get significant benefits in return: a leg up on the competition, a reason to believe for customers and stakeholders, an ability to control its future success, and the majority of the benefits listed earlier in the chapter.

Second, companies have to realize that brand building is a holistic effort. Every time someone internally or externally touches your brand, there is an opportunity to reinforce the brand's promise or denigrate it. Most companies do not realize they have this choice, let alone the ability to do anything about it. To succeed, companies not only need to know every way in which their brand touches their various stakeholders, but also how to manage it most effectively and consistently across brand touchpoints and across stakeholders. Most companies do not understand that this is how great brands are built. Unless these experiences or brand touchpoints are carefully managed, the brand will most likely be suboptimized.

Third, for this holistic approach to building the brand to take hold, all employees, within their respective roles, have to realize it is their responsibility to embrace and champion the brand. They must actively manage its various touchpoints in order to maximize their company's potential for long-term success. As a senior vice president of one of the big box retailers recently told us, "I can do everything perfect in my marketing role, but if the cashier is having a lousy day and the customer is impacted by that, then that will most likely be the last impression they have of my brand." All employees must believe that they can and do make a difference in bringing the brand to life.

The Organization Must Adopt a Holistic Brand Approach

If everyone in the organization does not understand his or her role in bringing the brand's promise to life every single day, the odds of suboptimizing brand performance are high. More important, the marketplace will recognize if you do not have your internal act together.

We saw this during the dot-com frenzy. Many dot-com businesses made external promises they were ill equipped to fulfill. We also saw it in a bigger way with United Airline's botched 1997 "Rising" campaign, which promised to fix business travelers' woes, from long lines to lack of overhead and foot space to poor communications. While United's researchers, marketers, and advertising agency should be applauded for understanding their customers, the company failed to follow through on the campaign's promises. Because of terrible internal preparation and poor operational execution, the ultimate impact was even worse than an ineffective "feel good" message. The company set expectations and did not meet them.

Disney, Dell, Nordstrom, The Four Seasons, BMW, Starbucks, Wal-Mart, and Southwest Airlines all have figured out that taking a holistic approach to building their brands, and making sure that every employee is helping to bring their brand promise to life every single day, is the surest way to market success.

One of our favorite companies is a Spokane-based company called Itron, which has seen the impact the brand can have on the performance of the company from several different perspectives. Back in 1999, Itron's CEO, LeRoy Nosbaum, realized that for his company to take its next big leap forward, he needed to lead the transformation of Itron from a meter reading company to a company that transformed the data it collected into valuable knowledge for its clients in the energy and water marketplace.

In doing this, marketing recommended and senior management embraced the notion that it had to shift both the position of the brand and the way in which the company managed it. Prior to the relaunch of the brand in the fall of 2000, Itron made sure that all employees were fully educated on the new brand strategy and its impact on their jobs. Importantly, Itron employees understood how their roles would help bring the new Itron brand to life, and senior management wisely tied brand metrics and profit sharing to the company's employees' ability to live the brand. The results for Itron could not tell a better brand story. In the first year since the brand focus was embraced, its stock has risen from $3.70 a share to over $32.00 a share, and employee morale has never been higher.

Senior Management Must Make a Dramatic Commitment to the Power of the Brand

Like Itron, some other companies are also very fortunate to have a CEO who has taken the role of being the ultimate brand builder within the company. When you ask John Chambers at Cisco who runs the brand there, he will quickly and emphatically retort, "I do." This is a significant development for those fortunate companies: there is no more powerful sign of commitment and belief in the brand than having the CEO or founder of the company (and not just the senior marketing executive) touting the virtues and importance of the brand.

In reality, it is only the CEO who can set the tone for the company and its brand, enforce whether there is truly a brand-based culture, and determine whether dollars and other resources put against the brand are deemed investments or expenses.

Companies that take brand building seriously generally have someone at the top who has made the brand the top priority. They have built and nurtured a brand-driven culture over time and consistently told all stakeholder groups, from Wall Street to their own employees, that the brand is the reason to believe. More often than not, they wear the brand on their shirtsleeves every single day (at Harley-Davidson, it may be a tattoo).

Conversely, think about all of the CEOs who have lost their jobs over the past few years. Certainly, many can be discounted as casualties of the dot-com debacle, but many powerful leaders, from Richard McGinn at Lucent to Durk Jager at Procter & Gamble to Doug Ivester at the Coca-Cola Company, were caught disregarding the company's brand and its valuable relationship to the customer. Instead, they focused their efforts fairly intensely (and some would argue exclusively) on the balance sheet.

Many of the great brand builders are well known: Jack Welch at GE, Meg Whitman at eBay, Lou Gerstner at IBM, Steven Jobs at Apple, Andy Grove at Intel, Jeff Bezos at Amazon.com, Fred Smith at FedEx, Howard Schultz at Starbucks, Richard Branson at Virgin, Gordon Bethune at Continental, Herb Kelleher at Southwest. None of these top-tier executives came into the job to build a brand. None came from a classical marketing position. However, each came into the job to build or strengthen a company and deliver on a promise that would allow them to differentiate their organization from the competition and create a value proposition that they could deliver consistently and in a customer-centric way.

Building the Brand Has to Go Beyond the CEO

The CEO has to be the ultimate brand ambassador, czar, or champion but cannot possibly build the brand alone. CEOs can provide the motivation, the spirit, and even the carrot and stick; however, they lack the widespread muscle required to bring the brand to life because their reach into the organization can go only so far. They have to have the right human and financial support and resources to back up their brand building.

In other words, the name of the game is to convert C-level executives from their stereotypical role as brand-building inhibitors and turn them into brand-building champions. Without them, brand building will fail. Why? Because these executives ultimately control whether brand building will get the right level of human and financial attention. For instance, we would contend that more than anyone else in the organization, the chief operating officer (COO) is becoming one of the most critical brand-building change agents to emerge over the past few years. By all accounts, getting the COO to embrace brand building and rally the troops to "live the brand" is arguably the single biggest brand-building enabler. In effect, the COO owns the employee base and thus has the ability and credibility to direct employees to bring their company's brand promise to life.

Other top executives are significant players as well. The chief financial officer (CFO) ultimately holds the purse strings to fund brand building and needs to understand the rationale for brand building and, more important, the return on investment to expect. The chief information officer (CIO) controls the ability to get the right information to make smart, brand-driven decisions. The senior vice president of human resources has to find and reward the talent, identify brand inhibitors, and establish career paths tied to building and driving the brand over time.

The Dialogue Has to Change

Although it is the CEO who can set the tone and make the promise, it is the other C-level executives who have a great deal of the ultimate accountability for bringing the brand to life. We believe that to get senior-level executives not only to buy into brand building but visibly and demonstrably support it, you have to change the dialogue from a "branding" dialogue to one that is more relevant to each senior executive's specific domain.

Too often, marketers want to build their brand case in language they are comfortable with, which is often laden with nomenclature that is not applicable to most within their organizations. In some cases, typical marketing terms, such as *brand equity, brand touchpoints, positioning, brand personality,* and *brand attributes,* can be alienating and condescending to marketing outsiders, depending on the organization's roots. In fact, at a recent Association of National Advertisers executive retreat, most senior marketing executives admitted that they rarely brought the COO or CFO into the brand discussion because they did not know how to talk to them in a meaningful way.

The solution, as many executives today are recognizing, is to change the brand dialogue. Do not talk about "unique value proposition" or "positioning" or "identity" to a CFO or a COO. Instead, talk to them in terms that resonate for them and the role they are playing within the organization. For instance, if you are talking about the brand to the CFO, you need to use investment and return terms (for example, "increasing the lifetime value or profitability of a customer"). With the senior vice president of research and development, talk about simplifying or streamlining the new product development process by using a new strategic screen (the brand) that will help determine which innovations to take forward. With the senior vice president of human resources, talk about attracting and retaining the top employees and maximizing the performance of your staff. And with the CIO, talk about increasing your ability to get the right data to infuse into your CRM efforts through deeper customer relationships (that is, brand loyalty).

The bottom line here is to change the dialogue. Get out of your comfort zone of marketing-speak and talk to other executives about brand issues in a way that is relevant to them. We believe there is no better time to start to shift this dialogue and bring brand front and center than to start to talk about brand and corporate strategy as one.

CHAPTER TWO

Connecting Business Strategy to Brand Strategy

R ecently, we had a conversation with the vice chairman of a Global Fortune 100 company. For the first fifteen minutes of the conversation, this thirty-five-year veteran did nothing but apologize for how little he felt he had to contribute to a conversation about the company's brand. However, as soon as we redirected the conversation toward customers, R&D partners, distribution relationships, the company's reputation, and the like, he came alive and captivated us with his insight and his vision.

He understood these issues intuitively, was able to talk about them in the context of the competition, and understood that there may be significant gaps between internal and external perceptions of the company and its brand. Most important, he realized that all along we were talking about the brand. At the end of the interview, we asked him, slightly tongue-in-cheek, if he still thought he had nothing meaningful to contribute to a conversation about the company's brand.

It is our view that discussions on and strategies about customers, distribution, pricing, and communications are what connect business and brand strategy. Think of the demand side of your company's value equation and, in particular, the offensive elements of your strategy;

each has to be inextricably connected to the company's brand strategy. These are natural things for CEOs and boards of directors to discuss and support our belief that brand and business strategy are one.

Our hypothesis is simple: companies that cultivate great strategic brand skills, develop integrated business and brand strategies, and are then able to operationalize these strategies—and thus the brand—will effectively win the battle for customers and profitability.

As markets move, new competitors enter, or customer needs change, companies may have to move through this cycle again and in some industries frequently. But get the basic components right, and you have a recipe for long-term business and brand success.

Operationalizing the brand effectively and efficiently is not an easy thing to do, and it is not as marketing-driven or as intuitive as some might think. That is why we spend the bulk of this book, Chapters Three through Nine, discussing it in greater detail. To set the stage for these chapters, we must start with strategy.

BRAND NEEDS A VOICE IN STRATEGIC DISCUSSIONS

For brand building to credibly take hold in an organization, it needs a voice at the highest level. Without this high-level support, most brand-building efforts will fail.

This means that CEOs, presidents, COOs, operating division heads, strategic planners, CFOs, corporate development specialists, and corporate marketing and acquisitions specialists need to develop a deeper understanding of brand and its role within strategy. Just as these individuals are comfortable reading pro forma income statements, negotiating complex legal contracts, and approving technology investments, they will also need to be comfortable with the tools of measuring and strengthening their brands and leveraging them in the marketplace. As long as this muscle remains underdeveloped at this level of a company's leadership, a company will continue to minimize its strategic decision making and brand-building capacity.

Refining Your Brand Lens

The ability to bring a brand-based perspective to a company's critical business issues is what we call applying a strategic brand lens, which helps senior leaders and strategic thinkers integrate the brand into their approach to strategy. For example, with a well-defined brand identity and positioning, a company should be able to determine the fit of any major new product launch or potential acquisition. In addition, questions such as "Do we have credibility in this category?" and "How does our new presence in this category affect our image in other categories?" are far less complicated if a brand lens is used to determine what is in and what is out.

To achieve senior-level understanding of brand constructs, we need to make them seem less alien, more accessible, and more relevant to a company's leadership. In most organizations, brand admittedly comes with a fair amount of baggage. For some, it is Wall Street's buzzword du jour, for others it is marketing on steroids, and for a disgruntled few it is a way for companies that are not good at "real" things like technology, operations, engineering, or design to find a way to stay in business.

Much of the current language that brand and marketing professionals use does more harm than good at times as it is the outgrowth of legions of bright, verbal people wrestling with intangible, subtle concepts. And much of the content is restricted to the narrow set of operations traditionally defined as marketing communications. For example, in Prophet's 2002 Best Practices study, despite an overwhelming belief in the impact of personal contact, we found that only 41 percent of managers considered investment in customer service an important part of their brand-building efforts.

Going Beyond Branding Artifacts: The Tail Wagging the Dog

Given the current state of the dialogue, it is not surprising that many senior executives have an exceedingly narrow preconception about what it means to be focused on brand building. Usually, the artifacts of brand expression—colors, logos, names, taglines, or advertising—get confused with the fundamental principles that enable brand building to translate into sustainable and profitable growth. Nowhere is this truer than in the executive suite. How often have you heard statements like, "Brand has become important to us lately," or "We have started to invest in brand building"? What exactly does that mean?

Many executives treat the word *brand* as a slightly alien concept, primarily because they continue to confuse it with advertising or logo designs. This was observed at Amazon, as Allan Brown, former chief marketing officer, noted: "The problem is that a lot of senior executives equate brand to advertising. We needed to get people to understand that brand is a promise, and all the advertising isn't anything unless they deliver on the promise."

DEVELOPING A BRAND LENS REQUIRES A LEADERSHIP MIND-SET SHIFT

We do not want to underestimate the conceptual and cultural shift required to embrace this type of strategic role for brand. The full extent of this context shift will be discussed in Chapter Nine, so for now, we will focus on just the strategic implications. There are two aspects to this: balancing short-term and long-term company priorities and being unable to control all aspects of how your brand is built and experienced.

A Longer Outlook

Brand building is long term in nature. The interplay between brand management and resulting customer perceptions could evolve over a long period of time, especially given people's increasingly rushed, crowded, time-starved, and complex lives. Moreover, some actions, if memorable enough (positive or negative), can live in customers' minds and hearts for significantly longer than most companies' institutional memory, especially in these days of downsizing and high turnover rates.

Thus the prerequisites for a high-impact, brand-informed approach to strategy can be perceived as being in conflict with the short-term, quarter-to-quarter pressures that often dominate, especially in publicly traded companies. Before you get caught in that trap, shift the leadership mind-set and acknowledge that short-term actions, while understandable, could have long-term ramifications. The goal should be to promote a balance between short-term and long-term objectives and priorities, maintaining an equilibrium in decision making. Even with this change in philosophy agreed on, often the short-term priorities win, but at least the decisions are made with knowledge and, ideally, within the context of a longer-term vision for what you are trying to build through the brand.

Wrestling with Intangibles: That Uncomfortable Feeling

The other main stumbling block for senior management involves embracing and actively wrestling with the brand's intangibles, like customer perceptions, which are the driving force in defining a brand.

The fact is that management can control only certain company actions (such as marketing, advertising, product packaging, customer service call routing, and which employee is at the cash register). Management cannot control customer perceptions as a result of these actions.

Unfortunately, there is very rarely total congruence among company actions, their intended impact on others, and the way they are perceived. From our experience, these intangibles often make the Type A personalities who run most major enterprises uncomfortable. Helping senior management overcome this kind of discomfort will help set the stage for success.

Developing a Brand Lens Given a Company's Cultural Heritage

A company's cultural heritage is an important determinant in how a brand mind-set shift will be received and often sets the tone for its overall strategic agenda. Sales-driven cultures tend to be short term, tactically driven, and deal oriented. Motivating the sales force to produce more volume is the key cultural driver, even if it is counterbalanced with longer-term, relationship-oriented account management activities.

Engineering-driven cultures tend to value hard-core technical or scientific skills, whether leveraged in the name of basic technology or R&D or along more applied product or process lines. For them, it is generally about the drill bit and not the hole. These cultures tend to be deeply suspicious of marketing or brand-related concepts, most likely because they are totally foreign to their base of expertise.

Operationally driven cultures, whether the focus is on manufacturing, logistics, or distribution, are pragmatic, cost-focused, and execution-oriented. They see marketing as overly simplistic and not relevant. Planning-driven cultures tend to have more of a cautious, analytical, process-intensive, corporate-staff-driven feel. Creatively driven cultures value big ideas, vision, intuition, and inspiration.

You may recognize elements of these cultures within your own company. We are not saying that any of these are inherently wrong, just that they encourage an inside-out orientation. In other words, the company's internal culture and mind-set, whether they are driven through an engineer's product design, a merchant's intuition, or a COO's operational improvement measures, become the overriding driver of strategic decisions, with minimal external data, customer perspectives, or brand perceptions infused in the dialogue. Bringing a brand lens into these types of organizations can ultimately help cut through the clutter and make strategic decisions in support of your brand-building efforts.

Moving Beyond an Inside-Out Orientation

If an appropriate mind-set shift is made and cultural challenges are mitigated, there are a few leadership tools that help to incorporate brand into strategy discussions better. The first is the CEO's checklist, which describes the key organizational capabilities necessary to build a brand-driven business. The second is a conceptual framework, which we refer to as the credibility footprint, which can serve as a simple but powerful metaphor for the role of brand within business strategy. Third, we have identified a set of practical techniques that have worked with our clients for jump-starting a brand-driven approach to strategy. These techniques help to highlight both the enablers as well as the inhibitors experienced by some of the most successful and most challenged global industry brands.

THE CEO'S CHECKLIST: WHAT IS REQUIRED TO BRAND-ENABLE YOUR ORGANIZATION

The CEO needs to ensure that the organization is armed with the appropriate foundation for effective brand building. Regardless of where your company is starting, the CEO's checklist can serve as a snapshot of where you are trying to head: brand-driven success. It itemizes the critical capabilities required to brand-enable your organization and leverage your brand to realize your corporate vision. At the simplest level, it says you need to balance an ability to think strategically and operationalize consistently. "Think strategically" is shorthand for all the ways an organization applies world-class strategic brand thinking to market opportunities and business challenges. And "operationalize consistently" is shorthand for all the things an organization must do to deliver the brand and its promise consistently.

Your company needs to be able to balance both types of activities if you are to drive sustainable competitive advantage through your brand. And because the CEO is responsible for ensuring these capabilities are built, it is important that he or she understands the role brand plays in achieving business success.

The CEO's checklist for building a brand-driven business is set out in Figure 2.1. To develop it, we have drawn on the rich thinking of well-known brand strategists, including David Aaker, and distilled five key strategic capabilities for building a brand-driven business. These capabilities need to be developed so that they can be applied consistently over increasingly complex business domains and with a speed that was unthinkable as recently as ten or fifteen years ago. Because Chapters Three through Nine focus explicitly on operationalizing the brand, the rest of this chapter examines solely the "think strategically" component of the CEO's checklist.

Dynamic Customer Modeling

Dynamic customer modeling involves conducting analysis around customer segmentation, customer need states, customer behaviors, and influence patterns across different types of participants in a purchase process.

Although many companies understand the value of thinking about their customers, surprisingly few companies take the same rigorous approach to understanding their customers. "Businesses must find better ways to mirror their customers—big or small, sophisticated or casual, service-conscious or price-sensitive, occasional buyer or soul mate. There are countless ways to segment customers and address their specific needs. Start thinking about them."[1]

Think Strategically	Reference
• Dynamic customer modeling	Chapter Two
• Brand identity and positioning development	Chapter Two
• Brand portfolio management (architecture)	Chapter Two
• Multidisciplinary, general management perspective	Chapter Two
• Maintain brand portfolio relevance over time	Chapter Two

Operationalize Consistently	Reference
• Brand touchpoint analysis and prioritization	Chapter Three
• Multichannel marketing execution	Chapter Four
• Purchase and post-purchase brand delivery	Chapters Five and Six
• Brand-driven reengineering and brand metrics	Chapters Seven and Eight
• Employee brand assimilation and culture	Chapters Eight and Nine

Figure 2.1.   CEO's Checklist.

The challenge, as noted by James Champy, a pioneer of the reengineering movement, is that many companies believe that segmentation efforts alone equal customer modeling. The problem with this is that traditional segmentation is often static, somewhat superficial, and based on impersonal demographics. Going forward, a dynamic and compelling customer model has to be developed, which includes insight into how customers think and act within a category, make purchase decisions, use products or services, and see your brands fitting into their lives. With this type of information, you can make smart customer-driven decisions tied to bringing your brand's strategy to life.

Brand Identity and Positioning Development

Brand identity and positioning involves what many think of as traditional marketing skills. This includes an ability to distinguish features from benefits, an understanding of the interplay between rational, emotional, and self-expressive benefits, and an acknowledgment that positioning concepts should be differentiated (from competitors), relevant and compelling (to target customers and stakeholders), and ultimately ownable (for the company and brand trying to claim it). David Aaker's concept of brand identity recognizes that it is important for a firm to approach short-term positioning opportunities in the context of a longer-term aspirational vision for the brand.

Brand Portfolio Management

Brand portfolio management is the capability to manage multiple brands, subbrands, and other brand assets with potentially complex interrelationships and dependencies, in a way that provides optimal flexibility and leverage, given a company's growth objectives. A good example is from Denise Yohn, vice president of segment marketing and brand planning at Sony:

> There never has been a real marketing program for the Sony corporate brand. We continue to speak about Sony through its subbrands. We are trying to make these subbrands more emotive, connected to lifestyles, toward certain types of consumers rather than soley product oriented. For example, we are evolving the Walkman brand from meaning portable audio to a lifestyle brand for Gen Y. But the question remains: How do we develop platform brands that are all about creating customer value, and what product names should be underneath the platforms?

As the Sony experience indicates, managing a portfolio of multilevel brand relationships is difficult. It requires a solid understanding of the existing and potential boundaries of current brands and the ability to make in-the-portfolio investments, with an eye on all brands in the portfolio simultaneously.

In the past, many organizations have not managed their brand portfolios very strategically. Rather, their portfolios often just evolved, based on a series of ad hoc product launches (requiring a new brand launch) or organizational restructurings ("We separated the brands because that was how we were set up"). As a result, many brand expenditures and initiatives get overly expensive or redundant. Since brand portfolio management is an underdeveloped concept in so many companies, a company that develops this capability to its fullest extent has the potential to gain a significant edge over the competition.

Multidisciplinary, General Management Perspective

The fourth capability is well developed in companies with sophisticated brand management cultures like Anheuser-Busch, Disney, and Coca-Cola. In those companies, "brand people" are businesspeople. They are rigorously trained to understand the connections among financial, operational, and strategic priorities and brand strategy. They understand the ramifications of culture and organizational structure on effective brand building. Most important, they can bring well-balanced perspectives to bear, crafting multidisciplinary paths across all elements of a company's value chain. To be effective, every organization will need individuals with this type of strategic and brand-based capability.

Maintaining Brand Portfolio Relevance over Time

The fifth capability, an ability to maintain brand portfolio relevance over time, is the holy grail of brand management. Relevance is a key driver of whether a company can extract real economic value from its brand at any time. However, maintaining relevance over extended periods of time is a capability that even some of the greatest brand-driven businesses find difficult to achieve consistently. To succeed, it is necessary to weigh short-term brand leverage against the dangers of medium-term overextension like the Gap experienced in the early 2000s. Also required is a willingness to consider timely retirement of brands that are no longer relevant, like Oldsmobile. As Paula Dumas, director and vice president of marketing and development at Kodak, told us, Kodak understands the risks and opportunities and is tackling this issue head on:

> As with any other leading brand, the greatest threat for us is apathy and a failure to keep the brand relevant. My role is to redefine the Kodak brand within what we are now calling "info imaging sciences." The trend from traditional to digital is a dramatic change that will continue to be dramatic over the next twenty years. But a great brand can transcend technological change as long as its attributes are relevant.

Coke's performance in the late 1990s should serve as another cautionary tale around the dangers of complacency. Coke has been accused of focusing too much on short-term deal-making and financial reengineering at the expense of brand building, marketing, and new products, because it was lulled into believing that Pepsi, by the mid-1990s, was on an irreparable slide into irrelevancy. With Coke turning its back on brand building and thus its roots, Pepsi has been gaining brand relevancy and market share with younger consumers via products such as Mountain Dew, Code Red, and Sierra Mist and with health-conscious consumers through its Tropicana, Gatorade, and Aquafina brands.

THE CREDIBILITY FOOTPRINT: CREATING AN EXPLICIT ROLE FOR BRAND IN A COMPANY'S STRATEGIC DIALOGUE

Now we get to the most important issue: how to use these strategic brand constructs to change the way you approach business strategy within your company to create a high-priority and explicit role for brand in its strategic dialogue.

Standard Corporate Strategy Constructs

When done correctly, corporate strategy is ultimately about articulating a road map that is often bold and visionary yet attainable and tells a story about how a company plans to achieve continued profitable growth over time.

At the most basic level, most corporate strategy frameworks have two fundamental inputs: market opportunities and organizational competencies. Market opportunities are real or potential growth areas based on a careful analysis of competitor, customer, and market factors, as well as technological, environmental, and regulatory trends. These opportunities can be found within the core business, adjacent to the core business, or far afield from anything the company is currently doing.

Organizational competencies reflect what a company does well, focused on a combination of people, processes, and capabilities. A deep assessment of core competencies, highlighting points of leverage, opportunity, and fit, should start to point you to the unique and defensible competencies you have to leverage to give you a sustainable competitive advantage.

After this assessment is completed, the strategic debate should then center on which choices are available that best align attractive market opportunities with organizational competencies and, most important, whether any represent significant sources of competitive advantage.

Brand Portfolio Relevance

While these are often robust discussions, we think they could be improved by taking a key concept that may be buried deep in the analysis and making it explicit: brand portfolio relevance. Brand portfolio relevance is defined as the existing customer and stakeholder equity (meaningful feelings, thoughts, perceptions, or motivational power) resident in each of the company's brands. The most important reason for considering brand portfolio relevance as a critical input into strategic discussions is to get executives to consider the possibility that a more systematic, coordinated effort at leveraging the company's brand assets can actually enhance the company's ability to achieve its corporate strategy. By introducing brand portfolio relevance as a critical growth enabler, you should see your strategic growth options in a new light, as well as highlight opportunity areas that may not have even been under consideration.

Brand portfolio leverage becomes the extent to which that equity is externally perceived as relevant and credible and a basis for meaningful differentiation, in various contexts ranging from new opportunity areas for the firm to those which are on target with current, mainstream cash cow businesses.

We believe that by integrating a systematic and deep understanding of existing (and future) customer opportunities with the organization's commitment to build on its core competencies, a company has the potential to achieve the following goals:

- Meet its strategic objectives in a shorter time frame
- Lower the risk around particular strategic directions
- Uncover areas where extending the brand's leverage would provide strong ROI
- Uncover areas where extending the organizational competencies could provide strong ROI
- More quickly shed nonstrategic brand or competency initiatives

Put simply, the company will come up with better, more actionable, and more compelling strategy, led by the brand.

The Credibility Footprint

The credibility footprint becomes the intersection where brand portfolio relevance, organizational competencies, and market opportunities optimally align (see Figure 2.2). Understanding the existing credibility footprint as well as the potential directions that it can evolve in becomes the basis for assessing various strategic growth options that best help to achieve longer-term financial and strategic objectives. Clearly, the wider the credibility footprint is, the more strategic flexibility a business has. However, a company can get there only if it is continuously extending and strengthening its brand portfolio relevance and consistently aligning its organizational competencies with high-potential market opportunities.

Ultimately, all strategy conversations need to be about focus and prioritization. By introducing the concept of brand portfolio relevance, the conversation can be focused on how to move the company's present credibility footprint along four worthy exploration paths, all of which could end up helping a company achieve its longer-term strategy.

Path 1: Strengthen the Core

Be like Wal-Mart. Be like Southwest. Be like MTV. Be like Asahi. Be like Volkswagen.

You could choose to compete strategically by keeping your focus solely on your core business and continuing to be your best at it. Wal-Mart

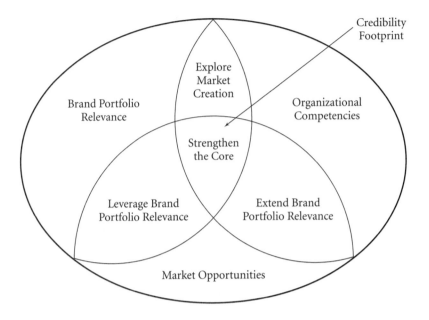

Figure 2.2.   The Credibility Footprint.

has focused ruthlessly on its core business, anchoring its brand around consistent low prices and friendly, approachable customer service, enshrined in ideas like Wal-Mart founder Sam Walton's "10-Foot Rule" ("I want you to promise that whenever you come within 10 feet of a customer, you will look him in the eye, greet him and ask him if you can help him").

In order to deliver against that brand promise, Wal-Mart developed a set of core processes and systems to drive efficiency throughout its entire operation. Incremental yet organic growth has come from rolling that model out into new areas in North America and gradually overseas. In addition, Wal-Mart has capitalized on its credibility around low prices to add additional profitable product lines like fresh groceries and electronics to its successful retail model.

When a company focuses on strengthening its core business and competencies, incremental growth opportunities can come in a variety of forms—for example:

• Taking existing concepts, products, or offers into new geographies (Southwest Airlines)

- Launching next-generation products or services that naturally strengthen the existing positioning of a company in its traditional markets (Volkswagen)
- Stealing market share from competitors by incrementally redefining the category in a way that allows you to capitalize on some new demographic or market trend (Asahi with the launch of Asahi Dry in the domestic Japanese beer market)

The life cycle of the company or offering, changes in customer motivations, and the dynamism of the competitive landscape will help effectively prioritize strategic growth opportunities. To do this, your company will need to sharpen its pencil, get alignment around its core competencies and best strategic opportunities, and develop specific strategies designed to deepen and strengthen the core brand.

Path 2: Extend Brand Portfolio Relevance

Be like Williams-Sonoma. Be like IBM. Be like Pepsi.

You could also choose to focus on growth opportunities in areas where you already have organizational competencies and an immediate market opportunity but minimal or no brand relevance. There are a number of paths to extend your brand relevance within your brand portfolio:

- Launching a new brand or subbrand (Oncor)
- Acquiring a brand that gives you credibility in that market space (Pepsi's acquisition of Gatorade)
- Actively repositioning an existing brand or subbrand to build credibility in that space (Sara Lee's Earthgrains brand)
- Some combination of all of these paths

These types of decisions get at the heart of brand portfolio management, the third capability on the CEO's checklist.

Companies like the Gap and Williams-Sonoma have leveraged existing competencies in specialty merchandising and developing retail concept stores to seize a market opportunity for reaching a more price-sensitive segment than was addressed by their namesake brands—thus launching Old Navy and Pottery Barn, respectively. Both thought that their existing brands would be stretched too far and spread too thin if they tried to attack this new market opportunity under the Gap or Williams-Sonoma brands.

In contrast, during the 1990s, IBM extended its brand portfolio relevance to take advantage of a market opportunity in information technology services and the Internet. IBM saw great market opportunities that aligned with its core competencies, understood that it needed to pursue this under the IBM brand (since it was selling to the same core enterprise information technology customer), but knew it could not do it without a major brand repositioning.

H&R Block saw similar challenges in its move toward offering a more diverse set of financial services to higher income clients. Karl Ploeger, vice president of creative service and brand management, states:

> As a company we had wonderful equity, but we're kind of a dusty brand. As our business model changes and we want to attract higher-income clients and prepare more complicated tax returns, we needed to refresh the brand, or we would hurt our ability to be successful.

Regardless of the brand portfolio strategy you deploy to achieve your objectives, failing to prove your brand relevance can be costly. Companies like Cadillac (low-end Cimarron), Xerox (personal computers), Clorox (laundry detergent), and legions of others can all speak to failed product launches and costly strategic retrenchments that resulted from having inadequate customer credibility and brand relevance to play in those markets. This is despite the fact that they had strong internal competencies and the market opportunity was fairly attractive.

Path 3: Leverage Brand Portfolio Relevance

Be like Home Depot. Be like Disney. Be like Virgin.

Alternatively, you could be in a position to leverage your brand relevance to take advantage of an existing market opportunity, but you may not currently have the necessary mix of organizational competencies to pursue this strategic alternative. This evolutionary path highlights future opportunities for your brand portfolio, especially if you believe that the necessary organizational competencies could be organically built over time, acquired, or obtained through partnering.

Home Depot, for example, is building on the most recognizable U.S. brand in home improvement by introducing a number of other concepts, notably EXPO Design Center, Villager's Hardware, and Home Depot Floor Store, each of which targets slightly different audiences and requires slightly different core competencies, which the company is growing organically. Disney leveraged its brand to move its business from animation to family entertainment through organic and acquisitive growth around competencies as diverse as land-based entertainment, travel, hospitality, PG- and R-rated movies, and specialty retailing. And Virgin leveraged its brand into industries as diverse as music, airlines, and water.

The question to ask is this: Given the relevancy of our current brand portfolio and our position with customers, where do we have credibility and permission to go in the future? This question alone may open up some new possibilities that shake up the conventional wisdom inside your firm.

Path 4: Explore (or Monitor) Market Development

Be like BP Solar. Be like IBM. Be like Sun.

Another option is to explore strategic paths that involve emerging market opportunities, which link back to your customer credibility and leverage the requisite organizational competencies. While the market opportunity itself has not yet fully taken form and the risk for you is that it may never materialize, if you immediately write the opportunity off, you will never know whether you could have influenced the shape, direction, or speed of the market evolution through your brand.

The bet that companies like BP and Shell are making in renewable-energy categories like wind and solar reflects this type of approach. Both in large part are focusing their efforts around creating new markets. These types of behaviors manifest themselves in high-technology categories all the time, as when Sun made significant bets to become the "dot" in "dot-com" (serving as the host for all Web sites) or with what Cisco is currently trying to do with voice-over Internet protocol. IBM's recent push around outsourced computing as the next utility is another attempt to create a new market. If you believe that through these sorts of activities you can change the pace of market evolution and you believe that you have a high probability of capturing the economic benefits and have them accrue to your brand portfolio, this could be an exciting and opportunistic place to play.

USING BRAND TO INFORM OTHER STRATEGIC PRIORITIES

Our guess is that you are probably thinking: "Great, I get it, and I see how this type of thinking could benefit my business. But how can I make room for brand on an already crowded strategic agenda?" This is a fair concern. Senior management is already addressing a host of pressing issues such as continuous innovation, cost cutting, value chain integration, leadership development, CRM, reengineering, globalization, and e-business.

But being able to apply a brand lens to strategic issues such as operational optimization, innovation, or value chain integration increases the probability that your efforts will ultimately be value creating instead of value destroying. Applying a brand lens will allow you to keep your focus sharp (see Figure 2.3) and drive toward better results. We will discuss two interesting examples, one around cost cutting and the other around networked organizational models, to bring this brand-driven point to life.

Marrying Brand and Cost-Cutting Initiatives Leads to Better Outcomes

On the surface, it may be counterintuitive to think of focusing simultaneously on operational optimization and strategic brand building. Operational optimization, at its worst, is seen as a euphemism for ruthless cost cutting and appears diametrically opposed to brand building,

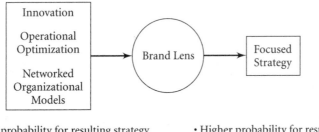

• Higher probability for resulting strategy to be neutral or value destroying
• Higher risk

• Higher probability for resulting strategy to be value creating
• Lower risk

Figure 2.3.   Using a Brand Lens to Inform Other Strategic Priorities.

which to most CFOs is about incremental spending. But by applying a brand lens to those strategic decisions, you will stay focused on optimizing the right value drivers while pruning away less relevant but equally costly activities.

The best example of this that surfaced in Prophet's 2002 Best Practices study was Amazon's efforts around customer service. The mandate was simple: customer service costs were too high on an absolute basis as well as on a cost-to-serve per order basis; find a way to lower them! There were many approaches that the team could have taken that would have generated short-term cost savings. (For example, Amazon could have reduced the number of customer service representatives, shut down a call center, and put more barriers between the customer and access to service, but all of these options would have been at the expense of long-term brand equity and, likely, growth.

This team, however, had internalized the implications of Amazon's brand promise, which is about friendly, accessible, reliable, and personalized access to product at a fair price. Rather than take one of the easy paths, they employed a rigorous process designed to identify the root causes of customer service requests and look for opportunities to reengineer these issues, always keeping the brand front and center. What Amazon found, for example, was that the confirmation e-mail promise of shipment within two to four days produced a fair number of inbound service requests from customers who wanted greater specificity. If Amazon could uncover a way to narrow that shipment window and communicate it clearly, it could achieve a significant reduction in that type of customer service request. So Amazon attacked that issue head on.

This process was repeated over and over again, ultimately resulting in a complete overhaul of the customer service process, with significantly more self-service components. Costs were reduced, operations were optimized, the customer on average felt well served, and Amazon's brand relevance was strengthened. The process may not always be this clean, but the lesson is clear. Applying a brand lens to operational optimization processes can help ensure their long-term effectiveness.

Brand and Networked Organizational Models

As more companies experiment with looser affiliations of networked organizational relationships, value chains are being reconfigured and companies are outsourcing more significant business processes. The benefits of focus, speed, flexibility, and leverage in the networked organization have been much discussed. But with these benefits come a new set of challenges around things like control, consistency, coordination, and communication. Because these challenges strike right at the heart of effective long-term brand building, pursuing networked organizational initiatives without a parallel strategic focus on brand impact would be a very dangerous path to move down.

IBM's January 2002 decision to pull out of personal computer manufacturing with its $5 billion outsourcing deal with Sanmina illuminates these interdependencies. IBM could have decided to get out of the PC business altogether, but it explicitly chose not to. Rather, senior management stated that it was important from a customer and brand relevance perspective for the IBM brand to stay in the PC business. IBM's decision allows it to "sell a full line of personal computers" while "still controlling marketing and design."[2] If IBM had not taken strategic brand considerations into account, its decision to get out of PC manufacturing could have been structured in very different, and ultimately unacceptable, ways, exposing the business to unnecessary levels of risk.

JUMP-STARTING A BRAND-INFORMED APPROACH TO STRATEGY

Over the past three to five years, companies as diverse as Goldman Sachs, Philips, Accenture, British Petroleum, and UBS have begun trying to integrate brand with strategy for the first time in either a new way or with renewed vigor. Since for many this has represented a fundamental shift in orientation, language, and behavior, these companies have had to experiment with many different ways of jump-starting this process and getting the changes to stick. Like any other organizational change effort, elevating the brand's presence in strategic discussions takes time, leadership, and patience.

Prophet's 2002 Best Practices study uncovered five jump-starting tactics that companies are using to infuse brand into strategy discussions:

- Turbo-charged marketing capability
- Cross-functional brand councils
- "Oscar-winning" strategic pilot initiatives
- Process assessment, innovation, and policing
- Senior leadership brand boot camp

Sometimes a tactic is used independently; sometimes it is used with others. But in aggregate, these represent a comprehensive set of approaches that CEOs should consider carefully in the context of the company's cultural starting point, its major areas of pain, and anticipated resistance to selling in the brand as a driver of business strategy.

Turbo-Charged Marketing Capability

This tactic involves elevating or redefining the role of the traditional marketing function. It may mean creating new brand management roles or new corporate brand teams, upgrading the quality of the people in the resulting organizations, and hiring in or promoting a strategic, executive-team-level individual into a CMO-like role. Often this means a dramatic evolution away from the current and often silo-focused marketing communications activities. All of these changes are designed to help drive effective brand building by allowing new entities to effect meaningful change.

One critical decision to make here is whether a strong insider or a strong outsider should take on the CMO role. Clearly, strong insiders bring personal relationships, organizational context, and industry expertise but may be lacking in sophisticated marketing or brand asset management knowledge. Insider or not, the individual should have a track record of innovation and be a high-energy change agent and a data-driven decision maker.

John Saunders, currently in charge of corporate marketing at T. Rowe Price, is finding himself in the role of strong outsider brought in as change agent, for the second time. The first time was his experience as head of strategic initiatives for Prudential. When asked about how both organizations strove to make brand-driven transformations, John was clear in that it started with "a commitment at the top" that dictated an external change agent be brought in "to run the play." He continued, "The initial phase would be the change agent aligning the disparate parts of the organization around the notion of brand. It would usually lead to some form of market-driven reorganization, which allowed us to service strategic customer segments better and more profitably."

Another important decision involves how much authority to give the turbo-charged function and how soon. Some of our clients have used a phased approach in which the turbo-charged role migrates from facilitator (no enforcement power, but bringing people together) to coordinator (has some veto power and resource allocation authority) to leader (holistically manages and controls everything that revolves around the brand). There are inherent dangers in either lingering too long at or accelerating too quickly through the facilitator or coordinator phase.

Centralized Versus Decentralized Approaches

The complexity in turbo-charging the marketing function is compounded when it involves the creation of a new role at corporate, especially in large decentralized organizations. Consistency is a critical success factor for effective long-term brand building and is ostensibly easier to achieve with strong centralization. Yet many companies have used decentralization to encourage market-focused entrepreneurial innovation and brand accountability, much to their credit and success. This tactic should not be seen as taking that away, but it must be properly positioned to the organization as an enabler in achieving longer-term goals and objectives and not as one more layer of hierarchy.

Again the experience of John Saunders at T. Rowe Price is instructive here:

> T. Rowe Price has typically let the divisions run relatively independently. At the onset of our brand initiative, the challenge was to overcome this silo mentality to arrive at one brand for the organization. T. Rowe Price also took a relatively large step to hire a head of corporate marketing. This was significant in the fact that T. Rowe Price has very few corporate roles. Thus by acknowledging that the marketing function has corporate oversight, the CEO was acknowledging the importance of brand consistency as a key strategic goal.

Cross-Functional Executive Brand Councils

Many companies are creating cross-functional executive brand councils (which will be discussed in more detail in Chapter Nine) as a way to drive strategic brand thinking deeper into the organization more quickly. These highly visible bodies can serve as effective two- to three-year bridging mechanisms until a brand-informed approach to strategy gains traction. By creating executive brand councils that include multiple functional areas, a very clear message is sent to the organization that says brand is the responsibility of the entire organization, not just marketing.

"Oscar-Winning" Strategic Pilot Initiatives

This involves selecting some highly visible strategic brand initiatives to push forward, allowing key people to experience the new brand-informed approach over time. Sometimes it works to take a more aggressive approach by focusing on articulating a brand vision, brand positioning, or brand architecture for the entire organization.

For some, though, this type of comprehensive brand approach may be the wrong place to start. We believe it can be just as effective to focus on very specific business problems—either a business or product line in crisis, a new growth segment or offering, a distribution channel in flux, or a new joint venture, partnering, or acquisition opportunity. Whatever the situation is, the goal is to demonstrate how attacking this strategic business issue in a brand-informed way leads to different and more productive ways of thinking about the specific brand challenges, as well as to a better overall outcome.

Process Assessment, Senior Leadership Boot Camp, and Other Tactics

Other companies have made a decision to lead brand-driven efforts with a focus on process or education. A process approach can involve picking specific elements of the brand plan, like global communications or new product or service development, and assessing employees' existing behaviors in the light of this new brand-informed approach to strategy.

At other times, brand education is a great place to start. A brand boot camp can be designed to equip senior management to be more effective in a brand-informed strategic environment, using some combination of outside reading, facilitated discussion, and hands-on problem solving. Brand immersion is a great learning vehicle, but while getting this kind of time commitment from executives would send a huge signal to the rest of the organization, the likelihood of making it happen for most is minimal.

COMMON ROADBLOCKS THAT PREVENT YOU FROM GETTING TO THE STARTING LINE

The jump-starting process, to be clear, refers to the beginning steps that a CEO can take to start cultivating a strategic brand competency inside the executive team. This alone does not guarantee that the company will become a brand-driven business but it will at least get you to the starting line. There are a number of common roadblocks that can prevent you from being successful in even this first step.

For instance, an organization's cultural heritage, especially as it relates to things like language, credibility, power, and the word brand, are sometimes the thorniest issues to manage. At TXU, a global energy provider, the word *brand* clearly did not work; people's eyes glazed over and the conversation shut down whenever it was brought up. But when the brand team started to speak to people in terms of "aligning inside behaviors with the personality of the company," people started to understand. To achieve this kind of shift, you need individuals championing the brand who understand the nuances of their organizational culture and thus are able to break down barriers and overcome inertia. In our 2002 Best Practices research, a participant from a major health insurance provider drove this home: "The CEO of Procter & Gamble may be very encouraged by what he can gain. The head of my company is more concerned by what he can lose. You need to use dialogue that the leader can understand. Otherwise they get overburdened with marketing-speak."

Organizational credibility is a tougher issue to manage. Sometimes this challenge can be handled in terms of how the role of brand is defined. If it continues to be too narrowly cast, as reflected in the vice chairman's story at the beginning of the chapter, you will be in trouble. Often, the issue is that the organization's brand activities revolve around "brand police" or "logo cops." If this becomes how others think of brand, then the predominant associations for brand asset management inside the firm will be negative, and your ability to leverage strategic brand thinking to develop your business will be minimal.

If organizational credibility remains an issue, maybe you have the wrong person in the job. If so, be ready to fix that, and as soon as possible. One or two highly visible failures may just reinforce preconceived notions that this "brand thing" was a waste of time.

CEO-LEVEL COMMITMENT TO A BRAND-INFORMED APPROACH TO STRATEGY

So what does CEO-level commitment to this new strategic thought process look like? It begins with the recognition that customers are complex and respond to situations, interactions, and relationships on many different levels—emotional, intellectual, rational, visceral, and social.

Some CEOs get this level of complexity and understand how to create room for it. At Xerox, the new CEO appears to be just such a person. She is elevating the brand voice throughout the value chain, mandating its involvement in the development of all current go-to-market strategies, and encouraging Xerox to have brand and research play a stronger role in new product development. Regardless of whether she believes that brand can be used to transform the entire organization, she sees how she can insert brand thinking into high-impact areas to drive out better results.

We believe a strategic focus on brand can and should drive sustainable growth and lasting change. As James Collins and Jerry Porras note in *Built to Last: Successful Habits of Visionary Companies,* "A company must have a core ideology to become a visionary company. It must also have an unrelenting drive for progress. And finally, it must be well designed as an organization to preserve and stimulate progress, with all key pieces working in alignment."[3]

Clearly, brand values and brand ideas need to form part of that core ideology. When done well, they inspire and become part of that vision and the unrelenting drive for progress. But just as important is the second part of the quotation, about the key pieces working in alignment: the best strategy in the world will fail without the ability to operationalize the brand effectively.

Part of this challenge, covered in the chapters in Part Two, will be to understand how to prioritize and operationalize the brand to drive long-term brand and company success.

Controlling Your Touchpoints by Operationalizing Your Brand

CHAPTER THREE

Understanding and Prioritizing High-Impact Brand Touchpoints

I magine you are in marketing at Whirlpool, attending an important meeting with the company's senior executives. Toward the end of the meeting, you are asked a simple question: "What are the different ways in which our brand interacts with the marketplace?" You get a little uncomfortable as you wonder to yourself, "Is this a trick question?" So, very deliberately, you start to list all of the brand-building activities that the company invests in and manages:

1. Print and television advertising that we use to promote our different models and appliances

2. In-store displays to help educate consumers at the point of sale

3. Our Web site, which helps to educate consumers before they make the purchase

4. Coupons and specials to drive more traffic into the store

5. Direct mail that we send out regularly, through our database marketing efforts, that helps us to keep our name in front of current customers

6. Our new e-mail-intensive communications plan, which enables us to communicate more frequently and cost-effectively with prospects and customers alike

7. Our retail partners, which actually have the most influence on the sale as they guide consumers through their decision process

Just as you think to yourself, "Well, that wasn't so bad!" the head of operations asks, "Is that it?" You think a little harder and remember a few more ways the marketplace interacts with your brand:

8. The bill that is sent out every month to customers on monthly pay plans

9. Service technicians who go out to homes to make repairs to appliances

10. Technicians who install the newly purchased appliance (arguably a walking billboard for Whirlpool, as they are in someone's home for many hours)

11. Customer service agents at the call center who handle all of the difficult questions that get asked

12. Other customer service representatives who are asked for helpful cooking hints to be used with their Whirlpool appliance

13. The person who sets up the financing of the appliance for customers buying on a payment plan

14. Partners like Proctor & Gamble and Tupperware that are going to market with our brand through co-branded partnerships

15. Whirlpool's vendors and suppliers, who can influence our image, directly and indirectly, through our relationships

16. Homebuilders, contractors, and architects, all of whom have a lot of influence on what appliance brand gets installed

"OK," you think to yourself, "now I've nailed it!" Then you hear from the head of human resources: "Is that it?" You think a little harder and remember still a few more:

17. Our sixty-one thousand employees who are in a position to tell at least a few new people every day that they work for Whirlpool

18. People who are being recruited on college and business school campuses around the world

19. Former company employees, who are now our alumni

Now you are getting a little exasperated. Every time you think you have the list complete, someone challenges you. The next is the head of global communications: "Is that it?" You think a little harder, and you realize you forgot some of the most important:

20. All of Whirlpool's community work with Habitat for Humanity, which generates a lot of favorable publicity

21. The day-to-day publicity that we secure for our senior executives in top-tier publications

22. The sponsorships, local and national, that help to build Whirlpool awareness

23. Our sales force, constantly in front of new distributors trying to sell the Whirlpool story

24. The dozens of analysts who track the company and issue reports on Whirlpool at least every quarter

25. All the speeches the executive team gives at branding, new product, and sales conferences

26. *Consumer Reports* and other magazines that rate our new products when they are launched

27. The annual meeting with shareholders and the CEO's and CFO's regular updates with analysts.

28. The annual report

29. The regular internal newsletters

Before you get challenged again, you come up with four more:

30. All of the new product launches brought out by R&D, like the Personal Valet, which help to create news and buzz

31. The Inspired Cooking class offered to help customers get the most out of their culinary experience

32. The customer satisfaction survey conducted after every purchase

33. The actual Whirlpool customers.

Almost immediately everyone starts to clap. You are the first to catalogue thirty-three ways that the Whirlpool brand touches its various stakeholders: consumers, employees, shareholders, analysts, media, partners, distributors, and others. You nailed it! You know deep inside that there are probably a few more, but you are pretty sure that the thirty-three you came up with is close to an exhaustive list.

As you get up to leave, you hear someone's voice and recognize that there is one last question coming. You rack your brains for an answer to another question regarding how the Whirlpool brand interacts with its customers and stakeholders. Instead, you hear the hardest question yet: "How well are we doing at prioritizing and managing those thirty-three interactions so that we are maximizing our brand's and business' performance?"

THE POWER OF BRAND TOUCHPOINTS

The dialogue that began this chapter is purely illustrative, but we do believe that it is the type of discussion that will become more commonplace as companies recognize that there are multiple ways of reaching or touching customers. We call each of these touches a *brand touchpoint*. A brand touchpoint is simply defined as all of the different ways that your brand interacts with, and makes an impression on, customers, employees, and other stakeholders. Every action, tactic, and strategy you undertake to reach customers and stakeholders, whether it is through advertising, a cashier, a customer service call, or a referral, represents a touchpoint.

For most companies, coming up with a list like Whirlpool's is challenging enough. Actually figuring out what to do with the list is even more daunting. Determining how to coordinate all of those brand touchpoints most likely feels impossible.

The important thing to remember is that all brand touchpoints leave an impression of your brand on customers, employees, or stakeholders, whether you want them to or not. The question that needs to be addressed then is this: Do you want to reinforce and strengthen what your brand stands for by identifying, prioritizing, and ultimately controlling *all* of your customer and stakeholder brand touchpoints, or do you want the brand touchpoints to control you and risk denigrating your brand and its promise?

This chapter is aimed at helping you begin to identify your current brand touchpoints, as well as how to prioritize and manage each within your organization. Importantly, the discussion will also help call out which touchpoints you should focus on in the future. This chapter is the foundation for the in-depth discussions we will have in Chapters Four through Six on specific brand touchpoint strategies and the most effective way to maximize your brand's (and your company's) chances for success.

A BRAND TOUCHPOINT OVERVIEW: THE FOUR BRAND TOUCHPOINT CATEGORIES

Touchpoints can be segmented into four somewhat distinct categories that generally represent the different dimensions of a brand's relationship with a customer:

• Pre-purchase touchpoints—a collection of brand touchpoints (the company employs) that significantly influences whether a prospect will place your brand into his or her final purchase consideration set on the way to making a purchase. Typical brand touchpoints here are advertising, word-of-mouth, direct mail, and the Internet.

• Purchase touchpoints—all of the brand touchpoints that move a customer from consideration of your brand to purchasing it. Typical brand touchpoints here are direct field sales, physical stores, and customer representative contact.

• Post-purchase touchpoints—all of the brand touchpoints that are leveraged after the sale, including the actual product or service usage, to help reinforce the purchase decision. Typical brand touchpoints here are installation, customer service, warranty and rebate activities, customer satisfaction surveys, regular maintenance, and reminders of product or service innovations that have taken place tied to your brand.

• Influencing touchpoints—all of the brand touchpoints that indirectly help to make an impression of the brand on its customers and various stakeholders such as annual reports, analysts' reports, current and past customers, and recruiting materials.

The Brand Touchpoint Wheel

These four brand touchpoint categories are represented in the brand touchpoint wheel (see Figure 3.1), in which the center of the wheel is divided into segments representing the pre-purchase, purchase, and post-purchase categories, with the influencing brand touchpoints encircling them.

There are many gray areas when you try to segment all of your brand touchpoints neatly into one of these four categories. For instance, where does community involvement go? Is community involvement used more to keep your brand top of mind and customers feeling good that they purchased a brand that has high values and morals? Or is it a pre-purchase touchpoint that influences a customer's decision to include your brand in the decision set? Are sales representatives relevant just during the purchase experience? Or are they equally relevant after the purchase in keeping up the relationship between the brand and the customer over time to guarantee future sales?

The answer is yes to all of the above questions. We have used the wheel metaphor to underscore the fact that the relationship a brand

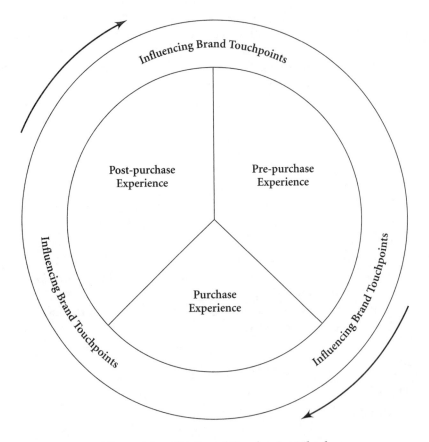

Figure 3.1.   The Brand Touchpoint Wheel.

has with a customer is ongoing and, you hope, never-ending. It is a never-ending journey to secure and maintain a deep and lasting relationship with a customer over time. We talk about this as the brand-customer relationship.

Regardless of which category each brand touchpoint fits into, prioritizing brand touchpoints will help you ensure that you are spending the right amount of attention and resources on those that your customers deem most important and relevant. This, in turn, will help in building longer-term brand relationships and deep brand loyalty, which ultimately affects the bottom line.

Figure 3.2 shows how we would categorize the thirty-three hypothetical Whirlpool brand touchpoints.

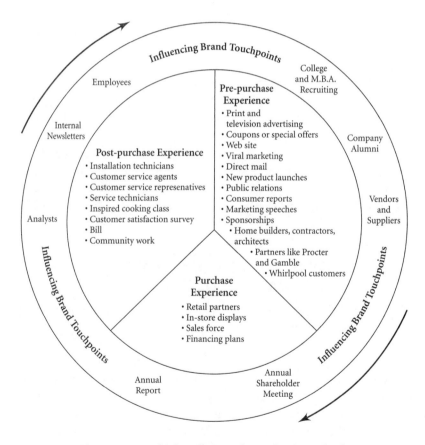

Figure 3.2.   Whirlpool's Brand Touchpoint Wheel.

At least half of the brand touchpoints we listed earlier may seem to belong in more than one place on the wheel. The primary concern, however, is not where each has landed but making sure that your list is complete and you have had an appropriate level of discussion about each touchpoint.

A Little More on Influencing Brand Touchpoints

In the definitions and the Whirlpool example, several of the brand touchpoints are lumped into a category called *influencing brand touchpoints.* Although we will not spend much time on this group of brand touchpoints in this chapter, we believe one of the bigger commitments a company has to make to build the brand over time is to look at all influencing brand touchpoints that may have an impact on your brand-building efforts. Although these influencing brand touchpoints are usually not given their just due in brand-building efforts, each can have a tremendous impact on both current and potential customers and stakeholders.

For instance, your employees are walking advertisements for your brand and thus could represent one of your more powerful influencing touchpoints as they talk about their job (the brand) to friends, family, and other colleagues regularly. Even more powerful for many companies, especially in service industries, is that employees are often the most visible representation of brand. Think about Southwest Airlines, Nordstrom, and American Express, where the delivery of the service is in reality the delivery of the brand.

BRINGING BRAND TOUCHPOINT ASSESSMENT, PRIORITIZATION, AND STRATEGY TO LIFE

The overall process for conducting companywide touchpoint assessment consists of four main steps:

1. *Internal assessment.* Identify high-level brand touchpoint priorities through an internal brand touchpoint assessment, aimed at eliciting internal perspectives regarding the most important brand touchpoints and assessing how well the company can deliver the brand via these touchpoints and specific capabilities required to succeed in the future.

2. *External assessment.* Conduct an external brand touchpoint needs and wants assessment, aimed at understanding what is most important to current and potential customers and stakeholders as they build a relationship with the company's brand. This includes a company versus competitor brand touchpoint assessment as a primary input.

3. *Analysis.* Map internal and external brand touchpoint assessments against one another to determine the current priority, performance, capability, and needs gaps that exist, as well as the primary areas to focus on going forward.

4. *Action plan.* Develop an overall brand touchpoint strategy, including identification of the internal resources and support needed to bring the brand touchpoint strategy to life, all aimed at helping the company reach its longer-term strategic goals and objectives.

This four-step brand touchpoint assessment and strategy process, set out in Figure 3.3, will help a company better understand how critical it is to uncover and manage every touchpoint its brand has in pursuit of making sure that every time current or potential customers or stakeholders touch the brand, they have the same experience, regardless of how they access the brand.

The assessment and strategy process can be completed in as little as three months or take as long as twelve, depending on the geographies and segments covered, the resources committed to the effort, and the buy-in process required to take action as a result of this effort.

For the rest of this chapter, as well as for Chapters Four through Six, we will continue to focus on implementing this brand touchpoint methodology for current and potential customers, since they are almost always the most important stakeholders a company is concerned about. However, if your company's success is highly dependent on your relationships with multiple stakeholders, we highly recommend conducting brand touchpoint assessments for each stakeholder entity.

Touchpoint Assessment and Strategy Team

To maximize effectiveness, we recommend a core team of three or four cross-functional individuals to drive the assessment process (see Figure 3.4). Ideally, each representative would be totally dedicated to the

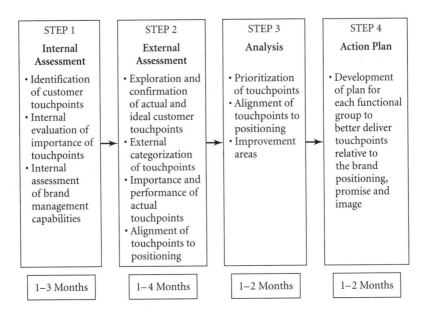

STEP 1	STEP 2	STEP 3	STEP 4
Internal Assessment	External Assessment	Analysis	Action Plan
• Identification of customer touchpoints • Internal evaluation of importance of touchpoints • Internal assessment of brand management capabilities	• Exploration and confirmation of actual and ideal customer touchpoints • External categorization of touchpoints • Importance and performance of actual touchpoints • Alignment of touchpoints to positioning	• Prioritization of touchpoints • Alignment of touchpoints to positioning • Improvement areas	• Development of plan for each functional group to better deliver touchpoints relative to the brand positioning, promise and image
1–3 Months	1–4 Months	1–2 Months	1–2 Months

Figure 3.3.   Brand Touchpoint Assessment and Strategy Process.

team while the brand touchpoint assessment is in process. Importantly, an extended team that is not fully dedicated to driving the process but still actively involved would also participate in the effort. This extended team would include all functional areas not represented by the core team. Finally, there would be an executive steering committee for this effort, made up of top executives within the company, that would provide overall direction, guidance, and governance to the process.

There are three primary benefits of having this type of representation and participation on your brand touchpoint assessment team:

- No one will be able to give better insights into a specific functional area's role relative to certain brand touchpoints than those who work in that area.

- Because the results of the brand touchpoint assessment must ultimately be activated by the functional areas, there is no better salesperson than a touchpoint team member from a specific functional area (such as customer service, sales, or marketing).

- Without senior management support and participation, this whole initiative will risk sitting on a shelf and not getting imple-

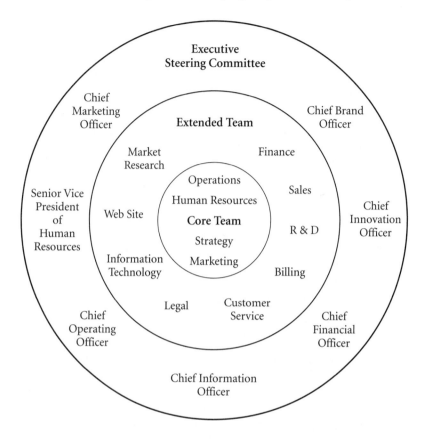

Figure 3.4.   Brand Touchpoint Assessment and Strategy Team Construct.

mented. With senior management support and participation, the likelihood that this type of investment will pay off is high.

STEP 1: CONDUCTING AN INTERNAL BRAND TOUCHPOINT ASSESSMENT

The first step in our four-step process is to conduct an internal touch-point assessment. This assessment helps elicit a view of brand touchpoints from within the organization and set up a gap analysis to compare what is learned internally with what the market tells you externally in Step 2.

To begin the internal assessment, it is important that the core and extended team try to capture all of the brand touchpoints your organization is currently leveraging, either explicitly (you are aware that you are leveraging this touchpoint and try to control it as best as possible) or implicitly (you are unaware you are leveraging this touchpoint and have no control over it).

By making an initial attempt at mapping your brand touchpoint wheel, you are achieving two important objectives. First, you are getting into the appropriate mind-set for conducting this kind of assessment. Second, you will use this brand touchpoint wheel as a template not only to share with other internal constituencies but also as the placeholder that continues to get filled in as you proceed through the four steps.

There are two parts to the internal brand touchpoint assessment that help shape an organization's understanding of the different touchpoints being employed. The first part includes conducting interviews with senior management and different functional areas within your company. The results of these interviews help to outline the different ways in which that functional area explicitly touches the customer in these day-to-day jobs.

The second part of the assessment involves integrating all of the senior management, functional area, and internal planning document review findings into a single point of view of the company's current and desired touchpoint strategies. This includes rating current effectiveness and uncovering gaps in perceptions, capabilities, and resources required to implement a successful brand touchpoint strategy. It is this second part of the assessment that indicates how close (or far) you are from being able to deliver on the eventual brand touchpoint recommendations and strategy.

Understanding All of the Brand Touchpoints That a Company Employs Today

The first part of the internal brand touchpoint assessment is aimed at answering the following companywide questions:

- What are all of the different ways in which your organization believes it touches the customer today?
- What are all of the different ways in which your organization would like to touch the customer going forward to achieve its longer-term corporate and brand goals and objectives?

- Who owns each brand touchpoint? How is each brand touchpoint managed today? Is the development of the brand touchpoint linked to the brand strategy?

- How does the organization overall, and each functional group owning the brand touchpoint, assess its performance on each brand touchpoint (1) relative to internal expectations, (2) relative to external expectations, (3) relative to the competition, and (4) relative to the stated goals and objectives?

- What will it take for the organization to improve its performance with respect to certain brand touchpoints to help close the gap between internal and current performance and market expectations?

SENIOR MANAGEMENT ASSESSMENT INTERVIEWS. With senior management, the objectives of the internal brand touchpoint assessment interviews are straightforward: you want them to articulate their perceptions of the strategy for the brand and how they envision the company bringing the brand to life today and tomorrow to meet longer-term goals and objectives. By virtue of the topics covered in these interviews, many senior executives may get uncomfortable in trying to answer all of the questions that follow. This is because they may not naturally think about the brand as an important strategic driver for achieving their longer-term strategic goals and objectives. In addition, the likelihood that they think and talk in terms of assessing brand touchpoints is low. But we contend that this is exactly the point of these interviews.

The initial questions to think about when you are conducting the internal brand touchpoint assessment with senior management should generally be broken down into three sections:

Brand Strategy Questions

- What are your specific goals and objectives for building the brand?

- What is your brand's image today, and how well does that align with what your brand is trying to achieve over the long term?

- What are your brand's strengths and weaknesses in relation to the competition?

- How well is your brand positioned today? Is your positioning relevant to customers and differentiated from the competition?

• How would you rate your brand-building efforts to date? What are your brand-building strengths and weaknesses?

Brand-Customer Target Segments

• What are the different market segments we serve?

• Which are the most important segments to focus on today? How might that change tomorrow?

• What do you think are the most effective ways to reach your target segments?

• How would you prioritize those target segments?

• What do you think are the key purchase drivers for each segment? What ultimately determines which brand they purchase?

• What do you believe are the key purchase influencers for this segment, meaning not necessarily a driver but something that helps influence the provider they want to be associated with?

• During the actual purchase process, what makes for a highly satisfactory purchase process versus an adequate purchase process versus a dissatisfying purchase process?

• In what ways are we continuing to build relationships with these customers after the sale?

• What are the direct drivers and indirect influencers with respect to brand loyalty?

The final part of these senior management interviews directly links back to the overall objectives of the internal touchpoint assessment. These questions specifically get back to what you are trying to achieve in the second part of Step 1: assessing the organization's ability to execute the eventual recommended brand touchpoint strategy.

Brand Touchpoint Effectiveness

• Who owns each brand touchpoint?

• How effectively is each brand touchpoint managed today relative to internal expectations?

• How effectively is each brand touchpoint managed today relative to external expectations?

• How effectively is each brand touchpoint managed today relative to the competition?

- How effectively is each brand touchpoint managed today relative to the stated goals and objectives?
- What will it take for the organization to improve its performance regarding certain brand touchpoints to help close the gap between the brand's internal and current performance and market expectations?

With the answers to all three types of questions in hand, you now have a good idea of what senior management is trying to achieve through their brand-building efforts—that is, you can see what senior management's specific brand-driven goals and objectives are. You also now know what brand touchpoints senior management believes either directly or indirectly influence the relationship that customers have with your brand.

At the end of these interviews, we suggest you create a touchpoint wheel, like the example shown in Figure 3.2, to help chart all of the brand touchpoints that senior management cited within their interviews.

FUNCTIONAL AREA ASSESSMENT INTERVIEWS. In addition to interviewing senior management, your assessment needs to include interviews with representatives from all of the organization's functional areas, as each touches the customer either directly or indirectly, albeit in different ways. These interviews should include discussions on the brand touchpoints that each specific functional area is responsible for developing and implementing. These discussions with functional area representatives have the following primary goals:

- Identification of all the different ways in which their functional area touches the customer
- Perceptions of the internal strengths and weaknesses in delivering their particular brand touchpoints to the customer
- The degree to which functional areas understand the company's longer-term corporate and brand strategies
- The degree to which functional areas understand the brand positioning
- The degree to which functional areas believe they are supplied with adequate resources, training, and support to deliver their brand touchpoints effectively

• The degree to which the functional areas include the brand
strategy in their annual planning processes

To get this information, you should ask questions similar to those
outlined for senior management.

In essence, you are trying to get a deep understanding of whether
the processes are in place to ensure that the brand is being incorporated into each functional area brand touchpoint. For example, when
talking to those responsible for Web site development, you would ask
how they are incorporating the brand vision, positioning, and identity in the annual planning process, the creative design, development,
testing, and tracking of the site.

Developing a Single Internal Point of View

Once all internal interviews are completed and analyzed, your goal in
part 2 is to integrate the senior management and functional area perspectives into a single snapshot of how the company manages and
controls its various brand touchpoints across customer segments. Obviously, there will be gaps between the senior management and functional area views at times, along with countless "I didn't know thats,"
as you get deeper into your integrated internal touchpoint assessment
and perspective.

Figure 3.5 shows how this integration might look, based on a project we conducted with a retail bank. For purposes of this book, we
included only a few of its touchpoints rather than them all. This figure categorizes the data from our interviews according to whether
a brand touchpoint had an impact on the pre-purchase, purchase,
or post-purchase experience or on an influencer segment. We used a
straightforward ranking system to assign a high, medium, or low effectiveness rating to each brand touchpoint and the representative
topic analyzed.

This type of rating scale will start to give an organization an idea
of how it is performing against the brand touchpoints that are deemed
most important (again from an internal perspective) and will provide
the basis to do a deeper analysis later in the process (once compared
to the external perspective).

Some interesting findings for this retail bank emerge from Figure 3.5:

• Overall, marketing appears to be much more prepared in terms
of brand strategy and positioning understanding to incorporate

Overall Organizational Scorecard

Functional Group	Respective Brand Touchpoints	Functional Area Assessment						Senior Management	
		Perceived Customer Delivery	Brand/Business Strategy Understanding	Positioning Understanding	Resources' Brand Support	Planning Process' Brand Alignment	Overall Rating as Improvement Area	Overall Touchpoint Effectiveness	Gap Identification
Pre-purchase Experience									
Account Management	Cold Calling	Low	Low	Medium	Low	Low	High	Medium	Medium
Marketing	Advertising	High	Medium	High	Medium	High	Low	High	Low
Marketing	Free Seminars	Medium	Medium	Medium	Low	High	Medium	High	Medium
Purchase Experience									
Account Management	One-on-One Meetings	High	Medium	Low	Low	Low	High	Low	High
Marketing	Marketing Collateral	Medium	High	Medium	High	Medium	Medium	Medium	Low
Marketing	Product and Service Assortment	Low	Medium	Medium	High	Medium	Medium	Medium	Low
Post-purchase Experience									
Customer Service	Client Support	Medium	Low	Low	High	Low	High	Low	High
Information Technology	CRM Life Event Triggers	High	Low	Low	Medium	Low	High	Medium	Medium
Web Site Development	Web Site	Medium	Medium	Low	Medium	Medium	Medium	High	Medium
Influence									
Human Resources	Recruiting	High	Medium	Medium	Medium	Low	Medium	High	Medium
Legal	Litigation Cases	Low	Low	Low	Low	Low	High	High	High
Investor Relations	Annual Report	Low	Medium	Low	Low	Medium	High	High	High

High ● Medium ◐ Low ○

Figure 3.5. Integrating Internal Points of View into a Single Point of View.

it into the touchpoints it is responsible for compared to other functional areas.

- Significant disconnects appear between senior management's view of touchpoint effectiveness versus the viewpoints of those responsible for the touchpoints.

- Support groups, such as human resources, legal, and investor relations, appear to have little knowledge of the brand strategy and feel they are given few resources to learn about it. This manifests itself in the minimal role that brand plays in the planning processes.

STEP 2: CONDUCTING AN EXTERNAL TOUCHPOINT ASSESSMENT

Learning the internal perceptions of the brand touchpoint strengths and priorities is important, but the understanding gained in the external assessment with customers is even more important. (We will focus on customers for the rest of this process discussion, but remember that depending on your situation, your conducting similar assessments with other stakeholders is also critical.) Your customers are the ones who are being most affected by your brand touchpoint efforts and are the only ones who can provide the organization with vital information:

- What their greatest needs are
- What affects them the most
- How to reach or interact with them most effectively
- How you are performing with respect to the brand touchpoints they deem most important relative to their expectations and the competition's performance

Determining External Brand Touchpoint Assessment Research Mix

The first task in successfully assessing external brand touchpoints is to identify the groups of customers that you believe will best help you get to the answer. While you might assume that current customers would most effectively and accurately help you determine and assess brand touchpoints, we believe that a combination of current, past or lost, and potential or future customers can provide the most thorough and accurate brand touchpoint insights. In general, we recommend a research mix of 25 percent past or lost customers, 25 percent potential or future customers, and 50 percent current customers.

Talking to past or lost customers can help you better pinpoint which brand touchpoints are having a negative impact and which competitor touchpoints are so effective that they induced a customer of yours to move to another brand (beyond the quality of the product or service itself). As a by-product of this assessment, you are in a better position to protect your current customers if you better understand what happened with past and lost customers.

Talking to potential or future customers can help you determine what is working well (or not) in the pre-purchase experience and purchase experience sections of the brand touchpoint wheel, as these customers are living through that now or might be soon. In addition, this group of customers can tell you what your competition is doing well (or not).

In researching current customers, we recommend dividing this group into a few categories. First, it is important to look at long-time, loyal customers. They can provide you with a lot of insight into what you are doing well (that is, which touchpoints have influenced them to stay loyal to your brand). One-time customers, who are in theory active with your brand today, can tell you why their participation with your brand has been limited. Newer customers, who have recently made the decision to buy your brand over others, can provide additional perspective on what won them over and how you are performing in the early stages of the relationship.

The appropriate research mix is highly dependent on whether you are a business-to-business or a business-to-consumer company. In addition, whether you offer products or services will influence how you conduct your research.

Research Goals

Data collection with these different customer groups should be tailored to the appropriate information they can provide. A simple 3-by-3 matrix helps to show you what research cells should be filled in through this external brand touchpoint assessment; Figure 3.6 provides an example.

	Pre-purchase Experience	Purchase Experience	Post-purchase Experience
Potential Customers	Primary Goal: Understand the criteria used to choose the brands in the consideration set Key Questions: • What criteria do you use to help you narrow down your selection of brands when purchasing X?	Primary Goal: Understand the ideal expectations around the purchase experience Key Questions: • What criteria is most important to you when making your final decision to purchase X?	Primary Goal: Understand how your brand is delivered to a potential customer Key Questions: • What types of expectations do you have around the usage of our brand? • What would we need to do to continue to keep you as a customer?
Current Customers	Primary Goal: Understand the drivers for putting your brand in the consideration set Key Questions: • What made you decide to put our brand into your final consideration set?	Primary Goal: Understand the strengths and weaknesses around the purchase process of your brand Key Questions: • What about our brand led you to purchase it? • What did you like about the purchase process? What would you change?	Primary Goal: Understand what touchpoints are instrumental in driving loyalty Key Questions: • Why do you continue to purchase our brand? • What could we do better?
Lost Customers	Primary Goal: Understand why your brand did not make it into the customer's final consideration set Key Questions: • What brands made it into your final considerations set? • Why did our brand not make it into that set?	Primary Goal: Understanding what ultimately drove the decision to purchase a competitive brand Key Questions: • What brand did you ultimately choose to purchase? • Why did you decide not to purchase our brand? • If you have ever been through our purchase experience, what would you change? What did you like?	Primary Goal: With those customers that have purchased your brand in the past, what about your brand failed to meet the expectations of what your brand promised Key Questions: • Why did you choose not to purchase our brand again? • What could we do better?

Figure 3.6. Mapping Customer Groups Against the Brand Touchpoint Experiences.

To help lead the dialogue with the different customer segments, you may want to use a brand touchpoint wheel. This will help guide them through the different areas you want to explore: pre-purchase, purchase, and post-purchase. In addition, you can start the discussion by asking them to write down all the interactions they have had with you and competitor companies in your industry during each brand touchpoint stage.

Following are some sample questions, which can be addressed qualitatively or quantitatively:

- What brands are you familiar with in this industry? How did you become familiar with these brands?

- When deciding to make a purchase in this industry, what criteria did you use to determine which brand you would purchase?

- After you decided to purchase a certain brand, what is most important part of the purchase and use experience, beyond the product or service performing as expected? What factors would trigger a repeat purchase of this brand?

- After you have used the product or service, what type of interaction do you have with the company that provided that product? How does the company maintain an ongoing relationship with you?

If possible, especially within focus groups, it is important not to mention your company's brand early on because you want to gain an overall understanding of the brand touchpoints in general for your industry and then specifically for your brand in an unbiased, unfiltered way.

Probing for Depth

Once your customer groups have identified all of the various brand touchpoints, you can start to probe which have the greatest impact relative to the following factors:

- What is most important to them
- What their specific needs and wants are
- Their expectations from a specific touchpoint, regardless of provider

• Their perceptions of the different brands they have
  interacted with

Another method of probing for richer data is to ask customers to place these interactions on a brand touchpoint wheel so they can visualize and describe the interrelationships among them.

As a general rule of thumb, always have customers describe brand touchpoints in their own words, so the organization better understands how they actually think about and define them. As you might suspect, many times customers define a brand touchpoint differently than the organization does. Thus it will be important for your company and employees to embrace new definitions or shift how you have traditionally thought about brand touchpoints to link better with how customers want to interact with them.

As you are going through this assessment of the various touchpoints customers have with your brand, you also need to consider how they view the competition in terms of the same brand touchpoints. Although the information you collect on your own brand is important, you are basically operating in a vacuum without a competitive reference point. We recommend getting competitive perspectives on at least two close-in competitors that you feel you directly compete with, plus one additional up-and-comer that is getting stronger every day and that you believe will be a competitive threat in the next few years.

Defining the Ideal Brand-Customer Relationship

The final aspect of conducting an external touchpoint assessment is to have customers articulate their perception of what the ideal relationship with the brand would be like for them. The hope is that there is a relevant example they can reference that comes close to this ideal (better yet, their ideal is their experience with you); trying to describe an ideal relationship or experience in the abstract is challenging.

Once you have this ideal description, you will now have the last piece of the puzzle from an external perspective. Ultimately, you will determine the gaps that exist between how customers and stakeholders are currently experiencing your brand, how they would like to experience your brand (tied to their ideal description), and how they experience the competition as well as the gap that exists between internal and external perceptions. Figure 3.7 pictorially brings all of the findings from Step 2 to life and illustrates a priority ranking for areas of improvement for the retail bank example shown in Figure 3.5.

Overall External Scorecard

Functional Group	Respective Brand Touchpoints	Current Usage	Ideal Importance	External Assessment — Company Performance	Competitive Performance	Overall Rating As Improvement Area
Pre-purchase Experience						
Account Management	Cold Calling	Medium	Low	Medium	High	Low
Marketing	Advertising	High	High	Medium	Medium	Medium
Marketing	Free Seminars	Medium	High	Medium	High	High
Purchase Experience						
Account Management	One-on-One Meetings	High	High	High	Medium	Low
Marketing	Marketing Collateral	Medium	Medium	High	High	Low
Marketing	Product and Service Assortment	Medium	High	Medium	High	High
Post-purchase Experience						
Customer Service	Client Support	Medium	Medium	Low	High	High
Information Technology	CRM Life Event Triggers	Medium	Medium	Low	High	High
Web Site Development	Web Site	Medium	Low	Medium	Medium	Low
Influence						
Human Resources	Recruiting	Medium	High	Medium	High	High
Legal	Litigation Cases	Medium	Low	Medium	Medium	Low
Investor Relations	Annual Report	High	Medium	Low	High	Medium

High ● Medium ◐ Low ○

Figure 3.7. External Brand Touchpoint Summary.

STEP 3: ANALYSIS: BRINGING IT ALL TOGETHER

Let's review where we have been up to this step. In Step 1, we conducted an internal assessment of the various ways the brand touches customers. This included looking at every possible brand touchpoint that influences the ultimate relationship between the brand and the customer. This also included brand touchpoints that influence the brand-customer relationship indirectly. In addition, we assessed these same brand touchpoints from a functional area perspective throughout the organization. In total, Step 1 provided an internally driven snapshot of how the brand-customer relationship works, tied to the various touchpoints they believe are in play today.

In Step 2, we assessed the role of the brand relative to the myriad of external touches the brand has with its customers. For Step 2 to be successful, not only is an exhaustive list of brand touchpoints required, but also a determination of how those brand touchpoints stack up to customer expectations, the competition and the ideal brand-customer relationship, and the respective gaps that exist between each.

We are now ready to analyze and integrate all of these data, relative to the brand-driven goals identified in Step 1, to develop a brand-customer touchpoint strategy.

Integrating Internal and External Touchpoint Assessments

To start Step 3, it is helpful to put all of the internal and external data into one matrix (see Figure 3.8) so that you can start to see where you need to focus your brand-building efforts going forward, versus where you are strong today and what your strengths are in relation to the competition. This is all examined relevant to how important the customer perceives specific touchpoints to be.

For instance, if customers have ranked a particular brand touchpoint high and your performance is strong in relation to your competition and the ideal, you probably do not need to focus on that brand touchpoint much in the future. However, you will probably want to spend some time trying to understand exactly what you are doing well with respect to that particular touchpoint so that you can mirror this behavior into other brand touchpoints where you might not be doing as well.

Integrated Brand Touchpoint Assessment

Functional Group	Respective Brand Touchpoints	Overall Rating as External Improvement Area	Overall Rating as Internal Improvement Area	Priority Area for Organizational Improvement
Pre-purchase Experience				
Account Management	Cold Calling	○	●	◐
Marketing	Advertising	◐	○	◐
Marketing	Free Seminars	●	◐	●
Purchase Experience				
Account Management	One-on-One Meetings	○	●	◐
Marketing	Marketing Collateral	○	◐	○
Marketing	Product and Service Assortment	●	◐	●
Post-purchase Experience				
Customer Service	Client Support	●	●	●
Information Technology	CRM Life Event Triggers	○	●	◐
Web Site Development	Web Site	◐	◐	◐
Influence				
Human Resources	Recruiting	●	◐	●
Legal	Litigation Cases	○	●	◐
Investor Relations	Annual Report	◐	●	●

High ● Medium ◐ Low ○

Figure 3.8. Integrated Brand Touchpoint Assessment.

After you have looked at all of the brand touchpoints and the gaps between internal and external perspectives, you can begin to prioritize which touchpoints require immediate attention. This is shown in the column in Figure 3.8 labeled "Priority Area for Organizational Improvement." Identifying priorities will help you develop a realistic plan of action for making sure that the critical touchpoints—those that either drive sales (or are driving away prospective customers) or retain current customers—are improved first.

The purpose of Step 3 is to provide you with a holistic assessment of your brand's relationship with customers based on the impact and performance of the various touchpoints your brand has. If you were to end the process here, you would have gained tremendous insight on internal and external perceptions of touchpoints, performance against internal expectations, customer expectations, and performance against competitors and the ideal. You now have a fuller understanding as to how all of these brand touchpoints interact with one another and also where the gaps and opportunities exist.

To reap the greatest benefit from this process, you have to take it one step further and link everything you just learned in Step 3 back to your specific brand goals and objectives. This will enable you to develop a brand touchpoint action plan.

STEP 4: DEVELOPING A BRAND TOUCHPOINT ACTION PLAN

After the analysis in Step 3 has been completed and you have a scorecard that shows which high-priority brand touchpoints the organization needs to improve on, it is time to develop an action plan and dedicate the resources and time to make sure the necessary changes are made. This is where most companies fall short. Most companies at this point do very little with the information provided in Steps 1 through 3.

To start Step 4, go back and review the brand goals and objectives uncovered in Step 1 and determine what exactly you are trying to achieve strategically with your brand for your company. This analysis will allow you to decide which specific brand touchpoints will have the greatest strategic impact and what you need to do to improve on those touchpoints to have the greatest impact on your brand and overall business performance.

For example, if you see that the external assessment of the advertising touchpoint yielded a high need for improvement and that the internal audit of the communications group showed that they also gave advertising a low score, you can start to conclude that perhaps the issue is that marketing has a poor understanding of how their brand should be positioned in the marketplace in relation to the competition and what is most important to customers. This might mean you need to conduct an in-depth assessment on the brand's strengths and weaknesses to determine a more effective identity and positioning for the future. Or if your awareness is high but overall trial is low, you may need to boost specific pre-purchase touchpoint activities through coupons, satisfaction guarantees, or possibly even word of mouth to help increase your conversion from awareness to purchase. If you discover that customers are not currently loyal to your brand and often go back into the pre-purchase cycle when making another purchase in your category, this may mean that your post-purchase experience efforts are falling short. This may also mean that you are spending scarce resources on marketing and selling to current and previous customers who could become loyal customers if you were to increase your post-purchase touchpoint activities, such as incentives, loyalty rewards, new product activity, or after-sale service.

This process may also tell you that there are five touchpoints that need serious attention and that they are all housed in a single functional area. Thus you will need to focus on shoring up that one functional area to achieve your goals and objectives. Or it may highlight you that senior management's goals for the brand may be too aggressive or improperly focused.

For every company and every brand, the actions you take to improve critical brand touchpoints are going to be very different. Figure 3.9 takes you through the high-level components of a touchpoint plan. The bottom line, though, is that you now have comprehensive, data-based knowledge to make the right decisions necessary to achieve your goals and objectives.

In addition to the overall action plan, we always recommend outlining a plan for each functional area relative to specific brand touchpoints they control. By doing this, you are committing to managing all of your touchpoints consistently day in and day out, functional area by functional area.

Some of the plans might be light ("We should just keep on doing what we are currently doing"), some might be heavier ("We need to overhaul the fulfillment team as it's not helping us satisfy our customers' needs"), some might be new ("We have not had to focus on CRM to date, but obviously this is important to our future success and

Brand Touchpoint Plan — Medium-Priority Improvement Areas

Brand Touchpoint Plan — High-Priority Improvement Areas

Pre-purchase Experience

Functional Group: Marketing

Respective Brand Touchpoints: Free seminars

Brand Objectives: To ease financial stress of our customers by delivering high-quality products and customer service

Need: Relative to the competition, we are underperforming on delivering free seminars to our customers, who view it as a very important touchpoint. This may be due to the lack of brand training and resources that those responsible for developing this touchpoint feel they are in need of.

Plan of Action:
- Develop brand seminars to train those responsible for this touchpoint on the brand strategy, brand vision, and brand positioning (March)
- Demonstrate how the brand can be incorporated into the free seminars and their daily jobs (April)
- Reinforce the brand strategy in all planning and update meetings (ongoing)
- Tie goals to an increase in the satisfaction rate of our free seminars by asking participants to rate overall satisfaction and brand understanding (March)

Investment Needed: $5,000

Purchase Experience

Functional Group: Marketing

Respective Brand Touchpoints: Product and Service Assortment

Brand Objectives: To ease financial stress of our customers by delivering high-quality products

Figure 3.9.   Brand Touchpoint Plan.

to our current customers"), and some may force more cross-functional activity than ever before ("We need a holistic account management process that includes sales reps from different divisions because our customers are getting too many mixed signals from us").

Regardless of what the specific brand touchpoint action plans are, you now have a brand touchpoint management process that most likely did not exist before. In addition, your organization's understanding of what to focus on to succeed and reach your strategic goals and objectives has probably never been clearer. Finally, to successfully implement functional area plans, you need to go back to one of the primary reasons you set up a cross-functional team at the beginning of this process. These individual representatives are best suited to both sell this process and its recommendation to their respective area and to provide the appropriate context for indicating how their respective actions fit into the bigger process. To succeed, though, they will need to keep their functional areas up to date on the overall touchpoint assessment process, so these recommendations are not viewed as an attack or a surprise but as an enabler for future success.

Once the action plans are finalized and agreed on, it is important for the CEO to reinforce his or her commitment to providing the entire organization with the right tools to bring the recommended action plans and strategies to life. The last thing that functional areas need to be told is that they need to improve on how they are building the brand (through their respective touchpoints) and not be reassured at the same time that the company is committed to supporting these improvements and investments. Through this commitment, the CEO and the executive team will prove to employees that they believe every brand touchpoint is critical in shaping every customer's relationship with the brand.

Finally, a single owner of the brand touchpoint action plan should be established to ensure that the plan is progressing. This person has to be high enough in the organization to be able to influence the actions of both functional area leaders and senior management.

INDUSTRY AND COMPANY VARIATIONS

This approach to assessing and prioritizing your brand touchpoints may differ depending on your industry, your clients and customers or consumers, and whether you are a global or a local organization. If your company is serving multiple customer groups, you may be required to conduct several brand touchpoint assessments, especially if the touch-points employed are dramatically different. Organizations such as financial services, utilities, and telecommunications may find that they have more brand touchpoint wheels due to the number of different customer groups that they provide services for.

For instance, in a recent utility project, we had to develop different brand touchpoint assessments for seven important entities (or stakeholder groups):

1. Large commercial and industrial customers

2. Small commercial and industrial customers

3. Residential customers

4. Brokers and traders

5. Sociopolitical and regulatory bodies

6. Suppliers and partners

7. Financial community

As another example, a financial investment firm may have a brand touchpoint wheel for its brokerage services customers, its asset management customers, and its retail branch customers.

If this is the case for your company, make sure to have a singular corporate view of brand touchpoints as the umbrella over all the various brand touchpoint assessments, as the likelihood that a single customer may access multiple services (and thus be included in multiple touchpoint assessments) is high. This is the same philosophy that exists for positioning a brand. A company can have only one corporationwide positioning; however, how that positioning comes to life for different stakeholders and customer segments may be very different.

In addition, global firms may have a more expanded process in trying to assess its touchpoints, both internally and externally, due to the number of locations that are either managing or experiencing the various touchpoints. For instance, a global firm that has marketing collateral developed in each of its countries will need to assess the consistency of this specific touchpoint across regions.

THE CHALLENGES AHEAD

It is important to acknowledge a few of the challenges that we have encountered in trying to conduct this sort of assessment with companies worldwide.

First, a shift in mind-set is often required to realize that purchase, post-purchase, and influencing touchpoints are vitally important to the overall experience and relationship a customer has with the brand. In reality, though, they rarely get as much attention as pre-purchase experience touchpoints because most organizations focus their resources and brand-building investments on advertising, collateral, and traditional marketing methods for attracting customers to their brand. Nevertheless, we believe that it is equally important to assess, prioritize, and manage all brand touchpoints consistently across the entire brand-customer relationship, to build customer retention, loyalty, and "share of wallet" over time.

Second, most companies have minimal experience and exposure to the concept of assessing and prioritizing their brand touchpoints. Going through this process can be fairly time and resource intensive. For some companies, the idea of going through another assessment can feel like a poor use of time and resources as, in the words of one person we interviewed, "that time could be better used to close some more sales."

As reengineering gained steam in the late 1980s and early 1990s as the right thing to do to ascertain where the fat in the company resided and as we have seen with the recent recession's silver lining of being able to trim employees who do not fit or are unproductive, the difficulties of conducting a brand touchpoint assessment, we believe, can be outweighed by the positive end results.

Determining how to deploy resources most effectively and efficiently to meet longer-term goals and objectives is a necessity in today's highly competitive, resource-constrained environment. The purpose of a brand touchpoint assessment is not the assessment itself but to hone the company's ability to manage the brand holistically as the critical asset that it is.

The third challenge is tied to ego management. An assessment by definition is an audit of current performance. For this to work, egos have to be checked at the door and negative assessments have to be looked at as an opportunity for future growth. Position the work as forward looking and focused on the collective future success of the brand. In addition, try to stay away from the actual rating (or grades) that the touchpoint was given, and focus instead on the recommended action items or shifts that have to be made to ensure future success.

Finally, we recommend that marketing not drive this process. It is important for everyone to understand that this is a companywide endeavor, and by having marketing drive the assessment and the strategy, you are reinforcing the silo mentality that already exists tied to brand. Marketing does not own the management of the brand. Every employee owns the management of the brand.

THE BENEFITS OF A BRAND TOUCHPOINT ASSESSMENT AND STRATEGY

The long-term benefits of assessing your organization and the importance of your company's brand touchpoints externally are enormous. With this knowledge, you can help build a powerful brand that is relevant and important in the minds of your employees and customers. In addition, once the infrastructure is set, the benefits of fully understanding and prioritizing your brand touchpoints outweigh the time and effort invested in the process.

Once this assessment is completed, the organization is now equipped to take control of interactions that customers have with the brand. You now know which touchpoints are most important to customers and which will help you drive success and improve your bottom line. With this knowledge, the organization can more effectively allocate both human and financial resources to maximize touchpoint success. From here, internal structures can be put in place to enable you to become a powerful brand asset management organization.

CHAPTER FOUR

The Pre-Purchase Experience

Making the Brand-Prospect Connection

I̶t is November, and you receive a survey about the new Lexus you bought last month. This survey is intended to help Lexus's parent company, Toyota, better understand everything you did prior to coming into its showroom and ultimately what influenced your decision to lease the car. As you think back, you realize that the actual purchase experience for you started twelve months ago, so you start to write down in chronological order what you did in preparation for purchasing your new car:

• *Twelve months prior to purchase:* You started to notice and pay attention to car advertisements for the first time since you leased your last car.
• *Nine months prior to purchase:* You started looking at cars in your office parking lot, noticing what models were represented there and, when you could, who was driving what.
• *Six months prior to purchase:* You started to get letters in the mail from Honda (you were driving an Accord at that time) offering you incentives to buy your car outright from Honda at the end of the lease.

Honda also sent you brochures and videos on new models and previewed next year's models coming out in October. You were impressed with what you saw; many improvements had been made to the Accord over the past three and a half years.

• *Five months prior to purchase:* You remember having discussions with your friends Emma and Ethan about different car models to consider, including the strengths and weaknesses of each.

• *Four months prior to purchase:* You decided to get smarter about what was available by going on-line to do some research. You went to *Motor Trend's* and *Car and Driver's* Web sites, as well as to MSN Carpoint.com and Autobytel.com. In addition, you went to several manufacturers' Web sites to see exactly what was available. You started to get familiar with all of the models and their prices.

At this point, you realized you were ready to step up to the next class of car. You had been promoted recently and knew you could afford a car in the $35,000 to $45,000 price range. In effect, you eliminated two-thirds of all automobile choices from your decision set.

You were excited for this next car to make a statement about you: the perceived status of the car you chose, its price point, and your ability to afford it. You decided to look specifically at Infiniti, Lincoln, BMW, Acura, Lexus, Volvo, and Saab. You visited their Web sites and did some price comparisons, and you received videos and brochures from each manufacturer. Honda actually called several times in June too, which reminded you that the company also produces the Acura.

• *Three months prior to purchase:* You attended the auto show in your area in July because a few manufacturers sent you free tickets to visit their booth. You loved this opportunity to see all of the cars you were interested in, in one location, without feeling any pressure to buy.

You now had all of the information you needed to make some decisions. You decided to narrow your list down to models of just a few brands—Lincoln, Acura, and Lexus. You started to ask your friends and even random people in parking lots and gas stations who drove any of those cars what their thoughts were about each.

• *Two months prior to purchase:* You bought more magazines, revisited the Web sites, and found out how independent third parties were rating your top three car choices. Some of the things they said were relevant, like performance when driving in the snow, and some were not, like child safety, because you do not have children.

You called the toll-free numbers provided by Lincoln, Acura, and Lexus to learn more about pricing options, buy versus lease options, credit policies, and incentives that might be offered that may coincide with your purchase date.

• *One month prior to purchase:* Through all of the conscious and subconscious research you did over the previous eleven months, you felt totally equipped to visit the Lincoln, Acura, and Lexus dealerships to start the process. You felt that you probably knew as much as or more than any of the sales representatives about the differences in features, benefits, and pricing options (retail versus list) of these three car brands. In fact, all you really needed to do at that point was to take a test drive, because you knew exactly what you wanted to pay for the car.

Consider another scenario. It is Sunday morning, an hour before game time, and you are in a hurry because you overslept and still need to get some food at the grocery store before the big game. You decide that you must have potato chips when your friends come over. You get to the store with your list of ten things you have to buy quickly.

You get to the potato chip aisle and stand there for twenty seconds, looking left and right and up and down the aisle. You reach for the Pringles but hesitate and step back, thinking that you want a better dip chip. You see the Kettle's, but they are too expensive. You see the store brand, but that is not the image you want to project. You see the Cape Cods, but they are too delicate and will break. You finally see the bags of Lay's and Ruffles potato chips. You put the Lay's in your cart and start walking away.

Within two seconds, though, you have a momentary flashback of watching the Chicago Bears when you were younger, with your parents and your younger brother Benjamin, and always having a bag of Ruffles and some popcorn as your game time snacks. So you go back to the potato chip aisle, put the Lay's back on the shelf, and grab the bag of Ruffles and toss it into your cart. Without realizing it, you go through variations of this potato chip purchase nine more times as you pick up the other items on your shopping list. Interestingly, you have not purchased any of the items yet, and thus no money has been exchanged, and it is certainly possible that you may change what is in your cart again.

Is there any substantial difference between the process you used to purchase the Lexus prospect and the process you used to buy the Ruffles? The steps you took were exactly the same. Each time, you had a goal in mind and then went through some conscious and unconscious steps, thinking about things like price, image, quality, and past experience.

One took twelve months and the other ten minutes, but the thought processes were basically the same.

DEFINING THE PRE-PURCHASE EXPERIENCE

Everything listed in the foregoing examples is tied to what we call the *pre-purchase experience,* which is defined as a collection of brand touch-points (that the company employs) and processes (that the prospect employs) that significantly influences whether a prospect will place your brand into his or her final purchase consideration set on the way to making an actual purchase.

Pre-Purchase Experience Goals: The Company's Perspective

A company's end goal in the pre-purchase experience is pretty straight-forward: to have its brand end up in a prospect's final brand consideration set. To accomplish this, the company has to employ an array of strategies and tactics that will help educate prospects about why its brand is better than competitor brands. In doing so, it has to determine what information will best help existing customers and potential new buyers through their pre-purchase process.

Thus a company is striving to achieve these specific goals in the pre-purchase phase:

1. Retaining current customers—keeping past customers loyal to your brand by continuing to remain relevant in their lives

Assuming that the company is also interested in attracting new customers, it will try to achieve these additional goals:

2. Heightening brand awareness—making prospects aware of your brand

3. Shaping brand perceptions and expectations—helping prospects understand the benefits your brand offers over competing brands

4. Underscoring brand relevance—ensuring that prospects link the benefits of your brand to their needs and wants and see the value your brand can offer

5. Driving brand consideration—driving the brand into
a prospect's consideration set

Another way of looking at these five goals is tied to the specific steps a company should take to achieve each goal and move onto the next (see Figure 4.1).

A company cannot choose which goals it needs to achieve because each one is critical to getting its brand into a prospect's final consideration set. We contend that you have to take a prospect through each of these steps in one way or another, and the only true variable is how much emphasis the company should be placing on one step over another. For instance, a company can have high levels of awareness but undifferentiated benefits with regard to the competition (as demonstrated by the "burger wars"). Or a company can have very differentiated benefits but be unsuccessful in making meaningful connections to prospects (examples include discount shoe stores such as Payless and lesser-known delivery providers like Yellow Freight versus UPS or FedEx).

Pre-Purchase Experience Goals:
The Prospect's Perspective

From a prospect's perspective, the purpose of the pre-purchase phase is to try to get smart about the various brand choices available within a category. The ultimate objective here is for prospects to feel confident that any brand ending up in their final purchase consideration set will satisfy their needs. Prospects also need to determine what information they need to understand the array of brand choices they have to choose from, as well as what specific information is required to make their final decision.

Thus prospects are trying to achieve the following specific goals in their pre-purchase experience:

1. Determining degree of loyalty to current brand—deciding if other brands should be considered beyond the one with which they have experience

If prospects are either new to the category or reassessing which brands best fit their needs, then the goals include these:

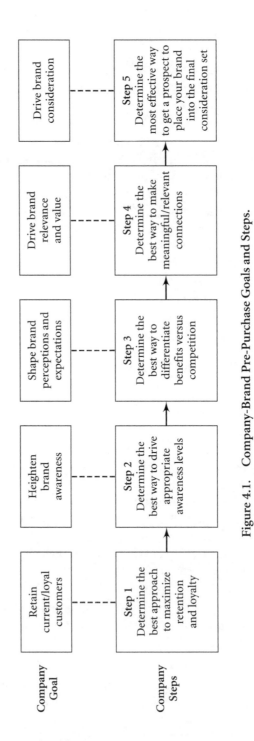

Figure 4.1. Company-Brand Pre-Purchase Goals and Steps.

2. Increasing brand awareness—becoming aware of the different brands that exist within the category of interest

3. Differentiating brand promises—gaining knowledge about a particular brand's benefits and the degree to which those benefits resonate with what that prospect is looking for

4. Clarifying brand value—seeking to understand the differences in benefits and value that various brands have over one another and which brands start to align more closely with a prospect's needs and wants

5. Narrowing brand considerations—narrowing their choice of brands down to a few that will be entered into their final consideration set based on a level of confidence that each can satisfy their purchase needs to one degree or another

Another way of looking at these goals and steps is depicted in Figure 4.2.

A prospect who is extremely loyal to a specific brand, as determined in Step 1, will generally bypass the remaining four steps. A prospect who is dissatisfied with the brand or is reassessing brand options for other reasons or is a new prospect to the category will then go through Steps 2 through 5. For a brand to succeed in making it through Steps 2 through 5, the company needs to be intimately aware of how prospects in the category think and what triggers a prospect to move from one step to another.

In-depth customer research will probably be necessary to understand a prospect's purchase process and purchase drivers within your specific industry. (A methodology is discussed in Chapter Four of *Brand Asset Management*.) This research will allow you to determine which brand touchpoints will be most effective with the different customer and prospect segments you serve and are tied to the steps these consumers go through in the pre-purchase experience. Once a company understands the customer and prospect dynamics within its category, the ways to align company goals and objectives with brand touchpoint goals and objectives should become clear.

In general, prospects are knowledge seekers in the pre-purchase experience: they are trying to gather, assess, and distill a lot of information to help them home in on a few brands to consider for purchase. It is important to note that although their financial expenditures are minimal in the pre-purchase experience, prospects do pay in terms of their time.

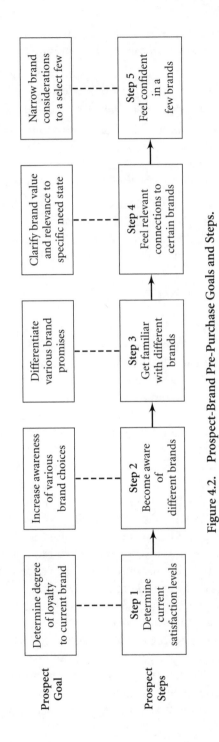

Figure 4.2. Prospect-Brand Pre-Purchase Goals and Steps.

Aligning Prospect and Company Goals

As you can see from the Lexus example at the beginning of the chapter, the alignment between what a prospect and company are trying to achieve in the pre-purchase phase is pretty straightforward. In addition, there is close linkage between the company's brand touchpoints and the prospect's actions in relation to these goals:

COMPANY BRAND TOUCHPOINTS		GOALS	PROSPECT ACTION
Offer incentives to buy again ←	Retain current customers	Determine degree of → loyalty	Assess satisfaction level
Provide the right on-line ← information	Heighten awareness	Increase → awareness	Visit Web site
Train call center representatives ←	Shape perceptions	Differentiate brand → promises	Call toll-free number
Provide value ← added at trade show	Drive relevance	Clarify brand value →	Visit trade show
Continue to delight current owners ←	Drive consideration	Narrow → consideration	Talk to current owners

WHICH ARE THE RIGHT PRE-PURCHASE EXPERIENCE TOUCHPOINTS FOR YOUR BRAND?

Did you ever think about questions like the following?

- Why BMW thought that a short, on-line movie series was worth the high costs of producing it?
- Why CIGNA decided to leverage a "power of caring" sponsorship that never talked about the products or services it offered?

- Why Panasonic developed the Jam Cam to monitor traffic in New York City?
- Why Procter & Gamble thought it was appropriate for Tide to sponsor NASCAR?
- Why Pepsi spent a huge amount of money on the 2002 Super Bowl when it already had 100 percent awareness?
- Why Allstate decided to sponsor the 2002 Winter Olympics?
- Why Dove Soap gave away a free pack of Dove Cleansing Wipes with its soap?
- Why Kellogg's decided to do a huge promotion with American Airlines?
- Why McDonald's decided to co-brand with Disney on Happy Meals?
- Why Maytag agreed to loan the lonely repairman to Chevrolet in a recent ad campaign?
- Why Volkswagen included a new Trek bike when it relaunched the Beetle a few years ago?

While we cannot totally be sure of their reasons, we assume that several strategic questions were most likely addressed to determine which brand touchpoints would help each company most effectively achieve its specific brand goals and objectives.

Our strong belief is that most companies are not very strategic in the way they choose one brand touchpoint over another, and for the most part, they rely on history, their advertising agency, and possibly their egos to determine which brand touchpoints to pursue. The reality is that most companies are desperately in need of having some method to help them prioritize brand touchpoint options and make sure they are spending their valuable dollars on only those touchpoints with the greatest potential impact.

While most companies generally think about only two areas when they are trying to determine the right brand touchpoints to employ ("Which will help me achieve my brand goals, and how do I stay within budget?"), we believe that in deciding which pre-purchase experience brand touchpoints are appropriate for your brand, there are several categories of questions you should consider. Each of these questions is aimed at addressing how well the specific brand touchpoint you are considering fits not just with your brand objectives, but also with your corporate strategy, customer thought process, positioning in relation to the competition, and other areas. The answers to how well the specific pre-purchase experience brand touchpoint fits across these issue areas will start to shed light on which brand touchpoints are on-brand versus off-brand.

Pre-Purchase Experience Brand Touchpoint Categories of Questions to Address

The typical issues we try to help our clients think through when evaluating pre-purchase experience brand touchpoints cut across six critical categories. Within each category, we have included several potential questions to address.

1. Does the brand touchpoint we are considering fit with our business strategy?

    Help achieve longer-term goals and objectives?

    Stay consistent with our corporate mission, vision, and values?

    Help us achieve our revenue and margin goals?

    Help with our market expansion plans?

    Allow us to extend our brand into new areas?

    Leverage co-branding and partnership opportunities?

2. Does the brand touchpoint we are considering fit with our brand strategy?

    Stay consistent with our brand promise?

    Help deliver our brand positioning?

    Support our brand identity?

    Enhance our brand image?

    Drive the brand's personality through association?

    Fit within our budget parameters?

    Drive new sales leads?

3. Does the brand touchpoint we are considering fit with our customer model?

    Help us address our desired target segments?

Align with the key purchase criteria of our target segments?

Support the customer's overall purchase process?

Address both purchase influencers and decision makers?

4. Does the brand touchpoint we are considering fit with our category dynamics?

Address major trends within category?

Allow us to support our current category position (for example, trendsetter versus fast follower)?

Stay consistent with customer perceptions of the category?

5. Does the brand touchpoint we are considering differentiate us from competitor approaches?

Help mitigate other potential substitutes (for example, Coke's biggest competitor is tap water, not Pepsi)?

Help us thwart future competitor moves?

6. Does the brand touchpoint we are considering fit with our distribution scheme?

Stay consistent with our current distribution strategy— direct versus indirect?

Satisfy channel partner needs (that is, will it enable exclusive product lines to be sold with key partners)?

Help us acquire and maintain multiple points of access?

The importance of addressing as many of these issue areas as possible relative to the fit of the potential brand touchpoints you are considering cannot be overstated.

The Master Brand Touchpoint Priority Matrix

To make sense of the answers to all of these questions, we suggest a method that we call the master brand touchpoint priority matrix (see Figure 4.3). The vertical axis lists all of the touchpoints you are considering using; the six higher-order "fit" categories are listed on the horizontal axis. For every company, the composition of these six categories will change because certain questions will be more relevant than others depending on the company's overall goals and objectives.

Master Brand Touchpoint Priority Matrix

Example Fit with: Touchpoints	Business Strategy	Brand Strategy	Customer Model	Category Dynamics	Competitive Differentiation	Distribution Scheme	Overall Need
Socially Responsible Sponsorships							
Targeted Sponsorships							
Mass Appeal Sponsorships							
TV Advertising							
Print Advertising							
Billboard Advertising							
Direct Mail							
Web Site							
Sales Force							
Trade Shows							
Trade Show Booths							
Marketing Collateral							
In-Store Signage							
Packaging							
Product Placement							
Product Quality							

5 = High   3 = Medium   1 = Low

Figure 4.3.   Master Brand Touchpoint Priority Matrix.

The best way to fill out this master matrix successfully is to comprehensively address each of the six fit categories. This involves creating a mini brand touchpoint priority matrix for each of the six categories. Each lists the same brand touchpoints on the vertical axis but shows the more explicit subquestions for the category on the horizontal axis.

As an example, Figure 4.4 takes the brand strategy category from the master matrix and blows it out into a mini-matrix, listing across the top the seven subquestions that need to be addressed to answer whether a specific touchpoint fits with your overall brand strategy.

If appropriate, we suggest assigning different weightings to the fit categories that may be more relevant to your brand at a particular time. For example, because Tide is primarily a commodity purchase (like Clorox bleach and Windex), Procter & Gamble may have determined that its strategy was to reach the masses in a different way than competitors do. It may have placed a higher weighting on "differentiates from competitive approaches" as well as on "specific pre-purchase experience goal and objective."

Within each cell, we suggest that you assign a priority number for each brand touchpoint, relative to the specific fit question, on a 1–5 scale, with 5 indicating an excellent fit and 1 a poor one. Once you have a total score on each of the mini-matrices, then you can enter the overall score for that particular category into the master matrix to have an overall score for each brand touchpoint being considered, relative to the seven strategic categories. Once this is completed, you then can start to prioritize brand touchpoints relative to their respective fit with your overall strategy.

EXAMPLE: PANASONIC'S JAM CAM. Because Panasonic competes in the ultracompetitive consumer electronics industry, it needed to find a way to reach masses of potential buyers that was consistent with its pioneering electronic technology but did not cost massive amounts of money. Bob Greenberg, vice president of marketing at Panasonic, describes how he approached the issue:

> We have embraced the idea of using sponsorships strategically. Our philosophy is that they should be related to electronics and it should appear that Panasonic could've created the event or idea. For example, certain radio stations in New York City were having trouble with their traffic monitoring because of all of the tunnels, so we developed

Fit with: / Example Touchpoints	Consistent w/ brand promise? (x3)	Delivers brand positioning? (x3)	Supports brand identity? (x2)	Upholds brand image? (x2)	Drives brand personality through association? (x2)	Fits budget parameters? (x3)	Brings new sales leads? (x1)	Overall brand strategy fit
Weighting	(x3)	(x3)	(x2)	(x2)	(x2)	(x3)	(x1)	
Socially Responsible Sponsorships								
Targeted Sponsorships								
Mass Appeal Sponsorships								
TV Advertising								
Print Advertising								
Billboard Advertising								
Direct Mail								
Web Site								
Sales Force								
Trade Shows								
Trade Show Booths								
Marketing Collateral								
In-Store Signage								
Packaging								
Product Placement								
Product Quality								

5 = High   3 = Medium   1 = Low

Figure 4.4.   Mini Brand Touchpoint Priority Matrix.

a system where traffic reporters could sit in a room and monitor traffic through a camera that is always "watching the traffic." We traded the technology for airtime, so the radio station is always mentioning the Jam Cam by Panasonic. For instance, the traffic reporter on WABC-AM will say, "looking live from the Panasonic TrafficCam" or "looking live from the Panasonic Jam Cam atop the billboard at the Lincoln Tunnel, we can see a twenty-minute delay."

Panasonic developed this specific strategy:

- Increase brand awareness tied to frequency of hearing the Panasonic name
- Sustain brand presence and familiarity in strategic target markets
- Facilitate tie-ins with retailers in each target market individually
- Include Web site and toll-free numbers to help track responses

Each of these strategic objectives would have been housed within the six fit categories of the master brand touchpoint priority matrix, and no doubt each would have received ratings of 5. This pre-purchase experience strategy has been an overwhelming success for Panasonic, with the following results, among others:

- In New York City, 250,000 drivers every day see the camera atop the billboard, representing over 70 percent of the adult audience for thirteen radio stations.
- As a result of the success of the New York City program, Panasonic has rolled it out in sixteen other major markets, including Chicago, Boston, Dallas, and Los Angeles, resulting in millions of potential listeners per day.
- Follow-up inbound calls have well exceeded expectations.

We can speculate that Panasonic probably also gave the Jam Cam ratings of 4 or 5 in the following categories from the mini brand touchpoint priority matrix:

Supports or extends brand identity	5
Upholds brand image	5

Shift perception in regard to competitive brands	4
Drive personality through association	5
Extends your brand into new areas	5
Usurps future competitor moves	4

EXAMPLE: BMW'S "THE HIRE." BMW was looking for new and innovative ways to reach its target audience. Anyone who can afford a BMW is already aware of the brand, so BMW's goal was not to generate mass awareness but to drive greater interest and potentially the inclination to purchase.

Thus one of the most unusual buzz marketing (word-of-mouth marketing) examples over the past few years was BMWfilms.com's online movie series "The Hire." BMW underwrote a series of five short films by renowned directors such as Ang Lee and Guy Ritchie. The story line behind each of the shorts was tied to an incredible car chase involving, of course, a BMW.

The strategy was fairly simple in that BMW's target audience was hard to reach, as they are busy people, with minimal time spent in front of the television. It also helped that the target audience that goes on the Internet has similar demographic traits to those who might be interested in buying a BMW.

Bruce Bildsten, the creative director at Fallon, the agency behind the films, described the strategy in a recent *Brandweek* article as "a strategy of going from a whisper to a roar." BMW had more than 13 million views, and in a six-month period, more than 1.5 million people viewed the film clips. Jim McDowell, BMW's vice president of marketing, says the company is very pleased with the number of sales prospects gathered from the campaign. In addition, this campaign led to a large amount of new prospect and customer information that can be used in the future to target potential BMW consumers more accurately.

Although we cannot score every single fit category, you can bet that BMW gave this particular pre-purchase experience brand touchpoint of creating a short on-line movie series a 4 or 5 in the following categories:

Consistent with brand promise	5
Helps deliver brand positioning	5
Supports brand identity	5
Upholds brand image	5

Consistent with brand personality	5
Shifts perception in relation to competitive brands	4
Drives inclination to buy your product or service	5
Brings in new sales leads	4
Helps address desirable target segments	5

CHOOSING THE MOST EFFECTIVE PRE-PURCHASE EXPERIENCE BRAND TOUCHPOINTS, STEP BY STEP

With an understanding of how to determine which brand touchpoints fit a company's overall strategy better than others, we now need to shift our focus to determining which brand touchpoints will be most effective in achieving your company's specific pre-purchase experience goals.

If you start by thinking through how prospects approach buying a branded product or service, recall that they generally go through five steps (see Figure 4.2) to determine which brands they should consider purchasing. If you connect each step with how a company should respond, the touchpoints to employ become crystal clear. We believe that if you are able to help a prospect move through these pre-purchase experience steps, there is a high likelihood that a prospect will place your brand into the final consideration set for purchase.

Step 1: Determining Current Satisfaction Levels

Prospects who are past users of your brand have most likely formed fairly strong opinions of your brand tied to whether they would consider purchasing it again. A study referenced in *Brand Asset Management* showed that 70 percent of prospects want a brand to help guide their purchase decision, meaning that most purchase processes generally start with a few brands in mind.[1] Prospects who have had a good to excellent experience with your brand will most likely either consider your brand strongly for a repeat purchase or will automatically buy your brand.

Prospects who had only a fair to satisfactory experience with your brand or are seeking something different (remember our Lexus example at the beginning of the chapter) will most likely begin the pre-purchase experience cycle again.

As we mentioned in Chapter One, Robert Passikoff has documented that it takes seven to ten times the cost and effort to gain a new customer than it does to keep an old one and that an increase in customer loyalty of just 5 percent can result in an increase in customer profitability by as much as 95 percent.[2] For any company, the benefits of maintaining a high degree of loyalty cannot be argued.

Step 1 directly aligns with the company's goal of retaining current customers.

Step 2: Becoming Aware of Different Brands

While certain levels of awareness are important, especially in a brand's early life, to achieve critical mass acceptance among target prospects, the role the brand must achieve in this step is to create enough brand awareness that it starts to break through an increasingly cluttered array of options.

Prospects do not necessarily have to know intimately what the different value propositions between your brand and competitive brands are; they just need to notice that you are there and that your brand is interesting enough to warrant seeking further information. Generally, this requires the brand to visually or verbally break through the clutter and achieve appropriate levels of repeated exposure for it to get noticed, which does not necessarily require exorbitant amounts of advertising spending.

By last count, prospects are exposed to up to eleven thousand brand exposures per day. For your brand to achieve a respectable level of awareness, prospects must believe there is something interesting, unique, or special about your brand.

Examples of brands that do this well in the awareness-building stage are Chick-fil-A, Snapple, Cingular, SoBe, Apple, and IKEA. On the other hand, the dot-com implosion from 1998 to 2000 produced a multitude of examples of awareness building that were all for naught. For most, extraordinary levels of investment succeeded in creating high levels of awareness, but that did not translate into market success (remember pets.com), indicating that among other things, they had not provided prospects with a meaningful reason to inquire further.

Step 2 directly aligns with the company's goal of heightening awareness of the high-level differences among the brand choices.

Step 3: Getting Familiar with Different Brands

While individuals may be aware of your brand and cognizant of its existence, they become familiar with your brand's differences only when they can easily recognize and differentiate it within a crowd of similar brands.

We tell our clients that it is important to strive to have their brand stick out from the masses consistently and, if possible, to be where current customers and prospects are. In effect, we tell them that they need to find the intersection of where their prospects are and when they might be in the frame of mind for hearing or seeing the brand's message. We call this creating *moments of truth*, which is simply a label for how a company can try to differentiate itself in a more targeted way than mass advertising, as in the following examples:

- AOL sending out its latest version of software in the mail to certain postal code demographics
- Deloitte & Touche's ads touting its services at every major airport, where many business travelers are passing by daily
- Starbucks being on every major street corner in major cities

A strategy tied to familiarity most likely will not include Super Bowl, prime-time television, or high-profile magazine advertising. The chances of generating awareness in this way are high, but achieving higher levels of familiarity are not.

Step 3 directly aligns with the company's goal of shaping perceptions of its brand.

Step 4: Feeling Relevant Connections to Certain Brands

Prospects can get motivated to take action only if they feel they have some relevant connection to the brand. We believe this fourth step is where prospects take a big leap forward in their purchase process and start to whittle their way down to a few select brands. This is where most brands either make the initial cut or do not. For a brand to succeed in the pre-purchase experience, it has to make some sort of relevant connection to a prospect's life in order for it to move into the prospect's final consideration set.

To succeed in this stage, your brand must communicate multiple relevant benefits that resonate with target audiences on many levels. The benefits should include not only functional benefits to help satisfy a prospect's needs, but also some emotional and self-expressive benefits that help a prospect make a meaningful connection with your brand.

Brand Asset Management introduced the concept of the Brand Value Pyramid, which highlighted the fact that much like Maslow's hierarchy of needs, brands have the opportunity to go beyond satisfying basic needs and can, if they are positioned well, move up to more important and emotional benefits. This can result in a true point of differentiation from what most brands generally compete on: features and attributes.

The further up on the Brand Value Pyramid your brand goes, the more powerful it becomes and the harder it is for competitors to usurp your position and strengths. Figure 4.5 depicts this construct.

For instance, most Volvo owners did not buy their car because of its six-track CD player or because it has a V8 engine instead of a V6

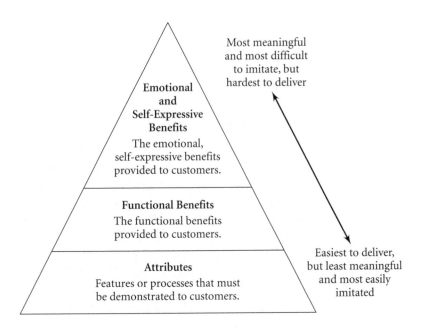

Figure 4.5.   Brand Value Pyramid.

or because it gets two additional miles to the gallon than the nearest competitor. Of course, these are all important features of the car, but most Volvo buyers have purchased that car because of its exceptional safety record. In buying "safety," you are really buying the best car for your family, which ultimately provides you with tremendous peace of mind. It is these last two—doing what is best for your family and achieving greater peace of mind—that are at the top of the brand value pyramid for Volvo.

The concept of the Brand Value Pyramid is often the missing link for companies trying to better understand how to leverage their brands most effectively, have their brand stand out from competitor brands, and make meaningful connections with prospects. It also helps in determining the most appropriate marketing mix and strategy for brands. Typically, functional benefits are usually communicated through obvious or overt messaging and marketing efforts. Emotional benefits can be conveyed in a much more creative way without ever explicitly talking about a specific feature or attribute.

A good example of a brand that has reached the pinnacle of the Brand Value Pyramid in terms of prestige is American Express. Others include Saturn (respect), Nordstrom (unconditional personal service), FedEx (peace of mind), and Polo Ralph Lauren (high self-esteem and self-worth).

Step 4 directly aligns with the company's goal of ensuring that the brand is relevant to the prospect's needs.

Step 5: Feeling Confident in a Few Brands

While feeling a connection to the brand may be considered the biggest challenge and goal within the pre-purchase experience, it is usually not enough to get your brand into the prospect's final purchase consideration set. Prospects might be aware of a thousand brands, familiar with a hundred of them, and connect with ten of them but can only manage to consider a handful seriously due to the limited capacity of the human brain to manage an overwhelming amount of information.

So what lies between connection and consideration? We believe a crucial requirement is for prospects to have a high level of confidence that your brand will be able to fulfill the needs it claims it can. How does your brand gain their confidence? We believe it is through your ability to convince prospects that your brand is more credible than competitor brands in providing the benefits it promises.

There are several ways for a brand to demonstrate credibility (and thus gain confidence), and most of these approaches can be defined within what we call the *Three E's of Credibility:*

- *Expounding* on the brand's history and stability. Expressing the heritage, stability, and integrity of the brand often leads to garnering a trust-based level of credibility.

- *Elaborating* on your brand's value and relevant experience. Provide proof points of your brand's abilities, successes, and points of difference in regard to the competition. Examples include other successful products under the brand umbrella and an impressive client list.

- *Endorsing* the brand through association. Associate the brand with a respected person or group (such as *Car and Driver*) or a credible and trustworthy one (think about Subway's spokesperson, Jared).

Prospects can be highly educated through their own research using the Internet, reading *Consumer Reports,* speaking with colleagues, and other means, but at some point, most purchase decisions require a leap of faith. This leap is much easier when prospects have a certain comfort level with the offering even though they may not have ever used it. This leap of faith is directly correlated to the credibility the brand does or does not have.

A high level of credibility is also the reason certain brands are so successful at new product introductions and get to bypass much of the pre-purchase experience process, as a prospect's leap of faith is often mitigated by the brand's track record and the credibility or endorsement earned by previous brand-based innovations. This is why Gillette's Venus shaving supplies for women and Mach 3 for men were instant successes. This is also why Sony and 3M have incredible innovation track records and why movie sequels and series such as *Star Wars, The Lord of the Rings,* and *Harry Potter* are so successful.

Step 5 directly aligns with the company's goal of driving the brand into the prospect's consideration set.

THE PROSPECT-COMPANY GOAL MATRIX

Effectively integrating prospect and company goals into an effective pre-purchase brand touchpoint strategy is where great companies start to differentiate themselves from the competition and break through the brand clutter.

The prospect-company goal matrix attempts to facilitate this integration by overlaying prospect and company goals together as one. This matrix has four columns, each tied to the intersection of the goals the prospect and the company are trying to accomplish within the pre-purchase experience (see Figure 4.6):

PROSPECT	COMPANY
1. Become aware	Drive awareness
2. Get familiar	Differentiate benefits
3. Feel relevant connections	Make meaningful connections
4. Feel confident in a few brands	Drive brand into consideration

This matrix allows a company to focus on the right touchpoint strategy for whichever prospects it is trying to reach, given whatever business constraints the company may be working under.

The biggest question for a company to address is not which column and commensurate brand touchpoints to focus on but what level of emphasis to place on each. We believe that all four columns need to be in play for a company at all times, as they are always in play for a prospect (remember the Lexus and Ruffles examples). The degree to which a company decides to focus on the particular touchpoints within each column will depend entirely on the specific brand goals and objectives it is trying to achieve.

As you can see from the matrix, the farther to the right you move, the more active the prospect generally becomes. We believe connections and confidence can be garnered only once the prospect has taken a more active role within the pre-purchase phase and moved from a potentially passive listener to a more active prospect.

Importantly, we have not included a loyalty column here in the pre-purchase experience, as we believe that loyalty is garnered through post-purchase brand touchpoints, a topic covered in Chapter Six. However, for existing customers, pre-purchase experience brand touchpoints can help strengthen existing levels of loyalty.

Figure 4.6, which shows the matrix, points to some of the most obvious and best examples of touchpoints to leverage within each of the complementary prospect-company goal columns. To be clear, the

Passive → Active

Prospect Is More:

Prospect Goal = Company Goal	Become Aware = Drive Awareness	Get Familiar = Differentiate Benefits	Feel Relevant Connections = Make Meaningful Connections	Feel Confident in a Few Brands = Drive Brand into Consideration Set
Advertising	X			
Promotions	X			
Marketing Collateral	X			
Direct Marketing		X		
Public Relations		X		
Web Site		X		
Sales Representatives			X	
Trade Shows			X	
Targeted Corporate Sponsorships			X	
Testimonials				X
Expertise Marketing				X
Buzz Marketing, Friends				X

Figure 4.6.   Prospect-Company Goal Matrix.

number of touchpoints in the pre-purchase experience approaches the thousands, as, for instance, there is not just "advertising," but print, television, radio, and billboard advertising. Within each of those types, there are different approaches to bringing the advertising to life tied to various target audiences and price points.

Although almost any of the touchpoints in Figure 4.6 can cut across all four pre-purchase experience columns and goals, advertising is generally assumed to work best at achieving mass levels of awareness. Similarly, direct mail is a great touchpoint to help achieve brand familiarity, trade shows are great ways to make pre-purchase experience connections, and testimonials are a powerful way to drive credibility. You see that as you move across the continuum from left (passive) to right (active), the touchpoints you will want to focus on will shift as your goal shifts with it. Let's take a deeper look at the four columns:

• Column 1: Become Aware/Drive Awareness. The goal of brands in column 1 is aimed at generating high levels of awareness for the brand across the general public. Brand touchpoints leveraged in this column are most effective when the product or service you are selling requires low involvement and entails a low level of risk for the prospect (examples are Pepsi, Taco Bell, and most new movies).

With a more complex or business-to-business purchase (such as a new computer, a vacation, or tax services), column 1 brand touchpoints may be leveraged to spark initial interest in a brand or generate curiosity tied to a new brand. This is what AT&T Wireless did with its vague "What is mLife?" campaign. The goal was to pique enough interest in the brand that prospects would take it upon themselves to seek out more information about the brand in question.

• Column 2: Get Familiar/Differentiate Benefits. Column 2 touchpoints are a bit more deliberate in nature, as the company is starting to target the brand to specific audiences. These brand touchpoints, however, are still fairly broad because the prospect is generally still a passive recipient of the brand information at this point.

Think about the difference between columns 1 and 2 from a mass marketer's perspective. Some mass marketers, like Publishers Clearing House, send their information to almost all households in the nation, whereas the *Harvard Business Review* and the *Wall Street Journal* will send out mailers targeting only households that fit a certain demographic profile or have displayed certain usage patterns in the past.

Column 2 is generally embraced by a company that wants to maximize its brand's potential for success by segmenting the prospects it targets, with the goal of prospects' getting to know more about the brand than just the message they may have heard on television. In this situation, a company is trading off mass awareness building and the potential for greater volume for a more targeted message and perhaps a higher success rate. Another example of a touchpoint in this column includes content-laden Web sites, as they can help a prospect become more familiar with the company.

In general, columns 1 and 2 are less effective at driving sales in complex buying situations, which include multiple purchase influences or purchase variables and in which information and time are important. The key point is that during this time, the prospect is not actively driving the purchase process, and thus the company has little control over what actions the prospect chooses to take or the success or outcome of whichever touchpoints are being activated. One can even argue that during this stage, the prospect is not really a prospect but just a consumer.

• Column 3: Feel Relevant Connections/Make Meaningful Connections. Column 3 is very different from column 1 in that the prospects in column 3 are doing all of the hard work. They are the ones seeking information about your category and your brand, which makes them active prospects. Your job in column 3 is to make sure you have the right message, coupled with the right touchpoint, to deliver your brand's message precisely when a prospect is seeking it.

An easy analogy is tied to purchasing a new computer. A prospect may first turn to *PC Reports* to see which PCs had the highest ranking. If the two with the highest ratings were Dell and IBM, the prospect might go to their respective Web sites to learn more about purchasing those systems. This may prompt a trip to Best Buy to see and interact with or test each model. As the company, you had everything to do with making sure that the active prospect was equipped with the right information and message to help her address her issues and questions. We believe that how a prospect narrows his or her brand options is determined by how well your brand touchpoints perform in column 3. This is also why brand touchpoints such as sales representatives and trade shows are so critical: strong connections are often made when another human being is involved.

• Column 4: Feel Confident in a Few Brands/Drive Brand into Consideration Set. Arguably, column 4 brand touchpoints are the most powerful of all in the pre-purchase experience, as they are driven by a prospect who is, more likely than not, serious about making a purchase in your category. The success of the brand touchpoints activated in this column will ultimately determine whether your brand will be placed in the prospect's final consideration set. The more targeted your approach to column 4 brand touchpoints is, the higher the likelihood is that you will be addressing prospects' individual needs in a meaningful and relevant way.

In column 4, sales representatives, who are responsible for the close, as well as testimonials and even buzz marketing, all provide powerful reasons to believe in your brand. They help prospects distill all the information available on the different brands in your category and help them differentiate category brands from one another.

Again, columns 3 and 4 differ from columns 1 and 2 in that potential buyers are actively seeking information about brands in your category. Thus you can assume that the purchase process has already started in their minds and that your job is to make sure they have the right information needed to place your brand into their final consideration set.

In summary, the prospect-company goal matrix aligns both company and prospect goals neatly into four categories, which should help you determine which brand touchpoints deserve the most attention. Again, you are not choosing among columns; both the prospect and the company will most likely go through all four columns. The question to address is which columns should receive more or less emphasis given the brand goals you are trying to achieve.

The pre-purchase experience brand touchpoint questions provide a tool that your marketing team, as well as your agency, has to use going forward. Without it, you are taking a leap of faith that the strategy you have employed is the one with the highest potential for success; we call this luck. With it, your luck not only turns into probability but, we would argue, a high probability for success.

THE ULTIMATE PRE-PURCHASE EXPERIENCE EXAMPLE: AMAZON.COM

Amazon.com provides an excellent example of a successfully integrated marketing strategy that relies on creating a holistic connection between its brand and its customers, starting in pre-purchase experience. Amazon.com uses a rich mix of on-line marketing, television advertising, catalogues, retail partnerships, customized e-mail messaging, and high levels of service to drive the pre-purchase experience, which in turn drives incredible amounts of usage and loyalty. Most impressive is the fact that Amazon continues to implement new strategies that further develop its power as the on-line retailer of choice.

Today, Amazon.com has a highly loyal customer base, which has resulted from the culmination of several powerful loyalty and pre-purchase tactics, including these:

- Providing pricing discounts and special offers using e-mail on a regular basis
- Providing page excerpts so potential buyers can read passages from a book, just as they could at a bookstore
- Providing book reviews by other Amazon customers
- Offering on-line Amazon.com gift certificates

Amazon's matrix is shown in Figure 4.7.

SOME FINAL PRE-PURCHASE EXPERIENCE BRAND TOUCHPOINT THOUGHTS

By now, you clearly understand that your pre-purchase experience brand touchpoints are the foundation for building a holistic brand-customer relationship. You also know that there are certain cognitive steps that prospects go through to move from initial awareness of a brand to purchase consideration. In addition, you know that there are several goals that a company is trying to achieve in the pre-purchase experience that line up almost one-for-one with the goals a prospect is trying to achieve. Knowing that the goals you are trying to accomplish in this phase are aligned with what a prospect is also trying to achieve should provide the right perspective to maximize your pre-purchase brand touchpoint strategy and get your brand into a prospect's final purchase consideration set.

Prospect Goal = Company Goal	Become Aware = Drive Awareness	Get Familiar = Differentiate Benefits	Feel Relevant Connections = Make Meaningful Connections	Feel Confident in a Few Brands = Drive Brand into Consideration Set
Mass				
TV Advertising	High	Medium	Low	Low
Mail Catalog	High	High	Medium	Low
Newspaper Inserts Catalog	High	Medium	Low	Low
Targeted				
Customized E-mails	Low	Medium	High	High
Discount Coupons and Special Offers via E-mail	Medium	Medium	High	High
Page Excerpts	Low	Low	Medium	High
Book Reviews	Low	Low	Medium	High
Offering On-Line Gift Certificates	Medium	Medium	High	High

Degree of Impact: High ● Medium ◉ Low ○

Figure 4.7. Amazon's Prospect-Company Goal Matrix.

CHAPTER FIVE

The Purchase Experience
The First Step in Delivering on the Promise

*C*hristine is the COO of a high-growth communications equipment manufacturer and has decided the company needs a more comprehensive view of its key customer relationships. Thus she starts to survey the market for technology solutions and issues a Request for Proposal to three software providers. Two key managers, along with an analyst and a database specialist from the information technology group, will drive the selection process. Fortunately for Christine, the entire effort has been endorsed by the heads of global sales, field support, and customer service, and all support the initiative and will cofund it. Even so, she is concerned about choosing the right supplier and having the project succeed. If the supplier she finally selects fails to meet the company's expectations and deliver the promised results, Christine fears it might take her career off track.

One supplier appears to stand above the rest. After only the second meeting at their technology demonstration center, the three-person sales team talks in a language that Christine understands and addresses her company's specific difficulties, including all of the critical systems integration and database questions. Furthermore, the supplier's CEO makes two offers for a face-to-face meeting to answer any lingering questions—two more attempts than any of the other contenders.

Christine's direct reports support this supplier, but the head of global sales is not sure, so Christine conducts a more thorough reference check, which makes her feel better about where she is heading with her decision. Once the head of global sales is on board, Christine turns to negotiating the price down to a level that meets her budget and will allow her to hire this supplier. When they meet her price, she gives a verbal agreement over the telephone to move forward. The next day, the key contact takes Christine to lunch and afterward has her ceremoniously sign two versions of the contract in the conference room outside Christine's office.

Christine decides to try and catch up on some personal to-do's and finally purchase furniture for her weekend house in Sonoma County. After spending a few weeks browsing through various catalogues, she narrows her choices to a few. First, she stops by her local Pottery Barn where the store associate is helpful but does not have a floor sample of the exact sofa that Christine is looking for. Being a good associate, he gives her all the additional information she needs: he confirms that the sofa is available for immediate shipment and that delivery can be arranged to fit specific windows in Christine's busy travel schedule. He also calls around to find out if any of the neighboring stores has a sample on the floor and gives her his business card as she leaves.

After she leaves Pottery Barn, Christine goes to Crate & Barrel's new flagship location at San Francisco's Union Square. The new four-story layout is spacious, and Christine is pleased to find the exact pieces she is looking for, laid out in a fully integrated floor plan. Christine is almost ready to buy, but the price is a little higher than she expected and the store associate is too busy to help her find an alternative solution.

Christine leaves, a little disgruntled, but committed to finalizing her purchase at home that night over the Internet after one last consultation with her sister. When her sister relates her experience with Pottery Barn—great service and a customer-focused return policy— Christine has more confidence about purchasing the Pottery Barn couch without seeing it live, so she goes on-line to place the order. On potterybarn.com, she searches for the couch using key word search, reviews the product and shipping information to make sure it was what she expected, puts the couch in her "shopping basket," and checks out by providing billing, shipping, and payment information.

DEFINING THE PURCHASE EXPERIENCE

Christine may be a busy person, but she is no different from anyone reading this book. Many of us are engaged in multiple and concurrent purchase cycles and thought processes every day. As the outgrowth of the pre-purchase experience, the purchase experience begins when someone moves from a final consideration set to making the purchase.

Some purchase processes are complex and multifaceted; others are brief and impulse driven. They can happen inside a single selling environment or multiple environments (channels), with visits to retail stores, conversations over the telephone, research over the Internet, or in-person interactions with a company's field sales force. According to a 2001 holiday shopping survey conducted by DoubleClick, Inc., over 45 percent of shoppers of high-ticket items tend to browse in one channel before purchasing in another.

Some marketers believe that the main point of their jobs is to get the brand into the prospect's final purchase consideration set, expecting someone else to convert that prospect into a customer. Although we fundamentally disagree with this perspective (as the sales and brand life cycle are ongoing), it is clear that what drives customer perceptions during the purchase cycle is traditionally managed by other parts of the company, outside marketing. Whether it is field sales, store operations, the customer contact center, the Internet team, or various channel partners, these people in effect become the brand at purchase.

Given that much of the purchase process is managed outside of the marketing department, it is important to get each of these entities to buy into the brand's promise and understand and fulfill their role in helping deliver the promise. Importantly, this also speaks to the fact that brand asset managers—the people in charge of managing the brand—are going to have to develop effective ways to collaborate with and influence those functional areas that have to deliver on the brand in order to truly drive long-term value. Most of this chapter focuses on just this issue by describing the major purchase touchpoint categories, assessing how the brand gets operationalized through these touchpoints, and articulating a clear role for the brand asset manager throughout the process.

The Company-Brand Perspective

Just as in the pre-purchase phase, the company's responsibility is to drive its brand into the prospect's final purchase consideration set. Thus the company has two primary goals during the purchase experience:

- How do I get the customer to buy my brand?
- How do I set the right tone for the rest of the brand-customer relationship?

Successfully addressing these questions will determine if you will accrue revenues (and margin). Your objective is to get the customer to open up his or her wallet, sign a contract, issue a purchase order, or proceed to the checkout line. Success in this step is a major defining moment for the brand as you strive to close the deal at the right price for your business rather than have to offer discounts, rebates, extra services, or other incentives, which may be off-brand, to get the prospect to commit.

This is an intensively competitive battlefield; category and industry fighting is fierce. Similar to the five steps of the pre-purchase experience, you need to address four critical issues that prospects will have:

- Instilling trust in the minds of the prospects about the brand
- Proving beyond a reasonable doubt that your offering is better than the others
- Reassuring prospects that this purchase will deliver the value they are expecting
- Helping prospects get comfortable with making a purchase

Just as important as addressing these four issues is determining how the purchase experience should set the tone for the rest of the brand-customer relationship. The actual purchase often provides the first real chance for an authentic relationship to be built with customers. Prospects turned customers will now see you up close for the first time and will judge for themselves whether your actions and deeds live up to the promise of your brand.

Two key obstacles can make the purchase process challenging. First, closing the transaction can be difficult because it often involves unpleasantries like asking for a commitment, negotiating price, and having prospects frankly say what they do and do not like about the brand. Second is focusing scarce resources on only the highest-probability prospects. Few companies can afford to do mass selling in hope of closing a certain percentage of business. Focusing on the right segments, with the right brand touchpoints, is the only solution for most companies.

Incentive systems are designed to address these issues, but they often lead to short-term behaviors that are neither customer focused nor brand consistent. Establishing clear guidelines for on-brand ways to deal with these compensation issues is critical for long-term, brand-driven success.

In order to meet these challenges and achieve its goals for the purchase experience, the company should set out to do the following things:

• Offer a branded value proposition to the customer that is both profitable and enduring (for example, Nordstrom's commitment to unconditional personal service).

• Create a differentiated purchase experience that is directly linked to your brand strategy and goals and is also relevant to your target audience.

• Deliver on the brand promise set up in the pre-purchase experience and follow through on building connections and credibility.

• Strive to have a deep, memorable impact on the prospect in a way that plants the seed for a long and profitable relationship.

• Make it easy for the prospect to commit, now and in the future.

The Customer's Perspective

Customers want to get comfortable with their purchase decision and make sure it matches both their conscious and subconscious expectations as well as the specific need they are trying to fulfill. For example, their goals for commodity, low involvement, or impulse purchases may be significantly different from those for capital-intensive, high-consideration, or highly personal purchases. At a minimum, customers want to

• Trust the brand

• Be confident that the brand purchased is the best offer given the kinds of benefits that they are expecting

• Feel reassured that the purchase is fair and they are getting the best value

• Feel good about their purchase by mitigating any lingering doubts

Because customers will require that your brand's purchase experience deliver on the expectations created during the pre-purchase experience, we believe that slightly overdelivering is a sure way to start garnering brand loyalty. With each purchase, customers will look for clues and subtle proof points in an attempt to understand what kind of relationship they are getting into. Providing an experience that is consistent, reassuring, and occasionally includes a small surprise is guaranteed to help you close the sale and build the relationship you aspire to have.

As also observed in the pre-purchase experience, the company's goals and the customer's goals are closely aligned in the purchase process:

COMPANY	CUSTOMER
Instill trust	Trust the brand
Provide the best offering	Select the best offering
Deliver value	Obtain the best value
Provide comfort about the purchase	Feel good about the purchase

SHAPING THE PURCHASE EXPERIENCE: HOW TO EXECUTE ACROSS DIFFERENT PURCHASE BRAND TOUCHPOINTS

In shaping the purchase experience, you are really shaping and managing your channel or distribution strategy and addressing the different ways in which you give prospects access to your products and services. Most often, a brand will go to market leveraging one (or a combination) of four primary touchpoint categories (see Figure 5.1), each shaped by the brand lens and credibility footprint discussed in Chapter Two:

- Stores and other physical environments
- Direct field sales
- Internet sites and virtual environments
- Customer contact centers

Each category requires unique core operating characteristics and organizational capabilities that we will highlight in our discussion. We

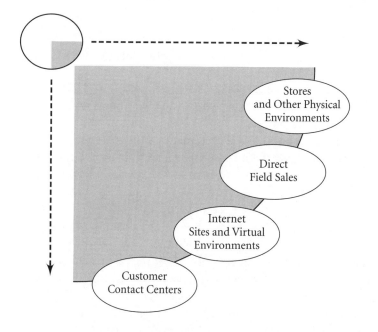

Figure 5.1.   Preliminary Purchase Experience Brand
Touchpoint Categories.

will also provide examples of tools to identify the full array of brand touchpoints that manifest themselves within a given approach and identify key strategic and operational issues that drive healthy, high-impact brand-customer relationships.

Stores and Other Branded Physical Environments

A retail store is the primary type of branded physical environment, although this category ranges from restaurants to gas stations, from bank branches to company conference rooms, from trade show booths to in-store kiosks. In any physical environment, there are generally four drivers of brand success:

- The location
- The environment itself
- The product or service offering
- The people

Even if you do not run a retail business, chances are high that you are bringing prospects into specific physical environments during the purchase cycle that ultimately play a role in the ultimate purchase decision.

CORE OPERATIONAL CHARACTERISTICS AND ORGANIZATIONAL CAPABILITIES. Delivering a purchase experience inside the context of a branded physical environment has a number of clear advantages. The brand has the ability to respond to the customer in a very personal and customized way, especially if your brand owns the environment (that is, if it is the only brand sold in that environment). In addition, you can simultaneously provide customers with an experiential brand interaction, as well as both a personal and verbal interaction.

To take advantage of these strengths, an organization needs to develop a set of interdependent core capabilities, none of which is more important than the environmental design of the physical format and the customer-facing employees who have to consistently display on-brand behaviors within that space. Because these capabilities can be expensive to acquire, you will have to balance efficiency and profitability concerns carefully with a desire to deliver a complete on-brand experience that delights the customer.

SPECIFIC FORMATS: FROM COMPANY OWNED TO THIRD PARTY. There are a number of types of branded physical environments that could be incorporated in your distribution mix (and thus your brand's purchase experience). As depicted in Figure 5.2, these can range from environments that are branded and controlled by the company to those that are branded and controlled by third parties, with various hybrids in between. As a brand asset manager, you need to identify which of these formats are most relevant and appropriate, given your specific brand promise.

At one end of the spectrum are traditional retailers like Wal-Mart and the Gap, which might have a mix of large and small format and outlet stores. At the other end of the spectrum are branded manufacturers or branded producers like the Coca-Cola Company, Palm, and Gillette, which sell their products only through third-party distributors such as grocery stores, convenience stores, specialty electronics retailers, and discounters. Many companies, like Kenneth Cole, a top U.S. fashion brand, have a presence across a variety of channels. For Kenneth Cole, these range from stand-alone Kenneth Cole stores in downtown urban locations (company owned and branded) to Ken-

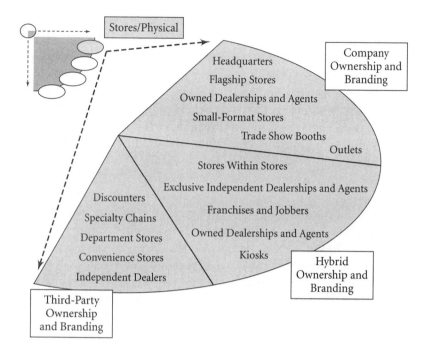

Figure 5.2.   Branded Physical Environment Formats.

neth Cole–branded boutiques or stores-within-stores in Macy's or Saks (hybrid formats) to Kenneth Cole products available through warehouse formats like Costco (third party owned and branded).

A DETAILED ANALYSIS OF A BRANDED PHYSICAL ENVIRONMENT: AVEDA FLAGSHIP STORE. The next step is deciding how to operationalize the brand within each format. Said another way, there is a series of discrete customer interactions or brand touchpoints that occur in the context of branded physical environments. Employees drive some of these interactions, whereas the environment or the merchandise itself may drive others. In a detailed analysis, all of these brand touchpoints are identified, studied, and prioritized (much as described in Chapter Four regarding the pre-purchase experience), resulting in a game plan that gets executed in a way that reinforces the brand identity, brand promise, the customer experience, and the desired brand-customer relationship.

Let's take Aveda as an example. Aveda is a high-end retailer of personal care products, ranging from hair care to aromatherapy. Figure 5.3 presents a detailed analysis for an Aveda Lifestyle Flagship Store, highlighting how a particular environment appears to be implemented to represent the Aveda brand identity, which is about blending nature, beauty, and health care. This type of analysis and planning goes into minute detail, covering brand touchpoints from the store associates' personalities to the service ethos, from the fixtures to the breadth of the assortment.

Once again, the brand is used as the touchstone for brainstorming and making decisions, not only on what touchpoints to include, but also how each touchpoint in the pre-purchase and purchase experience should come to life in the physical environment. Once you have decided on the right brand touchpoints, you then need to think through the cross-functional business issues that need to be addressed.

The Aveda example illustrates a company that is addressing these issues relatively well. Figure 5.3 addresses the key questions:

Customer Touchpoints	Aveda
Salesperson personality	Calm, curious, interested
Sales service ethos	Attentive, educational
Depth of product and service knowledge	Clear on nuances for product, ready to make recommendations based on customer needs
Breadth of assortment and services	Skin care, hair care, makeup, aromas, lifestyle products, stress-relieving services
Inventory depth	Well-stocked products displayed neatly on shelves
Price accessibility	High prices, clear listing of prices in mini frame hanging from shelf under product
Hours of operation and location	High-end malls and shopping streets, 10 A.M.–7 P.M., Monday through Saturday, 11 A.M.–6 P.M., Sunday
Fixtures, floor covering, lighting	Soft lighting, high-end wood fixtures and floor, stone garden, soothing waterfall, large candles, interactive touch screen to experience smells, mission statement hanging behind check-out area
Music, smells	Strong Aveda signature aroma, soft, soothing international (for example, Indian, African) music

Figure 5.3.   Sample Brand Touchpoints of Aveda Flagship Stores.

- What are all the brand touchpoints within this category?
- How is the customer experiencing each brand touchpoint?

You should conduct this same type of analysis with your own brand in conjunction with the brand touchpoint assessment described in Chapters Three and Four and then answer other key questions such as these:

- Is the brand coming to life in a way that is consistent with the brand strategy? How would you grade the company's delivery of the brand promise at each brand touchpoint?
- Have you leveraged all the brand touchpoints at your disposal to convey your brand in the best way possible?
- For the brand touchpoints where you are not performing as well as you would like, what is the action plan to rectify this situation?
- What are some of the tactics you could employ to ensure that other functional areas consistently deliver on the brand's promise?

Keep your company's goals and the goals of the customer in mind as you think through these questions. Similar to the Amazon example at the end of Chapter Four, Aveda leverages multiple brand touchpoints within its physical environment to achieve its goals and the customer's goals (see Figure 5.4).

In addressing these questions, you will also need to define your role in working with the other functional areas to ensure the brand is appropriately represented through the right touchpoints within the specific physical brand environment. For example, if the Aveda brand calls for calm and pleasant store associates and an attentive service ethos, then the brand asset manager needs to work with human resources to define the characteristics for recruiting and training employees with these profiles.

In the same way, a commitment to well-stocked products needs to be defined by the brand asset manager and then supported and brought to life by the merchandisers and inventory planners. To get to this level of brand touchpoint commitment, the brand asset manager will need to employ a wide range of tactics, such as participating in key meetings,

Prospect Goal = Company Goal	Trust the Brand = Instill Trust	Select the Best Offering = Provide Best Offering	Get the Best Value = Deliver Value	Feel Good About Purchase = Provide Comfort About Purchase
Salesperson personality	High	High	High	High
Sales service ethos	High	High	High	High
Depth of product and service knowledge	High	High	Medium	Medium
Breadth of assortment, service	Medium	High	Medium	Medium
Inventory depth	Low	Medium	Low	High
Price accessibility	Medium	Medium	High	Medium
Hours of operation, location	Medium	High	Medium	Medium
Fixtures, floor cover, lighting	Medium	Medium	Medium	Medium
Music, smells	Low	Medium	Medium	Medium

Degree of Impact: High ● Medium ◐ Low ○

Figure 5.4. Aveda Customer-Company Goal Matrix.

providing creative briefs, or educating colleagues in different departments to ensure that the brand is consistently understood and interpreted by all functional areas and any operational roadblocks are addressed.

THE BRAND ASSET MANAGER'S PLAYBOOK: HOW TO ANTICIPATE AND NAVIGATE THE TOUGH ISSUES WITH BRANDED PHYSICAL ENVIRONMENTS. Above and beyond these detailed efforts, which will provide insight and direction on operationalizing individual touchpoints, you will likely come across periodic strategic opportunities (like store renovations) and other operational and execution-oriented critical issues (like out-of-stock merchandise) that brand asset managers have to anticipate and be prepared for. Using our findings from Prophet's 2002 Best Practices study, Figure 5.5 shows that certain critical issue issues demand a brand-appropriate response. For each of these issues, there are a few different approaches a brand asset manager could take (indirectly influence, collaborate on, co-drive, or own and control), depending on the specific issue.

For example, inconsistent service is a current critical issue for both McDonald's and Home Depot.[1] One customer, bemoaning a "burgerless" Big Mac from a recent drive-through experience, now feels it is necessary to "double-check the bags" before leaving the store. Home Depot customers feel it is impossible to find "products in the cavernous stores," and the clerks seem just as "clueless."

Both companies claim to be trying to address their critical issues. McDonald's, for instance, is taking an "influencing" approach by introducing a nationwide toll-free number for customer complaints, mystery shopping its stores to evaluate employee performance, and installing new regional oversight positions for cleanliness and quality. Home Depot is taking a "collaborating" approach by increasing the number of floor employees on weekends and unpacking merchandise late in the evening to free up salespeople during prime shopping hours.

Direct Field Sales

When implemented effectively, direct field sales forces are powerful business and brand weapons that provide significant barriers to competitive entry, as IBM and Xerox did in the 1960s and 1970s and GE, Oracle, and Siebel did in the 1990s. Many companies in Prophet's 2002 Best Practices study ranked their sales force as their most effective brand-building tool, ahead of traditional tools such as advertising and marketing. Merck describes its sales force as "the face of the drug, making

Brand Touchpoint Critical Issues		Management and Influence Tactics
Format proliferation	Influence	1. Conduct risk assessment 2. Look for economic rationale and brand rationale for each new format 3. Strive to operationalize the brand similarly across formats
Store renovation, revitalization programs	Co-Drive	1. Insist on active participation in any such programs 2. Ground efforts in deep customer insight and experiential branding concepts 3. Test, test, test
High employee turnover, inconsistent service	Collaborate	1. Assess ramifications from customer and brand perspective 2. Evaluate underlying human resource policies 3. Pilot structured brand assimilation programs
Weak in-store environment, and presentation	Co-Drive	1. Quantify drag on sales and brand value 2. Partner with visual merchandising team, bringing deep customer insights to the table 3. Experiment, deploy, and measure
Out-of-stocks	Collaborate	1. Actively participate in inventory planning process 2. Align the depths of buys with customer insight and promotions plan 3. Advocate for systems that give associates better visibility into companywide inventory availability
"Big Bet" featured merchandise and seasonal themes	Co-Drive	1. Partner with merchandising team, bringing customer-data grounded insights to table (forward-looking as well as historical) 2. Think through marketing and promotions tie-ins 3. Be the reality check
Employee knowledgeablility, accessibility	Own and Control	1. Create the content; make it brand driven 2. Partner with store operations to deliver systematic training 3. Advocate for systems (intranets, TV/video networks) to streamline and invigorate process
Promotions, pricing cycle	Own and Control	1. Drive planning and keep it on strategy 2. Establish clear business rules for mark-down process; be pragmatic but hold your ground 3. Scenario plan competitor actions and prepare responses

Figure 5.5.   Brand Manager's Playbook in Company-Controlled and Branded Store and Other Physical Environments.

or breaking the reputation of the product." Another participant noted "that a greater percentage of brand decision-making power lies at the 3.5-foot level [the exact distance between a company's sales representative and a decision maker] than it does at the 30,000-foot traditional branding level!" Although it may be unusual to think about the sales force as a brand touchpoint, this group is arguably the most critical and vital touchpoint you have at your disposal.

Sometimes the sales force manages a complex process over long time periods, with sequential phases to the experience and with multiple stakeholders and influencers involved in the purchase decision. Other times the sales cycle is short and is simply about order taking. Sometimes the offering is commoditized, other times very customized. Sometimes the approach is tactical; the opportunity is a one-time, discrete transaction. Other times the opportunity is strategic, with the potential for repeat use and a long-term relationship. All of these opportunities are high-touch situations and usually relationship oriented (in that they often involve a sales representative rather than traditional "static" pre-purchase experience brand touchpoints), and they must be managed with the level of deftness and skill that the brand dictates.

For instance, as a prospect, I want a sales representative who understands my problem, uses language I can relate to and understand, and is able to access the right resources on my behalf to get the job done. As a company, I want someone who can sell and close effectively while hitting their numbers on a consistent basis.

CORE OPERATIONAL CHARACTERISTICS AND ORGANIZATIONAL CAPABILITIES. The core operational characteristics and competencies needed to go to market through a direct sales approach are fairly well understood. This is a high-touch, people-driven vehicle, where knowledge and interpersonal and closing skills are highly valued. Therefore, it is critical that your sales force has embraced your brand in a way that manifests itself in their selling behavior. As one individual from a company with a sales force in transition described, "The new CEO knew what to do in the field. Hire and train. Hire and train. Train and mentor and get them motivated. And hire and train." The key to success is to hire and train using a brand lens and structure the right incentives to keep the sales force properly motivated.

SPECIFIC VARIATIONS, FROM COMPANY OWNED TO THIRD PARTY. Companies and brands can employ a variety of forms of field sales organizations to drive purchase experiences on their behalf. These structures run the gamut from company owned and branded to third party owned and branded (see Figure 5.6).

A company such as Prophet has a simple model, where Prophet's partners and directors sell into specific geographical territories. Global behemoths like IBM and GE have highly complex direct sales models, with many different field sales organizations. Some focus on specific vertical industries like health care or government, while others focus on certain reseller channels, and still others have specific global or strategic customer accounts. Yet others represent integrated solutions covering a company's entire product line. It is essential to understand this complexity and visually map out your own structure to make sure you are managing your brand optimally within each.

For instance, it often makes sense to leverage the field sales organizations of third parties to take your brand to market. These reseller or channel relationships can provide long-term alternative distribu-

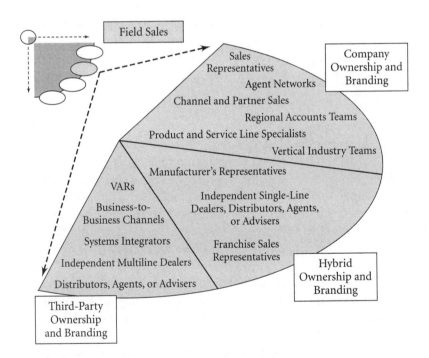

Figure 5.6.   Field Sales Variations.

tion for your brand in the way that the sales teams of technology consulting firms like EDS and CSC do for products from Sun, EMC, or Siebel. Of course, trying to get the attention of the salespeople inside these third parties to pay attention to your brand the same way you would is the most significant brand challenge most companies that use third-party distribution channels face within the purchase experience.

A DETAILED ANALYSIS OF FIELD SALES: GE POWER SYSTEMS. After you have mapped all of the various field sales structures that are at work in your business model, you must do a detailed analysis on the discrete brand touchpoints each structure provides. Figure 5.7 provides a sample for a regional accounts sales force, highlighting how specific brand touchpoints would manifest themselves given the brand identity of GE Power Systems, whose brand of products and services for the energy industry is grounded in partnership, heritage, trust, and technical superiority.

For GE Power Systems, a power plant's seven-year sales cycle could include initial discovery meetings, the Request for Proposal response, face-to-face specification meetings, facility tours, sell-in meetings with the company's various stakeholders, relationship building, price and volume conversations, informal and formal reference checking, and final contract negotiations.

GE Power Systems also focuses on building strategic relationships throughout the sales cycle, leveraging opportunities such as its "State of the Art" seminars, in which potential customers are educated on the latest diagnostics, monitoring systems, and products. Within each phase of the sales cycle, the brand gets a chance to be reinforced in the eyes of the prospect.

As your company tries to move from vendor to trusted adviser, from point products to integrated solutions, your field sales force is often leading the charge. Thinking about the following questions will help you develop a plan to equip them to be effective in their role.

- What lasting perceptions do you want the prospect to have from each interaction, and how does that support your business and brand objectives?
- How can you as a brand asset manager provide the tools, the training, or the support necessary to enable the field sales force to deliver those experiences?

Customer Touchpoints	GE Power Systems
Salesperson personality	Responsive, great communication skills, persistent and assertive; friends and partners
Sales and service ethos	Highest integrity; stick with clients through thick and thin
Sales team configuration	Sales team lead by account executives (AEs); maintain a single face to the customer
Depth of product and service knowledge	Technically deep knowledge
Product and service portfolio	Products ranging from power plants to day-to-day parts to emergency parts
Face-to-face meetings	Most AEs are located where the customer is, so they are in front of them all the time; deepen relationships at "State of the Art" conference
Product and service quality assurance	Spend significantly on upgrading products so never disadvantaged in the market; customer quality managers are assigned to twenty clients
Senior management participation	If a significant deal requires encouragement, GE senior management line up with senior management at prospect, and interface at conferences and social events
Pricing and discount strategy	Never cheaper in price; win all the ties
Payments, financing	Most customers do not need financing or capital; GE Capital structures creative financings on occasion, like lease airplanes of a customer

Figure 5.7.   Sample Brand Touchpoints of GE Systems' Regional Accounts Sales Team.

THE BRAND ASSET MANAGER'S PLAYBOOK: HOW TO ANTICIPATE AND NAVIGATE THE TOUGH ISSUES WITH FIELD SALES. To go beyond the deep dive, brand asset managers should anticipate and be prepared for certain types of overarching issues very specific to field sales that Prophet's 2002 Best Practices study unearthed. Figure 5.8 points to the fact that some critical issues cover periodic strategic opportunities (like sales force structure), while others call out operational and execution-oriented critical issues (like channel conflict or sales force education).

Sun Microsystems, for example, is working through a major repositioning of its direct sales force in an attempt to become more brand-

Brand Touchpoint Critical Issues		Management and Influence Tactics
Decisions around sales force structure (territories, product and service lines, incentive compensation)	Collaborate	1. Understand stresses in the system, internal and external 2. Bring market and customer perspectives on ease of access, intuitiveness of structure, other breakdowns 3. Advocate for solutions that serve customer and support brand priorities
Keeping the field sales force informed—offer, positioning, collateral, pricing	Own and control	1. Collaborate with product marketing, but own and integrate the content 2. Move toward dynamic, real-time media (flash, intranet sites, on-line learning modules) 3. Train, train, train
Channel conflict	Co-Drive	1. Identify whether it's causing material customer confusion 2. Quantify financial and brand equity damage 3. Uncover specific friction points and develop business rules to incent brand-appropriate behavior and make recommendations to restructure channel
Getting sales representatives from different product groups to work collaboratively on customer's behalf	Collaborate	1. Diagnose the root causes (training, education, incentives) 2. Identify whether this is causing material customer confusion or lost sales 3. Partner with the vice president of sales to brainstorm creative solutions (client advocates, integration specialists, sales force restructuring
No integrated view of customer's transaction history, product, or service requirements	Co-Drive	1. Document financial and brand impact (incremental revenues and lost sales) 2. Identify high return-on-investment areas (recent purchase history and recent service calls) for incremental improvement 3. Partner with sales, customer service, and information technology to drive phased solution
"Anything to close the deal" orientation versus brand values	Influence	1. Don't sound like a Pollyanna; be pragmatic 2. Identify key hot spots where people are doing things to close the deal that directly conflict with brand values 3. Be proactive in developing comprehensive solutions to these issues, while keeping feet to fire around out-of-bounds behavior

Figure 5.8. Brand Asset Manager's Playbook: Company-Controlled and Branded Field Sales.

centric. In the summer of 2001, it retrained its entire sales force to re-inforce the idea that it is not selling "a bunch of products" but rather "infrastructure that helps solve a customer's problem."[2]

Virtual Environments on the Internet

Branded virtual environments are a purchase experience vehicle made available by the explosion of the Internet in the late 1990s and will continue to evolve with the broadband and wireless boom. Although it is still in its infancy, this vehicle is already reshaping the brand-customer relationship in dramatic ways across diverse sectors, such as personal computers, stock purchasing, component replenishment, and travel. The strengths of branded virtual environments include customer control, ease of use, information richness, market aggregation, efficiency, and flexibility and have enabled companies like Travelocity, Dell, Staples, Schwab, and eBay to significantly differentiate their brands.

Having a virtual presence for many brands is now a requirement. The question is no longer whether but when and how. Articulating a clear role for this environment in the context of a customer's overall purchase experience is critical:

- Will it substitute and replace other purchase experience brand touchpoints?
- Will it be used as a complementary purchase vehicle, in conjunction with other purchase experiences?
- Will it vary by specific customer segments around specific use scenarios?
- How will we leverage it to deliver our brand promise?

These are important questions to answer, for they allow you to prioritize investments into this brand touchpoint category as well as understand how connected (or not) your on-line strategy is to your brand strategy.

CORE OPERATIONAL CHARACTERISTICS AND ORGANIZATIONAL CAPABILITIES. A number of organizational capabilities are required to operationalize this touchpoint category and make sure it is in line with your brand's promise.

Virtual environments can provide access to a broader customer base more quickly, since the Internet is everywhere and is always on. However, since few interactions need human intervention, this environment needs to stand on its own, delivering the brand promise with remarkable self-sufficiency. Customers have learned how to serve themselves, on their schedule, and at their own pace. You need to decide whether this customer-driven and -controlled environment is, first, aligned with your brand and, second, how the brand promise will be consistently delivered in this environment. Obviously, the intuitiveness and usability of the on-line experience are critical, as are speed, convenience, and accessibility. All of these together help bring the brand promise to life.

SPECIFIC VARIATIONS: FROM COMPANY OWNED TO THIRD PARTY. The obvious format in the company-owned category is a direct-to-customer branded site (of the format www.xyzcompany.com) that is available to the general public. The variations have to do with the creation of differentiated experiences (see Figure 5.9).

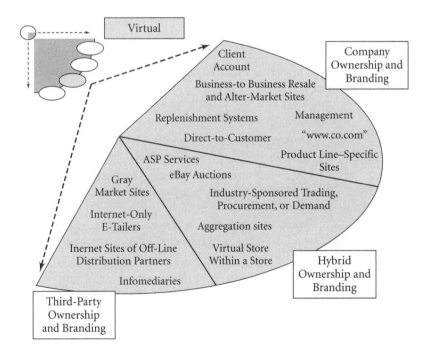

Figure 5.9. Virtual Environment Variations.

While some of the formats that appear in the hybrid or third-party-owned categories may just mirror your off-line format, some represent a new breed of Internet-specific alternatives. Most, like the auction sites (eBay), demand aggregators (Orbitz), Internet-only e-tailers (Amazon), and infomediaries (C-Net, My Simon), take advantage of the Internet's unique strengths to create new opportunities for the brand. The brand asset manager's job is to map out which formats are most appropriate tied to your business model, as well as those that will help support and strengthen your brand in the future.

A DETAILED ANALYSIS OF A VIRTUAL ENVIRONMENT: DELL'S PREMIER PROGRAM. Figure 5.10 shows a detailed analysis for a client account management Web site using Dell's Premier Program as the illustrative brand. Dell's brand is grounded in a belief in the strength of direct interaction with customers and in strong functional attributes around "price-for-performance, flexible customization, tailored service and support and the best customer experience."[3] Thus both the strategic decision to implement a premier program and the specific manner in which each of its touchpoints is designed is totally aligned with the brand. From its decision to allow the customer to list only preapproved configurations and SKUs to the ability to support work flow processes inside the customer's organization to get an end user's PC choice approved by his or her purchasing manager, Dell has achieved a true customer-centric approach, further building what the Dell brand stands for.

THE BRAND ASSET MANAGER'S PLAYBOOK: HOW TO ANTICIPATE AND NAVIGATE THE TOUGH ISSUES WITH VIRTUAL ENVIRONMENTS. Prophet's 2002 Best Practices study unearthed certain issues that brand asset managers should anticipate and be prepared for, listed in Figure 5.11. Some are strategic, like the decision to sell direct to customers, while others are more operationally oriented.

The decision to sell direct to customers creates an opportunity to better control and therefore truly deliver on the brand promise. For example, the U.S. airline industry is using this touchpoint to squeeze layers out of the value chain. By offering better pricing for flights purchased on their own Web sites, major airlines like United and Delta are encouraging customers to purchase directly from them. While this may feel unpleasant to the travel agents, it seems to be appealing to

Customer Touchpoints	Dell's Premier Program
Customer segmentation, needs-driven alternative shopping pathways	Information technology, purchasing manager, and end user needs addressed, "quick picks" for each user
Product selection and inventory depth	Create own store, with customer SKUs
Depth of product and service content	Deep, available if desired, "Ask Dudley"
Solution configuration alternatives	Robust solutions configuration tool; only preapproved configurations shown
Self-service shopping tools	Favorites list, preapproved lists
Site design and usability	Clean, uncluttered, intuitive
Speed, accessibility, and uptime	Fast, high uptime, flash, and HTML
Account-specific information and history; personalization	"Your prices, your configurations!"; dedicated account teams
Customer contact strategy: chat, e-mail, voiceover IP	E-mail alerts; Dell account team contact information, workflow approval and routing
On-site promotions	Employee home purchase, special offers
Customer payment	Paperless purchase orders, leasing/financing
"In-home" order receipt experience	Robust order tracking; Dell boxes

Figure 5.10.   Sample Brand Touchpoints of Dell's Premier Program Client Account Management Web Experiences.

the customers. A recent *New York Times* article mentioned that Southwest already sells 30 percent of its tickets on-line, and other major carriers, like Delta, hope to reach that level in the next three years.[4] This type of decision has huge ramifications on the brand-customer relationship for those companies.

Customer Contact Centers

The last major touchpoint category, customer contact centers, represents situations where remote telephone-based interactions are the primary drivers of the purchase experience. Major automated call centers dominate this category, and call center representatives—the voice on

Brand Touchpoint Critical Issues		Management and Influence Tactics
Decision to sell direct-to-customer (what products/ what offers)	Collaborate	1. Develop hypotheses around attractive opportunities 2. Partner with sales and business development to quantify financial and brand risk to "disrupting" existing channel relationships; look for win-win scenarios 3. Drive holistic cost-benefit analysis and present business case to management
Decision to support region-specific, product line–specific or division-specific sites	Own and control	1. Be proactive, using customer research to understand navigability; usability of existing Web site portfolio, before this mushrooms out of control 2. Drive alignment over firmwide information architecture 3. Develop business rules for when microsites can be deployed, with minimum integration standards
Site launches and upgrades	Co-drive	1. Partner with Internet team (business and technology) to establish rhythm and timing 2. Bring data-driven customer insights to drive feature design and prioritization 3. Support through usability testing and launch
Decision to develop customer segment-specific shopping and purchasing experiences	Own and control	1. Study segmentation strategies used in other channels; test applicability for Internet 2. Study the data around usage, lost sales, and customer satisfaction to uncover other opportunities 3. Develop business case and offer for specific hypotheses
Depth of customer-specific personalization and information	Co-drive	1. Partner with Internet team to understand what is technically feasible 2. Determine what level (for example, account history versus personalized product recommendations) is appropriate for the brand; do not automatically assume more is better 3. Design, deploy, measure, and reassess
Ability to operationalize customer contact and back-end distribution capabilities	Influence	1. Do a brand-driven assessment of existing capabilities and processes, unearthing high-risk areas 2. Work with cross-functional teams to troubleshoot key breakdowns 3. Guard against marketing/offer/brand promise getting ahead of operational capabilities

**Figure 5.11.   Brand Asset Manager's Playbook:
Company-Controlled and -Branded Web Sites.**

Use of portals, intermediaries, auction sites, or other native Internet brands	Own and control	1. Analyze the role that each could play for your brand; target customer overlap, economic attractiveness, brand fit 2. Develop clear business case for each tactic, don't overplay 3. Experiment with many different configurations; it is still a young medium and we have a lot of learning to do

Figure 5.11. (*continued*)

the other end of the telephone—dominate the experience. With the emergence of other communication options, such as e-mail, live chat, and voice-over Internet protocol, however, the telephone is only one of many contact channels that these representatives use to interact and build relationships with prospective customers.

CORE OPERATIONAL CHARACTERISTICS AND ORGANIZATIONAL CAPABILI-TIES. Unlike the other three touchpoint categories, customer contact centers are not often considered as a stand-alone purchase driver. Rather, they are used in conjunction with some other purchase driver, such as a visually attractive printed catalogue, a field sales team, or a rich Web experience to complete the purchase cycle. Because contact centers usually complement another touchpoint, there is significant emphasis here on cross-channel coordination.

Although they are expensive to build, contact centers offer a number of benefits. These include using a quality customer database and historical purchase knowledge on a real-time basis to help close a sale by better understanding the customers and allowing employees to personally deliver on the brand experience. Mitigating the risks of high employee turnover and the peaks and valleys of customer demand, you have the advantage of operating in one location, training centrally, and placing experienced people with inexperienced people to accelerate everyone's learning.

Sometimes there is still a fair amount of persuasive selling that happens during the interaction, and other times the interaction is more about order taking. Regardless, training and motivating the call center representatives to live the brand consistently is critical to the long-term success of this touchpoint. Finally, customer contact centers can often serve the dual purpose of handling post-purchase customer service requests (discussed in Chapter Six).

SPECIFIC VARIATIONS: FROM COMPANY OWNED TO THIRD PARTY. Although there are many types of remote telephone and Internet-assisted interaction variations presented in Figure 5.12, the major differences are whether calls are inbound or outbound and whether you have decided to outsource the function.

With inbound telesales, you wait for customers to call, usually using some type of direct marketing vehicle to drive them to call you. The vehicles you have used to market the brand will determine what tools to put at the representative's disposal (for example, assisted Web navigation or live chat). With outbound telesales, you are likely to be responding to a prospective customer's request for information (or you may be cold calling, which makes it a pre-purchase interaction). Regardless of the vehicle, the script has to be on-brand for the prospect to experience the brand consistently.

The outsourcing decision is equally interesting. Since contact centers are remote, the prospective customer may never know if it is outsourced. Many companies are exploring different options, including offshore providers, to drive down costs and garner better efficiencies.

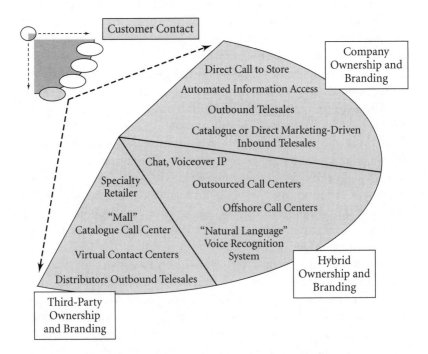

Figure 5.12. Customer Contact Center Variations.

Clearly, the contact center and the represented company need to work together closely to design a brand-driven training program and monitoring system to ensure accurate representation of the brand and the delivery of its promise.

A DETAILED ANALYSIS OF A TOLL-FREE NUMBER INBOUND CALL CENTER: 21ST CENTURY INSURANCE. Many of the specific brand touchpoints within a toll-free number purchase experience are comparable to those of in-store or Internet environments. The challenge for this brand touchpoint category is that you are completely reliant on the skills, personality, and flexibility of the customer service representative (CSR) to bring all of this to life. Clearly, you have some decisions to make about what kinds of training, tools, and incentives you provide them, but the CSRs make or break the interaction. In Figure 5.13, we provide an example of the analysis for 21st Century Insurance, a U.S. auto insurer brand that has thrived and survived on a toll-free number direct response system.

Customer Touchpoints	21st Century Insurance
Call associate personality	Perky; quick to respond; sense of humor
Shopping assistance, service ethos	Full service; honest; inquisitive; holistic
Depth of product, service knowledge	Involved; expansive, thorough
Hours of operation	24/7
Product selection, inventory depth	Focus on autos only; no new home policies
Price accessibility	Quote on phone and on Web
Phone number	1-800-211-SAVE
Transfer	Quick and efficient; no personal hand-off
Level of automation	Initial greeting automated; select "English" or "Spanish," "Home" or "Car" insurance
Level of customer knowledge	Collected basic information; tried to build customer profile; bad historical data
Hold music	Elevator music
Support of Web channel	Call center representatives subtly discourage use of Web site

Figure 5.13.   Sample Brand Touchpoints of 21st Century Insurance's Toll-Free Number Call Center.

THE BRAND ASSET MANAGER'S PLAYBOOK: HOW TO ANTICIPATE AND NAVIGATE THE TOUGH ISSUES WITH CUSTOMER CONTACT CENTERS. As a brand asset manager, you need to partner with those who control the customer contact center to guarantee that the company is delivering an on-brand experience here. Prophet's 2002 Best Practice study uncovered some typical challenges in the customer contact center world (see Figure 5.14).

A critical challenge involves striking the right balance between CSR productivity and high quality, on-brand interactions. Tension exists here because closing a sale quickly is often rewarded without regard to whether the CSR delivered an experience that will lead to a better brand-customer relationship and deliver greater revenues and profits over time.

BREADTH OF DISTRIBUTION VERSUS CONSISTENCY OF EXECUTION: THE TIGHTROPE WALK

Most organizations no longer have the luxury of "just" trying to optimize the purchase experience within a single distribution vehicle, in which they have complete control. In fact, our Best Practices study showed that most companies are increasing rather than decreasing the number and breadth of their purchase experience touchpoints. There is a sense of urgency to create ways for the customer to purchase the brand wherever, whenever, and however the customer pleases.

At the same time, companies are being pressured to make sure that each purchase format in use (for example, company owned, third party) represents the most effective way to reach those customers in a consistent, on-brand, and differentiated way. Xerox, for example, has large national accounts with a direct sales force, but it has also invested heavily in developing an exclusive dealer channel dedicated to working with small and middle-market businesses exclusively.

Given all these distribution choices, all businesses still need to answer the same fundamental questions by using their brand as a lens to determine the best strategies to pursue:

- How broad should our distribution be?
- How easy will it be for us to execute consistently across this breadth of brand touchpoints?
- How much of this distribution do we want or need to brand and control?

Brand Touchpoint Critical Issues		Management and Influence Tactics
Multichannel contact management	Co-Drive	1. Establish cross-channel task force 2. Identify other key points of communication and foster closer relationships 3. Align channels through collaboration and incentives
Load balancing and peak staffing issues	Influence	1. Capture and provide customer feedback from challenges that occur during peak times 2. Identify reason for high volume of calls 3. Align channels through collaboration and incentives
High employee turnover, inconsistent service	Collaborate	1. Focus on running centralized training programs on systems, behavior, brand, and products 2. Provide simple rules for employees to adhere to 3. Review profile of employee recruiting
Variable compensation	Influence	1. Work with the call center manager to understand compensation model 2. Don't make compensation formula too complex that employee does not understand it 3. Consider alternatives tied to brand or sales goals
Employee knowledgeability, accessibility	Own and control	1. Give employees tools to get their job done right 2. Consider appropriate level of product knowledge that reflects brand and offers return on investment 3. Institute formal knowledge management program
Balance between productivity and quality	Co-Drive	1. Closely monitor productivity by number of customers, dollar sold, and length of time on phone 2. Tape and monitor call to gain insight on quality 3. Track repeat sales, and conduct customer satisfaction surveys
Quality of customer information	Own and control	1. Do your best to create a single view of the customer 2. Put systems in place to clean data 3. Train on the importance of quality

Figure 5.14.   Brand Asset Manager's Playbook: Company-Branded Inbound Customer Contact Center.

With a better understanding of the major purchase touchpoint categories, you should be able to help your company answer these questions with the ultimate goal of developing sustainable brand-customer relationships.

How Much Breadth?

We advise taking a pragmatic approach here. Clearly, there are business and brand considerations that should be incorporated into how you answer these questions:

Business Questions

- How much up-front investment and cost is there to develop and operate the brand-customer experience we seek to deliver?
- How can we access core markets and customer segments?
- How mature is the distribution channel?
- Does it fit with our brand?
- Do we have the ability to deliver an on-brand purchase experience consistently?
- What is our expected margin profile in each channel?
- Do we have a differentiated value proposition relative to existing distribution choices?
- Do we have the ability to execute?
- What are other risk factors?

Brand Questions

- What are core customers expecting of our brand?
- Where would they expect to find us, and where would they not?
- How can we best reach them and make it easy for them to reach us?
- How would some of the new target customer segments that we are eyeing for future growth answer those same questions?

Sometimes the market, customers, or competition will dictate the answers for you, and your job will be to figure out how to respond efficiently and effectively. Obviously, making sure you have a compelling strategy to create the right brand presence is critical for success.

How Much Consistency?

Consistency is a fundamental requirement for strong brand-customer relationships, so you should be prepared to ask hard questions:

• What would it take to deliver against the brand promise consistently in a particular touchpoint or format?
• Can we do it?
• Can our distribution partner do it?

In the context of a multichannel, multiformat, or multilevel distribution strategy, achieving consistency is challenging. Basic intuition tells us that the more variables you add to the equation, the more difficult it will be to operationalize consistently. So the question becomes, "What type of incremental investment do we need to make in order to achieve the level of brand and channel consistency that we seek?"

Incremental investments in the name of consistency should always be grounded in the firm reality of customer expectations. If the same customer segment is accessing and purchasing your brand across different formats and vehicles that carry your brand (Pottery Barn stores, Pottery Barn catalogue and call center, and PotteryBarn.com), customer expectations for consistency are high. If different formats are focused at different segments (like the Xerox example above), with minimal customer crossover, overinvesting in consistency is unwarranted.

How Much Control?

The final issue is control. How much control and branding of the distribution do you really want or need to be successful, and at what price? Total control of distribution may not be necessary or desirable. Strong incumbents could already exist with solid relationships with your target customers, and in this situation, it makes more sense to go through them rather than around them. Or your model could be built exclusively around a third-party distribution strategy, such as Procter & Gamble or Pepsi. Or total control may not be an option because of your company's size, stage of development, capital structure, or regulatory category.

From a brand perspective, however, control clearly has its benefits because you have a better chance of delivering a consistent, on-brand purchase experience that will, it is hoped, turn into on-target profits.

You will also have direct access to the customer to develop a meaningful post-purchase relationship on terms that work for both of you.

There are various types of branded distribution vehicles (among them, franchises, dealerships, exclusive independent agent, or distributors) that strike a balance between these two extremes. Each has slightly different trade-offs around ownership, control, capital investment, and ease of execution, but in essence, the distribution channel carries your brand without requiring enormous capital outlays. Although coordination becomes more complex, you get the benefits of having a branded distribution relationship with customers. Of course, if a salesperson, a Web site, or a store carries the BP, McDonald's, Porsche, AT&T, or Allstate brand, customers are going to expect the same level of service, a comparable experience, and a hands-on ability to get problems resolved.

This whole conversation, of course, needs to be juxtaposed against what the customer is truly expecting of your brand in any particular purchase context. For instance, Kodak cannot be too concerned about its lack of control over Eckerd's counter personnel because it trusts that consumers can differentiate between what is being delivered by the Eckerd brand versus what is being delivered by the Kodak brand. Put another way, in traditional distribution formats, customers have the ability to distinguish between the role of the distribution brand and the role of the product or service brands.

Optimizing Your Brand's Purchase Experience Given Third-Party Distribution

Most companies have some percentage of third-party-controlled and -branded distribution in their overall purchase mix. If you can get exclusivity for your product line or brand with a given third-party relationship, go for it. It always helps to be the exclusive line that a third party carries.

Most third-party distribution relationships, however, are not willing to offer exclusivity because much of their value proposition has to do with giving customers a variety of brand choices. Thus many brands have no choice but to compete with other brands in the same purchase environment. For many categories, that is just standard operating procedure. As Bob Lachky, vice president of brand management at Anheuser-Busch, notes, "The retailer has a ton of power over a brand like ours. If they decide to promote you one weekend, it can make a huge difference. Their power has a lot to do with consumer choice. If you do not get the shelf space and you do not get the promotion, you will not be successful."

Nevertheless, a multitude of tactics can be used to influence a customer's interaction with the brand at purchase even when the company does not control the purchase environment. Clearly, pricing, packaging, point-of-purchase marketing, priority shelf space positioning (and its equivalent in a direct sales environment), as well as the product or service itself, are all different ways to compete. Jeff Herbert, president of Beverage Partners Worldwide, shares this approach:

> Different channels command different prices for our product just based on the channel's value proposition. In convenience stores, we can price at a premium because consumers are paying for, well, convenience. In supermarkets, we price low and stock high, and try to tie in with other things in grocery. In mass merchandise, our influence in having more space is greater, so we look at things like different holders and racks. We have a value chain for each channel, and we track the movement and payout on each channel investment. For each channel, we tailor the message and the promotions but not the brand personality.

It is obvious that to create the right win-win approach, brand asset managers need to find the right dollar-information incentive mix to continue to motivate third-party distributors.

IBM's Business Partner program provides a great example of how to get comparable third-party leverage in a business-to-business complex purchase model. IBM's PartnerWorld program provides extensive support to the channel in key value-added areas such as marketing and sales, education and certification, technical support, and customer financing. Partners can access this support on-line, over the telephone, or through their channel sales manager. All of these investments are designed to help the channel understand the IBM brand and better promote IBM's products and services, even though many IBM Business Partners also partner with Sun, Dell, and EMC.

Strategic Thinking at the Channel Level

Finally, be strategic in understanding how your brand adds to the channel's value proposition and experience. There is often a lack of distinctiveness in these third-party multibrand retailers or channel partners. The channel may need elements of differentiation that can set them apart, and your brands could provide some of that cachet and pull. By understanding the role your brands play in driving traffic and profit, as well as being an ingredient in the channel's overall offer, you are in a better position to effectively leverage your brand to drive purchase.

Allowing the channel to force your brand into becoming overly promotional at purchase can create bad expectations around discounting, which customers get used to. Hyatt and other travel brands worry about how this new class of Internet-based travel distributors, which sell strictly on price, and have the impact of commoditizing brand selection at purchase and thus commoditizing brands in this category overall. Approaching this challenge with an appropriate mix of short-term aggressive tactics and longer-term objectives is essential.

The objective should be to get the most appropriate leverage for your business and your brand at any given point in time. Obviously, the needs of your company may evolve as your brand evolves, so be ready to make the appropriate changes when the time comes. Flexibility is key.

FROM PURCHASE EXPERIENCE TO USAGE AND OPERATIONAL DELIVERY

In this chapter, we have demonstrated how to operationalize the brand during the purchase experience. For any given potential customer around any given purchase occasion, the purchase experience can be simple or complex, involving a few basic interactions or a whole series of different interactions in multiple purchase contexts. For any brand, the purchase contexts through which it is going to market can vary dramatically. In all of these situations, companies are trying to do things that help drive toward the right outcome, which is to get the customer to purchase the brand.

Even if Christine had not made purchases tied to the scenarios presented earlier, she still would have been left with a set of impressions, thoughts, and feelings that would become the basis for a possible future relationship. The worst-case scenario for the brand is that Christine did not make a purchase because she became frustrated during the purchase experience and thus the brand-customer relationship went negative.

But luckily, the software provider and Pottery Barn purchase experiences were successful, and Christine did buy. She would now move to the next phase of the brand-sales cycle, the post-purchase phase. The most important component of that is usually the usage or consumption experience: How does the brand really work, taste, perform, make my job easier, give me better answers, bring me joy, or deliver against any one of the myriad of conscious and unconscious expectations that I had about this brand and this purchase at the time that it was made? This is where the brand has the opportunity to deliver and create deep, rich, and meaningful relationships with customers that become the source of long-term sustainable value.

CHAPTER SIX

The Post-Purchase Experience

Solidifying the Brand-Customer Relationship

Sherwin started a new job as information technology director for a small services business over four years ago. Having a mountain of issues to take care of in starting a new job and relocating his family, he decided to simply roll over his Fidelity 401(k) portfolio into a program offered by his new employer, even though that program was managed by an unfamiliar company, ManuLife.

The paperwork that he needed to fill out to orchestrate the rollover was easy to understand, and the funds were transferred without a hitch. His company's human resource department gave him all of the supporting materials and a toll-free number that he could call to get direct information. The plan seemed to have a good variety of investment alternatives, some conservative and some aggressive, and the representative he spoke with on the telephone was very knowledgeable about the plan's strengths and weaknesses.

Since Sherwin had been investing in the stock market for a few years, he did not need that much advice (and the ManuLife people were not allowed to give it anyway). On his own, he got the information he needed, decided to allocate his money across four different mutual funds, communicated that decision to the representative, and got on with his life. The quarterly account statements were fairly detailed, and the funds' performance was better than he expected (at least for the first year). He also received a newsletter on retirement planning and investment strategies from ManuLife, which he read when he had time.

About two years ago, ManuLife launched a Web site designed to allow customers to manage their 401(k) investments, monitor performance more frequently, and reallocate existing funds and new contributions on a nearly real-time basis. Sherwin signed up immediately, got a password, and added the site to the "Favorites" list of his Web browser. He started visiting the site frequently because it was so easy to access, and thus gradually he started to think about ManuLife and his 401(k) account more often. As the stock market became unstable, he rebalanced his portfolio a few times, and while he still received paper statements, he was fully functioning as an on-line client. Today, he considers himself a very satisfied ManuLife client.

Within his work world, Sherwin is dealing with the usual problem of the day: another T1 connection went down. He has switched service providers three times recently, yet still cannot get a reliable connection for the company's New York office. He is on the telephone with his current provider more in a week than he is with most of his other vendors in a year. If the company needs to send one more crew out to the New York office to address issues with Sherwin's routers and physical infrastructure, he knows he will move on to provider number four quickly.

Even more frustrating is the fact that his current supplier had the nerve to send him a proposal four weeks ago suggesting it become the consolidated source for all of the company's voice and data traffic. Sherwin wonders to himself, "How can they even consider pitching more business when their performance is so lousy?"

DEFINING THE POST-PURCHASE EXPERIENCE

Whether in financial services or data networking, the post-purchase experience begins immediately when someone has purchased or provided a firm financial commitment to purchase and ends when the customer completely consumes, resells, retires, or otherwise stops using the product or service. Some brands have post-purchase experiences that are long, complex, and relationship driven (GE Aircraft

Engines is one of them). For other brands, the post-purchase experience is often brief and almost exclusively outside the company's direct ability to influence, control, or otherwise manage once the product has left the shelf (for example, Trident chewing gum).

Within the entire brand-customer relationship, the post-purchase experience remains one of the most underleveraged yet potentially powerful ways to drive sustainable, profitable, and long-term value back to the company. In Prophet's 2002 Best Practices study, the three brand-building tools deemed most effective at developing loyal customers in the context of post-purchase were product or service quality, the use experience, and positive word-of-mouth referrals. The brand's effectiveness is predicated on a single critical assumption: the product or service is completely delivering on the brand's promise and, on occasion, overdelivering and delighting customers beyond expectations.

The product or service needs to do what is expected, as expected, for as long as expected, from billing to account service to all communications throughout the post-purchase relationship. This obviously requires a level of commitment to the post-purchase experience that few companies think about outside the department involved. Many Prophet 2002 Best Practices study participants, however, from utilities to hotels to wireless companies to industrial conglomerates, acknowledged the importance of getting this right. These individuals discussed scenarios in which they could see themselves advocating pulling money away from their budgets (usually focused on pre-purchase marketing communications activities) and shifting it toward key post-purchase brand touchpoints, because, in the words of Susan Atteridge, TXU's chief communications officer, "Nothing works if usage and customer service are broken."

If your company and brand consistently deliver against expectations, then you are in a much better position to drive "share of wallet" (have current customers buy more items or make purchases more often) and mitigate the need for customers to have to go through the pre-purchase cycle again. In addition, outstanding post-purchase experiences generally lead to strong loyalty over time, which triggers customers to recommend or endorse your product or service to others.

Post-Purchase Experience Goals: The Company-Brand Perspective

A company's primary post-purchase objective is to increase the loyal portion of its user base because this is the group with which it will develop its most profitable relationships. Although there is a perception that brand loyalty is wavering, we have consistently found that the 80–20 rule still applies for most businesses: 80 percent of profits come from 20 percent of customers. Thus a company's post-purchase goals have to be aimed at increasing the likelihood of converting first-time buyers into the 20 percent of loyalists. To succeed in the post-purchase experience, a company needs to

- Understand the economics of loyalty
- Create an integrated and actionable view of the customer's post-purchase relationship with the company and the brand
- Leverage the brand to find new areas for growth

Understanding the Economics of Loyalty

Whereas most companies talk about post-purchase experience success as being tied to high levels of customer satisfaction, we would argue that you need to go beyond that mind-set and look at which post-purchase investments need to be made to maximize chances for success. An economic model has to be grounded in an understanding of how new and loyal customers can directly and indirectly influence the future economics of the business and the brand.

For example, BMW knows that "almost two-thirds of its current lease customers roll over into a new BMW, especially if it is a family under thirty-five with two adults working," according to the company's vice president of marketing for North America, Jim McDowell. Moreover, BMW knows that it sometimes loses customers in their mid-thirties when life changes force them to switch to a more family-friendly car (such as a mini-van), which BMW does not carry. These are great insights because they can drive or influence post-purchase experience communication and new product development efforts. BMW's ability to identify customers who have recently moved into the mini-van demographic and those who have not allows it to tailor its messaging strategy and level of investment to two very different segments: the one that might return to the BMW brand in ten or so years from now and the other that might stay in the BMW family, at the time of their next lease renewal, a mere six months from now.

To succeed in the post-purchase experience, every company needs to understand the key economic influences at work in its business model. This understanding should include traditional efforts, such as calculating the lifetime value of individual customer relationships compared to offsetting customer acquisition and retention costs. Indirect economic influences, such as word of mouth, a powerful driver of new sales, may also play a significant role. Developing this level of insight into customer behavior gives you an ability to prioritize where, how, and for whom your post-purchase investments will be made and how best to deepen the brand-customer relationship over time.

Integrated View of Customer Interactions

Companies have to strive for competent, consistent, and professional interactions with customers at all times, regardless of how and where the interaction is taking place. In many categories, it is not enough just to have good answers. What is also needed is for the employee interacting with a customer to have some knowledge of the customer's past interactions with the company, what went right, what went wrong, what the customer's preferences might be, and other insights that help to determine the strength of the customer's relationship with the brand.

With small businesses, that knowledge may be passed down informally and never codified. In large companies, with multiple parts of the organization touching the customer at different times and in different ways, that knowledge and insight need to get captured in user-friendly systems that are easy for employees to learn and use. Recent CRM-related technologies have helped many companies achieve this objective. For example, Amazon takes the opportunity to deepen its brand-customer relationship every time someone logs on to its Web site. With its ability to recommend new books to you, based on previous purchases, as well as its ability to let you know the status of your order, it is able to reassure you that you are being taken care of and provide you with a personalized reason to consider a new purchase.

Leveraging the Brand to Find New Areas of Growth

During the post-purchase experience, a company should exercise its ability to listen better and get deeper insights into the relationship a customer has with the brand. Thus the final goal during the post-purchase phase should be to capitalize on your customer relationship and high levels of satisfaction to find your next major source of growth. To succeed at locating this next source, you will find that getting intimately close with your customers, having high levels of customer and brand understanding, and developing strong innovation capabilities can help provide an insurmountable competitive advantage that most companies can only dream of. This is the magic that Sony, Disney, 3M, and Amazon have unleashed.

To meet these post-purchase goals, the company has to

- Deliver on the expectations promised by the brand in the pre-purchase and purchase experiences
- Deliver more brand value to the customer (with less resource spending)
- Deepen and expand the brand-customer relationship by continuing to delight the customer
- Increase brand loyalty and advocacy

Post-Purchase Experience Goals: The Customer's Perspective

The customer's main objective in the post-purchase experience, whether conscious or subconscious, is to have their decisions validated. To this end, the customer hopes to accomplish the following goals:

- Receive the level of service and support expected as promised in the pre-purchase and purchase experiences
- Experience high levels of satisfaction through a favorable usage experience
- Feel confident enough in the brand to purchase the brand again or recommend it to others (or both)

In order for these goals to be realized, the product or service needs to perform to expectations while delivering both the functional and emotional benefits promised by the brand during the pre-purchase and purchase phases. Thus the product or service being used or consumed needs to behave, taste, feel, work, sound, perform, or look exactly as the customer expected. Part of the customer's post-purchase satisfaction may also involve being positively recognized, acknowledged, and validated by friends, family members, or peers as having made a smart purchase decision.

If problems emerge that prevent the customer from having a satisfactory usage experience, the customer will expect the company to take full responsibility for resolving those issues, no matter how difficult they may be. The brand promises made during the previous two phases will drive exactly how the customer will expect the company to act. Thus successfully handling post-purchase experience issues and complaints may be all that is required to achieve high levels of customer satisfaction.

Here is how the company's and customer's goals are aligned in the post-purchase phase:

COMPANY	CUSTOMER
Deliver brand promises	Validate the decision
Deliver additional brand value	Receive expected service and support
Delight customers	Be satisfied with usage
Increase brand loyalty and advocacy	Feel confident in brand

SHAPING THE POST-PURCHASE EXPERIENCE: HOW TO EXECUTE AGAINST THE BRAND PROMISE ACROSS DIFFERENT POST-PURCHASE BRAND TOUCHPOINTS

There are four major categories of the post-purchase experience for companies to focus on post-purchase brand touchpoints (see Figure 6.1):

- The product or service usage experience itself
- Other operational delivery brand touchpoints
- Customer service
- Loyalty programs and continuous communications efforts

For each, we provide examples of the detailed analyses that should take place, as well as identify key strategic and operational issues in the form of a brand asset manager's playbook. Throughout, we weave in a discussion of the interdependencies across these brand touchpoints and specifically focus on the dangers of a disconnected brand experience. Although an inconsistent experience is a concern for a

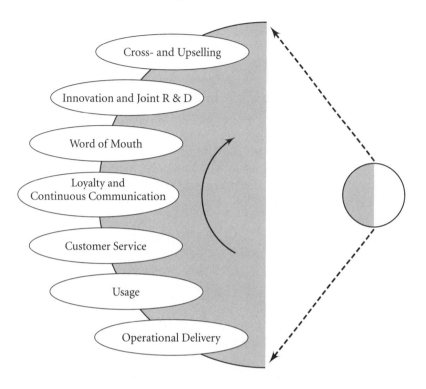

Figure 6.1.   Primary Post-Purchase Brand Touchpoint Categories.

brand during any phase of the brand-customer relationship, it is particularly troublesome when dealing with existing customers in the post-purchase phase. This is because you are trying to satisfy, build relationships with, and encourage customers to make a repeat purchase all at the same time.

The Usage Experience

The usage experience is the most important post-purchase experience brand touchpoint. BMW, for example, believes in the power of a compelling usage experience. In the words of marketing vice president Jim McDowell, "Nothing that we do is as convincing as having our potential customers behind the wheel. We show them that what your car does well, our car does brilliantly." Sony understands this as well. According to Denise Yohn, vice president of segment marketing and brand planning, for years the company focused exclusively on "making sure customers loved the products once they bought them."

Any experience that a customer has using or consuming the product or service—whether it is cooking dinner with that Calphalon pan, taking Tylenol, or executing an on-line sell order through a Schwab brokerage account—is covered in the usage experience.

CORE OPERATIONAL CHARACTERISTICS AND ORGANIZATIONAL CAPABILI-
TIES. Issues of quality, dependability, reliability, freshness, consistency, style, and effectiveness all become magnified in the usage experience. For example, with Hyatt, "the actual usage experience overrides any other post-purchase consideration, as it directly relates to future purchases. If the actual usage experience is unsatisfactory and the problem resolution is not satisfactory, people have many other choices beyond Hyatt," says Tom O'Toole, senior marketing vice president. Getting this right is critical for the long-term health of the business and the brand.

Thus to succeed, you need to understand what usage experience levers are most important for your brand. Here are some of the key questions that you should consider relative to usage experience success; many rely on capabilities highlighted in the CEO's checklist in Chapter Two:

- How will the product or service be used by the target customer? What types of functional and emotional benefits is the product or service expected to deliver?

- How significant a sum was spent (with significance defined as a percentage of disposable income or percentage of total budget or percentage of total category spent)?

- What is the life expectancy of the product or service? How long does any given customer expect to use it? What is the cycle time between purchases?

- Is this a single-use or multiple-use item? What is the frequency of expected usage?

- How much customization, configuration, or personalization is involved?

- In how many different types of situations or contexts (usage occasions) will the customer be using the product? Is the product used by a single person or multiple people?

- How much of a customer's usage experience is visible to (and tracked by) the company?
- How much of the usage experience involves company personnel (high touch)? How much does the product or service itself stand alone (low touch)?
- How critical is the product to the customer's life or operations? What are the switching costs and hurdles to move toward a different company or brand?

Ideally, you would have already asked prospects and customers these and other questions in the early steps of defining, designing, and developing the overall brand-customer experience.

We believe the usage experience represents a significant transition phase in the brand-customer relationship, where the customer starts to take control of and own the experience and the brand.

Robert Lachky, vice president of brand management for Anheuser-Busch, gives a good example of this in beer, which "is a fun social product, regardless if it is used with friends, family, or the softball team." Although the marketers at Anheuser-Busch know that they have minimal control over the usage experience, they can try to influence it through the programs they supply to wholesalers or through advertising. However, in the end, the customer creates the context for experiencing the brand.

DETAILED ANALYSIS OF THE USAGE EXPERIENCE: THREE EXAMPLES. Usage experience is a difficult brand touchpoint to talk about because it can vary so dramatically from category to category, product to service, and business to business. Some businesses have little or no ability to influence the usage experience directly once the product has been purchased (examples are Hugo Boss shoes and a Sony CD Walkman). For other businesses, the usage experience is highly dependent on a specific brand-customer interaction (examples are taking a JetBlue flight, eating a meal at McDonald's, or getting a haircut at Supercuts). Other categories require a fair amount of supporting operations to get a product or service installed and working (examples are Siebel's CRM system and a Merrill Lynch brokerage account), so operational delivery issues will drive a great deal of the usage experience. Some companies have a 100 percent accurate record of all of a customer's usage interactions (for example, an AT&T Wireless or Citibank account), and others have no direct visibility into when or how often their product is being used (for example, Porsche, Colgate, and Sara Lee).

To reflect these variations, we have outlined detailed analyses for three different types of usage experiences to address two primary questions:

- What are all the brand touchpoints within this category?

- How is the customer experiencing each brand touchpoint?

The three types of usage experiences represent three different ways in which the brand-customer relationship might be built:

- Through a series of one-time discrete service interactions (an airplane ride on JetBlue; see Figure 6.2)

- Through a multiuse product (E.P.T. home pregnancy test; see Figure 6.3)

- Through a long-term relationship built in a business-to-business environment (a consulting engagement with Prophet; see Figure 6.4)

Each of these examples illustrates how a company that is doing relatively well in its category provides an on-brand experience across a comprehensive set of brand touchpoints. This is the sort of analysis you should conduct with your own brand by asking key questions:

- Is the brand coming to life in a way that is consistent with the brand strategy? How would you grade the company's delivery of the brand's promise at each brand touchpoint?

- Have you leveraged all the brand touchpoints at your disposal to convey your brand best?

- For the brand touchpoints where you are not performing as well as you would like, what is the action plan to rectify this situation?

- What are some of the tactics you could employ to ensure that other functional areas consistently deliver on the brand strategy?

Your in-depth analysis could be worked on in conjunction with the brand touchpoint assessment described in Chapter Three.

Customer Touchpoints	JetBlue
Check-in process	Separate lines for people checking in with bags and without bags; somewhat frenetic
Seat assignment, upgrades	Single-class airplane, assigned seating; currently no opportunity to accrue frequent flyer miles
Timeliness of departure and arrival	Tightly run ship; generally on-time departures and always on-time (if not early) arrivals
Space for carry-on baggage	Sufficient luggage space; many people carry-on
Crew service ethos, personality	Fun, upbeat, cheeky, pleasant, casual, jokesters, very helpful; help people put bags overhead when getting seated; no frills
Seats	Comfortable leather seats; sufficient leg space; standard trays
Surrounding passengers	Lots of new and inexperienced flyers; many vacationers; somewhat rowdy group; planes always full
Pilot and crew communications	Instill confidence in experience and safety; announce closing of the Kevlar door to the cockpit at start of every flight; ensure people in emergency exit rows understand the obligation
Audio and visual entertainment	Free satellite TV on back of seat in front of each passenger; twenty-four channels including CNN, three ESPN channels, History channel
Food and beverage service	Drink orders taken like waiters instead of cluttering aisles with carts; no meals served but rather a selection of gourmet snacks including bagel chips, animal crackers; messaging at point of purchase to eat before the flight
Plane and interior design	Latest and greatest planes; clean; dark and light blues
Baggage timeliness, Sky Caps	Timely arrival of baggage in baggage claim; baggage handlers and Sky Cap personality consistent with flight crew; upbeat and helpful personality

**Figure 6.2.   Sample Brand Touchpoints
of Discrete Service Airline Usage Experience.**

Customer Touchpoints	E.P.T.
Packaging	Soft colors and fonts, but not too feminine; device individually wrapped in white foil; medical overtones
Instructions and education	One short page of "friendly," simple instructions on "How to Use" and "How to Read Results" with diagrams; device features also defined through diagram; straightforward answers to five frequently asked questions; English or Spanish
Device design	Advanced stick design provides easy handling; comfortable thumb grip; cap to keep results sterile; sealed splashguard protects results
Time to results	Three minutes
Reliability	Over 99 percent accurate in laboratory tests, typically used as a prescreen, and positive results are then tested by doctors; control window provides confidence that device is working
Expression of benefits	Access to information in the privacy of your own home; "The Most Certainty at a Time of Uncertainty"
Test results window	Easy-to-read; potential uncertainty reinforced through frequently asked questions
Toll-free number support	Registered nurses available from 8:30 A.M. to 5:00 P.M. Eastern Standard Time weekdays to answer questions; consumer specialists available until 8:00 P.M., recorded help available during off-hours

Figure 6.3.   Sample Brand Touchpoints
of Home Pregnancy Product Usage Experience.

As you can tell from the consulting example, where long-term relationships exist, the lines tend to get blurred between what might be
considered usage experience issues versus other supporting operational delivery issues. It matters less to pinpoint where the specific interaction may fall (usage or operational delivery) than to effectively
analyze, troubleshoot, and manage the touchpoint.

THE BRAND ASSET MANAGER'S PLAYBOOK: HOW TO NAVIGATE THE TOUGH
ISSUES WITHIN THE USAGE EXPERIENCE. Since product and service
usage is so important to the success of the overall brand-customer relationship, any breakdowns or disconnects need to be a top priority
for the brand asset manager. These problems can occur at any point

Customer Touchpoints	Prophet
Preengagement preparation	Good communications and focus on aligning and understanding client's objective; consultants get up-to-speed quickly
Kick-off and milestone meetings	Clean, well-managed agenda; collaborative dialogue, and exchange of information; sound expectation setting; ample visibility of project and progress
Brainstorming and insights	Fresh market-based perspective (customer, competitive, self) developed thought leadership, access to best practices, and proven models and frameworks; creative; relevant insight; customer focused
Interpersonal skills and relationship building	Candor, integrity, camaraderie, high energy, passion for brand; trusted adviser
Collaboration with client	Lively interaction; flexible in approach and level of client involvement; strong teaming skills; ask good questions and listen to answers
Responsiveness to client's issues	Very responsive; clear desire to deliver (if not overdeliver) on client expectations and create impact
Ability to navigate client's political and organizational waters	Seasoned professionals with deep cross-industry experience; savvy in working with senior leadership; communicate effectively using both brand and business language; able to facilitate conversation and move agenda forward
Project management, logistics, communication	Keep to schedule, provide regular status updates, complete legwork to make sponsor's job easier
Quality of written communications and presentations	Deliverables are packed with insights and clearly communicate argument leading to recommendation; offer new ways to think about challenges; presentations are lively and interactive
Recommendations	Recommendations are aligned with business goals and meet the needs of the client; dedicated to making recommendations actionable and achieve positive business results; strong in linking brand strategy to business objectives

Figure 6.4.   **Sample Brand Touchpoints of Business-to-Business Brand Consulting Usage Experience.**

within the post-purchase experience, so at a minimum, you must own and analyze all of the direct and indirect feedback around the usage experience that is coming into the organization.

When issues arise, you should help orchestrate an effective response. When there are opportunities to leverage and build on post-purchase experience brand touchpoints, you should focus on them and mobilize the organization to pursue them aggressively, regardless of which functional area needs to be tapped into. Kodak, for example, has recently given marketing shared responsibility for product usability, to maximize all usage experience opportunities. These and similar representative issues are identified in the playbook in Figure 6.5.

The general trend away from selling pure products toward services, information, and outsourcing presents a new brand touchpoint challenge for many companies, resulting in a tighter bond between usage experience and the brand. Xerox is trying to evolve customer perceptions of its brand and usage experience in an attempt to improve the overall level of satisfaction throughout the brand-customer experience. For instance, because most Xerox products are digital, they tend to break less and because the product is networked, you can sit in your office while making copies down the hall. In addition, Xerox can also perform remote diagnostics and do preventative maintenance on the machine.

The end result for Xerox is that fewer people are touching the machines anymore. Typical office professionals neither see nor interact with the product or customer service representatives. Although this configuration is less costly for Xerox to manage, the traditional usage experience, driven in large part by people and product interaction, has evaporated, leading to a Xerox identity crisis. Xerox's shift to becoming an outsourced service provider is one way to reinvent itself, as is a shift in advertising that moves away from paper and moves toward solutions (as IBM did in the early 1990s). Done well, a dramatic shift in usage experience can positively change the value that customers sense they are receiving, as well as their overall perceptions of the brand. But if such changes are not thoughtfully and aggressively managed, they can undermine the brand's promise and the overall brand-customer relationship.

Operational Delivery

Operational delivery brand touchpoints are a critical component of overall brand delivery, especially with the increased role of services and outsourcing in the economy. This section addresses critical post-purchase

Brand Touchpoint Critical Issues		Management and Influence Tactics
Next-generation product development	Co-Drive	1. Partner with R&D, identifying critical features, attributes, and drivers 2. Frequently expose target users to developing designs, using preproduction models, three-dimensional renderings, and focus groups 3. Beware of overengineering the offer with features and functions
Manufacturing, production, and engineering quality challenges	Collaborate	1. Partner with customer service and field resources to prioritize high-impact trouble areas 2. Implement proactive and forthright communications plan with customers (and broader stakeholder set) about steps for problem resolution, being prepared to pull product if necessary 3. Support the problem-solving process with detailed insights about customer situations and failure occasions
Getting systematic visibility into usage without direct customer access	Own and control	1. Develop consistent ways to gather this feedback from customers 2. Leverage traditional forms of customer surveys, focus groups, and other market research, but also blend in anthropological studies and other direct observation vehicles 3. Integrate this with other data sources from customer service, distribution partners, and field sales and communicate out regularly
Usability	Co-Drive	1. Develop a prioritized list of usage occasions and key brand benefits for the designers (industrial, food, software) to work with 2. Make sure that good design principles (consistent, well-organized controls, prominent display, good tactile and visual clues, positive feedback for actions taken) are used on behalf of the target customer 3. Deploy relevant, emotionally reactive, and ultimately intuitive usable interfaces
Employee knowledgability and service ethos	Influence	1. Work with the operational delivery teams to infuse the brand into core content and process training programs 2. Advocate for systems to streamline and invigorate process 3. Use a structured brand assimilation program to have customer-facing employees internalize how the brand values affect their job

Figure 6.5.   Brand Asset Manager's Playbook for Usage and Consumption Experience.

Move from "product" to "service"	Own and control	1 Map out how this transforms traditional usage experience
		2. Overcommunicate with company leadership to ensure that these ramifications are understood
		3. Identify and help orchestrate the key imperatives to support the transformation

Figure 6.5. (*continued*)

experience operational processes that have a customer-facing component and are often not considered in terms of how the customer perceives the usage experience.

CORE OPERATIONAL CHARACTERISTICS AND ORGANIZATIONAL CAPABILITIES. For many brands like FedEx, Grainger, and Ritz Carlton, stellar performance against key operational delivery brand touchpoints has provided a sustainable point of differentiation for their brands. Typical brand touchpoints to think about in operational delivery occur at any point during the post-purchase experience phase: pre-usage, usage, and post-usage:

Pre-Usage

- Account setup
- Instruction manuals
- Delivery process and communications

Usage

- Twenty-four-hour service
- On-line upgrades
- Account management

Post-Usage

- Account services
- Billing
- Loyalty program management
- Customer quality representatives

These brand touchpoints are often thought of as the supporting players, the infrastructure, or the "back office" for an organization rather than as customer-facing opportunities for brand building. However, each of these areas does touch the customer and can have a strong impact on brand perceptions. Without sustained focus on operational delivery, brand promises can ring hollow, and the brand may not be built in the way the company desires.

Operational delivery is generally a people- and service-intensive brand touchpoint category, which requires employees in different functional areas (for example, customer service, call center, and billing) to work together consistently and with precision. Strong coordination and communication across functional areas is crucial, given that many of these operational areas are so far removed from traditional marketing and brand management activities. To succeed, the broader organization must leverage the brand lens discussed earlier, which helps drive consistent brand practices and principles throughout the organization.

Pre-Usage Operational Delivery. In certain categories, a customer cannot succeed in the usage experience without going through some additional interaction with the brand beyond the actual purchase itself. Panasonic, for example, discovered that many customers are using their Internet product demonstrations after they purchase the product, not before. Bob Greenberg, the company's vice president for corporate brand marketing, noted, "It beats the hell out of looking through an instruction manual, as you can click on different parts of the product to show you the nuts and bolts of how it works."

Sometimes these brand touchpoint interactions go even deeper because the customization and configuration process is long (deploying SAP financials; customizing a Japan Airlines 777 from Boeing) or because the installation and setup process is complex (installing Applied Materials semiconductor manufacturing equipment; installing a magnetic resonance imaging machine from GE Medical Systems). It does not matter whether customers see these brand touchpoints as part of the usage experience itself or part of the pre-usage experience. You need to remember that these are important brand-building opportunities that further define the brand customer relationship. Do not let them slip through the cracks!

Post-Usage Operational Delivery. Another major area of operational delivery brand touchpoints occurs beyond the usage experience in areas such as account management, billing, and collections or with other support services critical to a successful usage experience. For companies with physical products, most customers clearly differentiate these activities from the usage experience. But for service businesses, like an advertising agency or accounting firm, some customers may see these brand touchpoints as part of the usage experience. Again, where to place them is less important than bringing these brand touchpoints to life in a consistent way that delivers value to the customer while reinforcing the brand promise.

A DETAILED ANALYSIS OF OPERATIONAL DELIVERY: DIRECTV. Given the diversity of operational delivery brand touchpoints, a detailed understanding of each executional element is critical to succeed. This clarity will generally show that most of these core elements lie outside the traditional purview of brand management and will most likely require a cross-functional but brand-driven approach to succeed.

In Figure 6.6 we illustrate a detailed analysis we conducted for DirecTV, a digital subscriber line (DSL) provider. The DSL category has historically been challenged in its operational delivery brand touchpoints. Some of these challenges included unclear ownership and accountability for the operational delivery infrastructure, an overly complex process that is not customer friendly, and poor coordination and communication across the different hand-off points in the value chain. The usual result was poor management of the brand and consistently unmet customer expectations. DirecTV appears to have learned from the mistakes of the first generation of DSL providers and has done a tremendous job at both meeting and overcoming these operational delivery hurdles.

THE BRAND ASSET MANAGER'S PLAYBOOK: HOW TO NAVIGATE THE TOUGH ISSUES WITH OPERATIONAL DELIVERY. As the DSL experience shows, operational delivery brand touchpoints are sometimes difficult for brand asset managers to get their arms around. These touchpoints are often loaded with issues that are far from a brand manager's comfort zone; involve complex, inflexible processes and systems; and appear difficult for a brand manager to control or change.

Decisions to outsource some or all of the operational delivery experience to third-party vendors or private-label outsourced service providers can exacerbate these challenges, as those service providers are one step further removed from the brand.

Customer Touchpoints	DirecTV
Initiate service	Once payment is made, customer is notified of time it will take (ranging from two to six weeks depending on third-party fulfillment, technical issues or other events) to connect DSL
Waiting period	Within the promised time frame (or better), DirecTV schedules appointment with phone company to establish outside connection, then works with them to complete the connection and hook up to DirecTV network (customer is not involved); once connection is made, DirecTV sends modem and software to use by two-day mail
Update notification	Should the timing change for that originally promised, customers are notified
Modem and software	Package arrives with black modem with DirecTV logo and CD with software also bearing the DirecTV logo (in some cases Telocity, the former name, still exists on the modem and software)
Self-install	User responsible for plugging in modem to the phone jack and USB or Ethernet port and install software onto computer; once complete, can access always-on DSL
Other benefits	Included in the package is information on using up to five e-mail addresses, five unique Web pages, and customized domain name
Assistance with install	If assistance is required, very short wait time for customer service representative to answer; very knowledgeable, pleasant representative could walk through install challenges with ease and speed

**Figure 6.6.   Sample Brand Touchpoints
of DSL Installation Operational Delivery.**

We highlight strategies for coping with some of the more challenging aspects of operational delivery in the brand asset manager's playbook in Figure 6.7. Although on-brand execution across these operational delivery brand touchpoints is often difficult, those that succeed automatically own a sustainable point of differentiation from the competition, helping to create customer loyalty and drive greater share of wallet.

Customer Support

A brand's customer support ethos is generally tied to areas like troubleshooting, problem resolution, and preventive maintenance. Although providing this type of customer support is a fairly standard operating procedure for many industrial and high-technology industries, now even service brands, like Hyatt, are allocating resources to this type of post-purchase experience brand touchpoint. Rather than just seeing it as a defensive measure, Hyatt believes that making these investments provides a greater opportunity for differentiation than allocating additional funds toward more traditional pre-purchase experience brand touchpoints.

CORE OPERATIONAL CHARACTERISTICS AND ORGANIZATIONAL CAPABILITIES. Customer support can be delivered in multiple contexts and environments: by telephone; over the Internet; in a retail store, dealership, or other branded physical environment; or through a channel partner. Sometimes the customer may come back to key purchase brand touchpoints and expect to satisfy his or her customer service needs there. Other times, companies are expected to bring customer support skills directly to the customer or administer customer support remotely.

In general, three types of customer support drive the post-purchase brand experience:

- Answering basic customer questions (delivery, installation, usability, configuration, billing, or others) and resolving specific problems
- Regularly scheduled maintenance activities
- Soliciting feedback and checking in with customers about quality, satisfaction levels, and other account service issues

Brand Touchpoint Critical Issues		Management and Influence Tactics
"Build versus buy" decisions across key elements of the operational delivery value chain	Collaborate	1. Given emphasis on cost-reduction and outsourcing, understand where company may be looking to reconfigure its value chain 2. Conduct a brand-customer risk assessment for each decision, establishing minimum on-brand service requirement 3. Drive brand architecture decision for each component
Coordination breakdowns across the delivery chain	Influence	1. Align players around the importance of the customer, inspiring an "all for one and one for all" attitude 2. Identify key coordination breakdowns that are occurring using a cross-functional task force 3. Develop short-term work-arounds, and then use a brand lens to help diagnose root causes and reengineer sustainable, on-brand people, process, and system improvements
Designing customer-friendly choices into product delivery process	Collaborate	1. Determine the customer need for delivery and do best to provide, applying the 80-20 rule 2. Explore holds for holidays or wedding registries, specific needs of goods, off hour delivery times, delivery to secure locations and other areas 3. Focus on most valuable customer and overcommunicate to best manage expectations
Redesign of key operational delivery touchpoints (billing, delivery process, installation	Co-Drive	1. Get assigned to "redesign" initiative, bringing relevant customer needs and brand data and serving as the voice of the customer 2. Understand the operating constraints and imperatives of your colleagues 3. Help drive toward win-win solutions that allow the company to do more for less and knock one out of the park for the brand
Inadequate display of "on-brand" behaviors and actions from operational delivery teams	Collaborate	1. Work with the operational delivery teams to infuse the brand into core content and process training program 2. Advocate for systems to streamline and invigorate education process 3. Use structured brand assimilation program to have employees internalize how the brand values affect their job

Figure 6.7. Brand Asset Manager's Playbook for Operational Delivery.

High conflict between account management and other operational delivery teams	Co-Drive	1. Understand the core source of tension, and the extent to which it is negatively impairing the brand-customer relationship 2. Look for incremental ways to remove tension from system (incentives, communication, training) 3. Explore creation of a pure customer advocacy function

Figure 6.7. (*continued*)

For many companies, customer support of the first type tends to be handled primarily by centralized customer service or support functions, with varying degrees of expertise, problem-solving authority, and awareness of their role in support of the brand. Sometimes there are dedicated teams and personal relationships with specific clients. In other situations, customer service representatives randomly accept any inbound caller.

Regardless of where and how customer service is delivered, these are high-stakes encounters for the brand because expectations have been set in the pre-purchase and purchase phases of the brand-customer relationship. A negative experience or an inability to resolve a problem in a timely manner will likely manifest itself in weakening the brand-customer relationship and either immediate or eventual loss of the customer. Some brands like Nordstrom and PeopleSoft are legendary for turning these types of encounters into credibility- and reputation-enhancing outcomes. For brands that are somewhat under siege, like McDonald's, nationwide quality hot lines have been established to give customers a way to be heard.

The second and third types of customer service are important but do not usually evoke the same level of emotional intensity. As long as customers do not have to wait an inordinately long time to get a maintenance appointment and are well communicated with before, during, and after a maintenance visit, most brands have the potential to deliver on their brand.

Lexus does better. It has demonstrated that excellent service can provide a strong point of brand differentiation. It has led all automakers in customer satisfaction for ten of the past eleven years in the United

States. It maintains this consistently high level of satisfaction by continuing to delight its customers: sending friendly service reminders, providing a loaner car to help customers run errands, washing the car and returning it cleaner than when it was brought in, and providing an overall superior level of service than the competition.

A DETAILED ANALYSIS OF CUSTOMER SERVICE: IBM THINKPAD'S TECHNICAL SUPPORT EXPERIENCE. As with other post-purchase brand touchpoints, customer service representatives, technical support teams, maintenance people, and other well-trained troubleshooters tend to dominate the customer's overall experience and perceptions of the brand. These individuals need to be "on" consistently for the post-purchase experience to succeed. The company must give them the resources, tools, training, and management support to allow them to spend the bulk of their time on delivering the brand experience that customers expect. For this to work, the brand asset manager has to deconstruct the service experience from the customer perspective into discrete components or customer-brand interactions. We have modeled a customer support experience in Figure 6.8, based on the technical support provided for IBM's ThinkPad laptop computer.

The IBM brand stands for reliability, responsiveness, trust, stability, heritage, and innovation. The ThinkPad subbrand, in particular, has played a pivotal role in helping the IBM master brand shed some of its traditional "big box" associations and become more relevant in the world of decentralized computing. Most of the discrete brand touchpoints in the technical support experience have been executed to reinforce these brand associations.

To begin with, the skill levels of IBM's technical support representatives are high. Second, the twin pillars of responsiveness and follow-up are emphasized and tracked at every opportunity, such as voicemail or e-mail follow-ups one day after a service interaction, customer satisfaction surveys, and ongoing service check-ins. Third, IBM appears to understand the extent to which third-party business partners often play an indispensable role in delivering against the overall IBM brand experience. If Airborne Express started to be unreliable with regard to timely customer pickups, both the IBM and the ThinkPad brands would suffer.

THE BRAND ASSET MANAGER'S PLAYBOOK: HOW TO NAVIGATE THE TOUGH ISSUES WITH CUSTOMER SERVICE. Because bad experiences in customer

Customer Touchpoints	IBM ThinkPad Technical Support
Toll-free number	Clear messaging around the toll-free number to call in case of problem with ThinkPad under warranty; phone calls received go directly to technical support representative to help customers through the problem
Customer service representative	Highly knowledgeable, well-trained, friendly, patient customer service representative listens to problem and works with customer to troubleshoot; customer gets immediate service and is never passed around from one representative to the next
Follow-up e-mail or letter	If the problem is resolved, the next day the customer service representative sends an e-mail or letter inquiring if the problem was indeed solved to satisfaction and requesting that the customer fill out a customer satisfaction survey
Replacement part delivery	If a part needed to be replaced, the new part is sent overnight via Airborne Express to the caller for replacement
Defective part return packaging	Included in the package with the replacement part are packaging and a prepaid self-addressed airbill for the return of the defective part to IBM; customer is only required to call Airborne Express for pickup
Shipping box delivery	If the ThinkPad needs to be repaired, a prepaid, self-addressed laptop shipping box is sent overnight to the customer, who puts the laptop in the box and calls Airborne Express for pickup
Equipment return	The laptop is repaired in one day and returned the following day via Airborne Express to the customer
Service report	Included with the repaired laptop is a letter detailing the corrective action taken on the computer for the customer's records
Follow-up e-mail or letter	After a replacement or a repair, the customer service representative mails out a customer satisfaction survey

Figure 6.8.   Sample Brand Touchpoints
of Technical Support Customer Service Experiences.

service and support can cause negative word-of-mouth that can spread like wildfire, courtesy of e-mail and message boards, you need to anticipate trouble spots in order to protect and steward the brand. Sometimes customers fail to understand where to go for support or are frustrated when they realize a customer service representative lacks decision-making authority because of a co-branded relationship, such as a Samsung cell phone using Sprint PCS service. These and other tough issues are identified in the playbook in Figure 6.9, as are tactics for approaching these issues in your specific context.

One interesting trend in customer support has been the rise of self-service support. Many customers dislike waiting on hold for service representatives or not being able to speak with a live person except from 9:00 A.M. to 5:00 P.M. Self-service components of customer service, like the ability to access frequently asked questions, on-line answer wizards, automated call centers, and helpful instruction guides, not only save the company significant money but are also perceived as more convenient and brand-centric because they let customers control when and how they access the service center.

Brand Loyalty Programs and Continuous Communications Efforts

Brand loyalty programs and other investments in communication with customers are designed to allow loyal customers, in particular, to have an ongoing relationship with the brand. This brand touchpoint generally allows a company to get to know the customer better or more specifically focus on encouraging repeat purchases and a long relationship with customers. Unlike other post-purchase brand touchpoints, marketing often directly controls this area because it is generally directly linked to outbound communications. Obviously, this may present an issue if marketing has not been involved in the relationship since the pre-purchase phase.

CORE OPERATIONAL CHARACTERISTICS AND ORGANIZATIONAL CAPABILITIES. The dominant form of this brand touchpoint is the traditional loyalty program, which usually includes some type of membership or reward-based promotional appeal, with the goal of encouraging frequent purchases and building a greater share of wallet. The airlines' frequent flyer programs have set the standard for using these programs to drive brand loyalty.

Brand Touchpoint Critical Issues		Management and Influence Tactics
Knowledge depth, service ethos, and action orientation of employees	Collaborate	1. Work to develop training program for service representatives 2. Include modules on product, brand, and corporate values 3. Teach representatives to respond in ways that make the customer happy
Quality, amount, and level of integration of customer-specific data	Own and control	1. Identify all areas where customer data are collected and assess ability to integrate 80 percent or 50 percent of the information and expected return from such integration 2. Keep the data fresh and clean 3. Manage expectations of the customer
Use of self-service elements in overall service mix	Co-Drive	1. Use historical data or capture new data to help assess opportunities for self-service 2. Talk to target customer to understand desire and adaptability to self-service 3. Ensure that level of self-service is consistent with brand strategy
Perceived service gaps created by co-branded products or third-party distribution	Own and control	1. Review obligation under contracts and enforce based on what is stated there 2. Collect and provide information about service gaps for customers and resulting reduction of sales 3. Make specific recommendations for improvement based on customer knowledge
Managing product recall or other crisis situations	Influence	1. Respond immediately to crises, taking responsibility within reason 2. Assess the long-term risk of short-term inaction, especially as it relates to brand 3. Create a solution that makes it easy for the customer to execute against and forgive
Customer service "triage"—treating some customers differently	Own and control	1. Recognize that all customers are not created equal, and reward those customers who are your best 2. Ensure that systems or top salespeople have the tools to know who the best customers are 3. Provide clear, on-brand simple guidelines to empower employees to act

Figure 6.9.   Brand Asset Manager's Playbook for Customer Service.

Many other categories, such as supermarkets, specialty retailers, quick-service food, and credit cards, have implemented loyalty programs with increasing popular appeal. In fact, a recent article in *Chain Leader* observed that "55% of the U.S. population is now believed to carry some type of frequent-shopper card. Of those who belong to a frequency program, 43% say that they believe the program causes them to purchase more from that one brand. Finally, once a customer joins a loyalty program, they tend to increase spending on that brand by an average of 27%."[1]

There are other examples of brand loyalty activities:

- Deepening the relationship through one-to-one marketing, newsletters, and user groups and by introducing value-added services like Harley-Davidson's and Porsche's driving clubs

- Lowering replenishment or repeat purchase barriers through convenience-oriented brand touchpoints like Amazon's one-click program and RedEnvelope's gift reminder service

Although event-based activities still play a significant role, the emergence of an inexpensive, noninvasive targeted communication medium such as the Internet and e-mail has dramatically changed the economics of these types of programs. There are now huge new opportunities for brands to stay connected with customers with timely, key, and potentially customized information.

Sony, for example, launched a CRM effort a few years ago to support its Vaio personal computer brand. Although the early efforts were promotional in nature, with the company sending special offers and discounts by e-mail, Sony felt the real opportunity was to leverage its relationship with customers to help them better understand all of the great things that they can do with a Vaio. This provides a deeper level of brand-customer engagement, which Sony hopes will drive deeper levels of loyalty over time.

A DETAILED ANALYSIS OF A LOYALTY PROGRAM: LETTUCE ENTERTAIN YOU. Figure 6.10 provides an in-depth analysis of a fairly traditional frequent purchase loyalty program with a slight twist: the program itself serves as an endorser to the underlying restaurant destinations—the brands—that are part of the network. Many of the traditional brand touchpoints for programs such as these—the enrollment process, the supporting marketing materials, the usage process, and the reward and redemption process—are illustrated. In particular, we highlight how these have been designed and executed to reinforce Lettuce's brand associations of newness; a sense of adventure; modern, creative, and upbeat ambiance; and quality service.

THE BRAND ASSET MANAGER'S PLAYBOOK: HOW TO NAVIGATE THE TOUGH ISSUES WITH LOYALTY AND CONTINUOUS COMMUNICATIONS PROGRAMS. We recommend that brand asset managers develop a portfolio approach to this brand touchpoint. In other words, you need to understand what is the right mix of activities (communication driven versus event driven) so that you are creating opportunities for customers to participate in, learn from, and celebrate the brand, and leveraging your emerging brand-customer relationship to remind customers gently and periodically to think about you and keep you at the top of their mind. You want to strike the right balance such that you have adequate coverage across your most important customer segments, relative to both the number of brand touchpoints they access, as well as your ability to deliver on the required experience.

In coming up with innovative ways to connect with the customer through this brand touchpoint category, remember to make sure that each vehicle serves a clear need, provides a clear benefit, and is perceived as both differentiated and relevant to the target. These brand touchpoints and critical issues are highlighted in Figure 6.11.

A Word About Word-of-Mouth
and Joint R&D and Innovation

Two other important types of post-purchase brand touchpoints deserve a brief mention. The first, word of mouth, happens outside the company's purview and control, but is often a huge driver of brand perceptions. Existing customers are the biggest and most legitimate generators of both good and bad word of mouth about brand encounters.

Many studies have demonstrated that, at least in Western cultures, people are likely to tell a story about a bad brand experience eight times more frequently than one about a positive experience. Companies can most directly influence word of mouth by executing well against the most critical customer-driven brand touchpoints. You can also indirectly influence public discourse through public relations, advertising, and other mass and grassroots communications activities.

Customer Touchpoints	Lettuce Entertain You Enterprises Frequent Dining Program, Chicago
Entrance and exit signage	Lettuce's logo prominently displayed at entrance/exit indicating membership to the network of sixty-two midscale, casual upscale, and fine dining establishments that offer a wide range of cuisines, creative themes, quality food, and upbeat, helpful wait-staff
Display at each restaurant	Small, colorful promotional information cards presented in Lettuce's signature display at all restaurants depicting the variety within the network; display includes frequent dining brochure
Program introduction	Simple program structure easily explained over the phone, through brochures, on Web site; simple point structure with one point earned for every dollar spent (minus tip and tax); crossing certain thresholds allows for faster accumulation of points
Enrollment	Easy to enroll using phone, mail, fax, or Internet; $25 enrollment fee returned in the form of a restaurant gift certificate after three uses of the card; can enroll jointly with spouse, automatic renewal
Enrollment form	Collecting information such as name, birthday, spouse name, birthday, home address, daytime phone number, e-mail addresses, and number of times member dines out at full-service restaurants
Membership card	Arrives within four weeks of submitting enrollment, including more information on the program
Restaurant visits	Provide membership card when paying bill and wait-staff instantaneously recognize customer and applies reward through new point-of-sale terminals; current account balance reported at end of meal
Account summary	Mailed quarterly, immediate access by toll-free number and Web site
Point redemption	Reward certificates sent automatically each month (or once earned, if requested) and can be redeemed for future meals (except on Saturday or holidays), United Airline tickets, and gym memberships
Newsletter	*The Last Dish* newsletter provides updates on latest happenings at restaurants; mailed quarterly with account summary, e-mailed monthly with more real-time information when e-mail address is on file
Periodic invitations	Wine tasting, chef chats, and other restaurant-sponsored events; birthday cards inviting you to a free meal to celebrate

Figure 6.10. Sample Brand Touchpoints of an Entertainment Loyalty Program.

Brand Touchpoint Critical Issues		Management and Influence Tactics
The scope and complexity of any loyalty-focused efforts	Own and control	1. Conduct customer research to understand key needs and benefits 2. Agree on objectives for the program and how it will provide value to customers 3. Use simple guiding principles to shape the program
Multichannel program	Collaborate	1. Give customers options to interface with program in any way they want 2. Work with information technology to build a system to support multiple channels, acknowledging its operational complexity 3. Create consistency with brand and functionality across channels where possible
Third-party partner selection and integration logistics (for example, rewards, operational logistics)	Co-Drive	1. Identify partners that are on-brand for customers and company 2. Ensure that goals are common and both are incented to work together 3. Test integration with each partner before launching
Capture, manage, and access data	Co-Drive	1. Capture actionable information that will be used in the loyalty program and beyond 2. Work with database developers to identify the key ways marketing will want to access and integrate the data 3. Develop systems for multifunctional users
From customer activity tracking to predictive modeling	Own and control	1. Tread cautiously in efforts to move from basic customer activity tracking to predictive modeling with personalized and targeted offers 2. Do not be presumptuous; many customers find it off-putting 3. Test the efforts judiciously, measuring and evaluating before large-scale roll-out
Frequency and rhythm of outbound contracts	Own and control	1. Develop an integrated view of all out-bound contracts to customer 2. Determine the right balance between promotional and brand-building/educational content 3. Explore variations by customer segment
Privacy policy	Own and control	1. Ensure that the information you collect is used in accordance with the privacy policy 2. Make communications relevant and value add to loyal customers 3. Be sensitive to number of contacts

Figure 6.11.   Brand Asset Manager's Playbook for Loyalty
and CRM Efforts.

The second type of post-purchase interaction occurs when a company decides to collaborate with existing customers in the development and design of its next generation of products and services. This type of collaboration can require varying degrees of time, resources, and financial investment but can often form the basis of the next wave of innovation and, more important, drive a deeper brand-customer relationship.

FLIPPING THE SWITCH: MOVING FROM SERVICING TO SELLING: CROSS-SELLING AND UP-SELLING

Much of the initial emphasis during the post-purchase experience is on servicing the customer. You do your best to guarantee that the customer is getting what he or she expects from the brand. In other words, your first objective is a satisfied customer who feels good about the brand, will say good things about it if asked, and will perhaps passionately endorse the brand in an unsolicited manner.

Your next objective is to get the customer to become a repeat purchaser of the brand and eventually get the customer to concentrate all spending in the category with your brand. To do this, you may look for ways to increase the customer's usage frequency (from one to two decaffeinated skim lattes per day) or amounts (supersize that!). Or you may identify new usage occasions or need states (aspirin reduces heart attack risk) or find ways to encourage the customer to substitute spending in other adjacent categories for spending in yours (deploying a Sun server to avoid ordering new IBM mainframes). If you have multiple product and service lines or multiple brands and sub-brands, your ultimate objective may be to get the customer to buy from all of your lines and brands repeatedly.

The question is how to get the customer to begin another journey through the purchase cycle and not consider another brand along the way. You would hope that the brand-customer relationship is strong enough that the customer already prefers your brand or may trust you enough to help with the next set of problems because he or she believes that you have something relevant to offer. Other times, however, you may need to prompt the customer with useful or interesting information or targeted discounts or promotions. And other times you just need to be more assertive, leveraging explicit interactions designed to cross-sell, up-sell, or otherwise engage the customer in a dialogue about future needs.

Unlike leveraging passive pre-purchase brand touchpoints, these post-purchase brand touchpoints are executed more aggressively and in the context of an existing and emerging relationship. Often companies will discover new ways to leverage information the company already has about a particular customer and project the practicality and importance of other post-purchase brand touchpoints in the quest to drive loyalty. Understanding how and when you have permission to draw on that customer information and begin to sell the "next thing" is the basis of maintaining and building (and not exploiting) the long-term health of the brand-customer relationship.

For instance, one multichannel retailer in Prophet's 2002 Best Practices study recounted an example of how it struggled with the business unit's general manager, who had grown accustomed to relying on using the entire customer database through e-mail offers to pump up revenues at the end of each quarter. Since the incremental cost was negligible, the higher the absolute number of e-mails sent out, the higher was the probability of hitting the numbers.

But what was good for that particular general manager's profit and loss statement for a particular quarter was not necessarily good for the brand over the long term. Running a product-line-specific promotion against the entire customer database was likely to offend a number of customers who had no interest in receiving these offers. The result was that a disturbingly high percentage of highly loyal high-value customers opted out after they received a promotion they deemed irrelevant to their interests. The trickle-down effect was for many brand-customer relationships to go dormant.

DEEPENING THE BRAND-CUSTOMER RELATIONSHIP

Building a brand-driven business requires your company to take a comprehensive view of the post-purchase experience and develop a coordinated effort to drive customer satisfaction, customer retention, and customer loyalty. This will allow your company to set up the conditions for a continuous, never-ending brand-customer relationship, whereby satisfied customers deepen their relationship with the brand while simultaneously driving new customers into the franchise, who then become satisfied customers, who then deepen their relationship with the brand, and so on.

Companies that have a clear strategy and vision for how to achieve this can effectively guide an integrated effort across all post-purchase brand touchpoints. There are many ways to accomplish this, and we will present two different examples of companies with an integrated approach to post-purchase brand touchpoints.

BMW: The Ultimate Driving Machine Embraces Its Owners

The "what your car does well, ours does brilliantly" quotation earlier in the chapter highlights how BMW has focused on designing, engineering, and delivering a compelling usage experience. For BMW, product is king, and most people inside the company would continue to overallocate resources to its cars at the expense of many other things, if that is what it would take to continue to deliver against this promise. But that does not mean that BMW assumes that a compelling usage experience can stand on its own and guarantee delivering repeat customers to the brand.

Rather, BMW wraps the usage experience with other well-thought-out post-purchase brand touchpoints aimed at reinforcing and supporting the brand. As a backdrop, BMW wants to be perceived as a low-hassle company that values first-time customers. All of BMW's cars are designed not to need service for at least the first fifteen thousand miles, so a BMW buyer may go a full year without interacting with the company. When a customer does have a problem, BMW aims to fix it right the first time and quickly, no questions asked. The company invests extensively in training for its dealers and its mechanics to ensure that this is the experience that BMW owners consistently have.

Given this infrequent interaction pattern, BMW wanted a way to touch customers more often. Thus it developed a concierge service to provide high-touch and relevant interactions for customers who want it. Within BMW's Web site is a special feature, the Owner's Circle, where owners can register their vehicles and enter key data about their car (model, customization, date purchased, leased or owned, type of lease) and about their personal interest areas. BMW can then provide targeted, relevant e-mail communications about the car, its service needs, upcoming BMW events in the area, and new product launches that a current owner may find interesting. Owner's Circle members also get prioritized service on the toll-free number, and since BMW knows that the majority of its customers prefer e-mail as the primary means of communication, it prioritizes its post-purchase dollars toward e-mail, even though it understands that its toll-free-number service is not yet best-in-class.

This integrated approach to usage, operational delivery, customer service, and loyalty brand touchpoints has huge economic benefits for the business: more customers stay with the BMW brand the next time they are ready to purchase. As noted earlier, over two-thirds of BMW's leases in North America roll over into new leases every year. By contacting current owners six months before the lease ends, asking them what they want in their next BMW, and giving them many customization alternatives, BMW capitalizes on an already effective post-purchase relationship to seal the deal, increase brand advocates, and create customers for life. Similar to the matrices for Amazon.com in Chapter Four and Aveda in Chapter Five, Figure 6.12 is an illustrative look at BMW's post-purchase experience brand touchpoints.

GE's Major Technology Business:
Product Leadership Coupled with Care and Service

GE has three major technology businesses: power systems, medical systems, and airline engines. Because the buyers in these markets are fairly concentrated, GE, with its strong market position, has an active, ongoing relationship with most potential customers. Like BMW, it wants long-term relationships with these customers and uses an integrated approach to managing the post-purchase experience as the best means for achieving this.

According to GE Power Systems regional leader Don Lucas, GE's post-purchase experience includes executing against its primary business and brand objective—"to improve penetration of the customer"—by "providing the customer with the technology and service required to encourage them to buy more and stay with GE longer." As a result, GE continues to invest in integrating its technology and solutions with the right levels of customer care and service to maximize the brand-customer experience. GE also understands the brand ramifications of these business objectives: if the customer is going to invest $10 million or $100 million on equipment and technology, "he or she needs to feel safe and believe that GE will never leave him or her stranded with antiquated technology and that GE will never walk away from a problem or a request," Lucas says.

With Power Systems, GE has developed a comprehensive post-purchase experience that is designed to increase its offering as the customer grows its business. When customers are ready to build new plants, GE's on-the-ground account team wants to know about those plans

Customer Goal = Company Goal	Validate Decision To Buy = Deliver on Brand Promises	Receive Good Service/Support = Deliver Additional Brand Value	Be Satisfied with Usage = Delight Customers	Feel Confident in Brand = Increase Brand Loyalty and Advocacy
Exceptional Ride	High	Medium	High	High
Luxurious Interior	High	Medium	High	High
Minimal Service Needs in First Year	Medium	High	Medium	Medium
Efficient Quality Repair Service	Medium	High	Medium	Medium
Concierge Service	Medium	High	High	Medium
"Owner's Circle" Web Site	Low	Medium	Medium	Medium
Relevant E-mail Communications	Low	High	Medium	Medium
BMW Events	Low	Medium	High	Medium
"Owner's Circle" Member Toll-Free Number	Low	Medium	Medium	Low

High ● Medium ● Low ○

Figure 6.12. BMW's Customer-Company Goal Matrix.

a year or two before the customer is ready to move. When customers are not buying new equipment, GE's account team is there to help solve problems with their current offerings and continuously provide value-added services.

To succeed, GE leverages an integrated account team, which serves as the epicenter for the brand-customer relationship. An account executive generally coordinates the activities of this team on a global basis and includes representatives from sales, operations, technical support, and quality. In addition, GE has a multilevel relationship-building plan, with CEO-level interactions for its top executives, vice president of construction and engineering relationships for its account executives, and bottom-up relationships with engineers and middle managers for its technical team. Many of these people are tenured, having been with GE and the customer for twenty or thirty years. If someone from one of GE's other business units wants to sell something new to the customer, the global account executive makes sure that his GE colleague has a warm introduction and that the pitch is focused on strengthening the customer relationship and implementing GE's business strategy.

GE's winning post-purchase experience formula includes constantly developing new diagnostics, new monitoring systems, and new business products designed to lower ongoing operating costs and reduce downtime through more scheduled dates for preventive maintenance. Customers have frequent access to educational and technical information through the Web, seminars, and an annual "State of the Art" customer conference. When the customer does have a short-term operational problem or crisis, GE's technical engineers are responsible for running diagnostics and quickly deploying a team to solve the problem, regardless of which product line it is.

In addition, to increase post-purchase satisfaction even more, GE designated a new role, customer quality manager, who works at the client site, side by side with the client on a daily basis, and works to expedite and resolve all client-GE issues. This manager goes to staff meetings, learns about customer issues, helps get the immediate issue addressed, and, importantly, goes back to GE with process suggestions designed to tackle the root cause of the customer's problems (which is then deployed on behalf of other customers on a global basis). These individuals have developed a reputation for being top performers as they solve lots of issues on behalf of customers with great energy, integrity, and communication skills. They are explicitly not brought into the sales cycle for new efforts, because it is important for the brand to "keep them pure."

With GE medical systems, GE follows a similar strategy, not only supplying the customer with a customized system but also helping design the supporting suite of system enablers to allow remote diagnostic tracking of that machine. This helps improve overall customer quality and reduce costs. So while the system itself may be the core of the GE-customer relationship, increasingly GE is starting to supply complete solutions for customers' business. This may include partnering with customers on the R&D side and trying to determine better what is most important to them: giving GE the inputs for the next generation of solutions the customer may be seeking.

In each of these businesses, GE combines technology leadership and a focus on providing complete solutions with its ongoing customer care and service to provide a highly satisfactory, loyalty-inducing relationship with its customers. With its long heritage and incredible staying power, GE, the brand and the company, has positioned itself as the smartest, safest, and best overall option by operationalizing the brand in a way that epitomizes its spirit: technically knowledgeable, assertive, persistent, responsive, communicative, and, most of all, trustworthy. As Don Lucas sums it up: "Why would the customer want to go anywhere else?"

WRAPPING UP BRAND TOUCHPOINTS

Chapters Four through Six guided you through a systematic way to take a detailed look at every possible touchpoint your brand may have with a prospect or customer over the life of the brand-customer relationship. Our goal has been to help you to recognize that they exist and manage them in a consistent and holistic way to maximize the overall relationship between the brand and the customer.

Chapters Seven through Nine now focus on bringing this mind-set to life, across the employee base and over the long haul, so that operationalizing the brand is a permanent shift in the way a company builds its brand-driven business.

PART THREE

Organizing Your Company Around the Brand

CHAPTER SEVEN

Developing a Brand Metrics System

Driving Brand Building by What You Measure

A s the first chief marketing officer (CMO) of your organization, you realize you have to set the right example for the rest of the executive team in working through the annual planning and budgeting process. You know this means being as strategic as possible about next year's goals. You also know that next year, all of your hard-fought marketing battles and plans will start to pay off. Your recent promotion has come as a result of those past wins but is also heavily tied to future expectations.

As you look back over the past five years, you realize that the goals you set out to achieve when you were first hired are now within reach:

Mission: Move this company from a commodity-based, price-driven player to one that is not only superior to the competition but provides value above and beyond the commodity.

Year I: Better understand the company's strengths and weaknesses and identify where brand building could most effectively help the company reach its longer-term goals and objectives.

Year II: Educate senior management and the employees on how the company could leverage the brand to achieve its goals.

Year III: Implement some operations, marketing, and communications changes that more closely align the organization with its brand.

Year IV [last year]: Build a marketing department to execute marketing-specific strategies.

Year V [the past eight months]: Focus on the repositioning and relaunch of the brand to demonstrate the true value your company offers the market.

Next year has to be about results. Although you are the CMO, you still need to get budget approval from the executive team and prove your case. Last year, your $8 million budget was approved because the executive team bought into the fact that the company had to execute the brand launch in a robust way or not do it all. This year, you are seeking a jump to $20 million to help extend your brand-building activities beyond the pre-purchase experience phase.

You decide to have lunch with the CFO to bounce this budget increase off her. She proceeds to ask a number of questions that she believes the executive team will ask you when you submit your request:

"Why do you need the increase in budget?"

"What has been the impact of the dollars you have already spent to date?"

"Have our awareness levels gone up as promised at last year's budget meeting?"

"We thought that your efforts were going to result directly in increased sales, but our revenues and profitability actually declined this year. We know your marketing expenditures had a direct impact on the profitability decline. How do we make sure that does not happen again?"

"Has this relaunch had any impact on our loyal customers? How about our perceptions relative to the competition?"

You are not able to answer these questions; in fact, you don't even know where to start. You have been in the brand-building execution mode for so long that you have not even thought about brand metrics. You start to wonder what to do next.

You gather your composure and openly admit to the CFO that you have yet not thought about measuring the impact of the strategies you have employed over the past eighteen months. You assure her (and yourself) that you will use every day until the plans and budgets are due to get your story together.

WHAT IS NOT MEASURED IS NOT MANAGED

Bringing the brand to life within your organization has to include establishing brand metrics, both internal and external. (Internal metrics are discussed in Chapter Eight. This chapter is focused on external metrics.) With a clear set of strategic brand metrics, managers and senior management know exactly where they should be focusing their efforts, what actions are required to succeed, and ultimately how they will be judged relative to their efforts.

A set of brand metrics, consistently tracked over time, allows your organization to develop its brand strategically in a number of ways:

- Providing insight into how your brand is performing externally versus customer expectations and competitor actions
- Helping you understand how your brand is performing internally compared to previous efforts (benchmark against past performance)
- Providing information on ROI by tracking a return on overall marketing and brand programs
- Helping sustain organizational focus and consistent communications
- Helping you allocate resources more effectively in the future
- Providing information that can be used for employees' bonus criteria

The good news is that when you develop your strategy for the brand, you have essentially established brand metrics at the same time. Think about a particular goal or objective your management team has established for your brand, and you can easily see the metric that would go along with it—for instance:

- Increase customers' recognition of what our brand offers (brand recognition)
- Increase customers' likelihood of considering our brand when purchasing in our category (brand consideration)
- Increase customers' preference of our brand over other options (brand preference)
- Increase customers' use of our brand's products (brand share of wallet)
- Increase customers' advocacy of our brand to other potential customers (brand advocacy)
- Increase customers' belief in our ability to extend our brand's reach into new areas (brand stretch)

With a set of well-defined brand metrics, there is a high probability that you know exactly what role the brand should play in reaching your company's longer-term goals and objectives. Without one, it is likely that you do not have a real brand strategy established and agreed on. Remember that what is not measured is not managed.

THE STATE OF BRAND METRICS TODAY

The reality is that very few companies are actually putting brand metrics into practice. In fact, Prophet's 2002 Best Practices study showed that only one-third of the companies surveyed measure the performance of their brand. It is encouraging to note, however, of those companies that do measure brand performance, the measures they employ generally go beyond the traditional brand measures of awareness and recall and start to address strategic issues and brand touchpoint–specific questions (see Figure 7.1).

In times of great economic uncertainty, it makes sense that the role of brand has been elevated to a level never seen before. Senior executives are recognizing, often for the first time, that true financial value can be derived from their brands. More important, many CEOs now realize that the brand is an asset, with an inherent value that is comparable to traditional tangible assets like plants, machinery, and humans.

Many companies that appreciate and think of the brand as an asset also recognize that metrics have to be employed in order to better understand brand performance and its impact on the bottom line. TXU

Measure	Percentage of Respondents
Customer satisfaction	96
Recall and awareness levels	83
Repeat purchase	79
Intent to purchase	79
Returns on brand investments	75
Annual profits	71
Market share	63
Annual revenue	63
Brand stability and longevity	63
Stock price	48
Price premium over private label	46
Financial impact of withdrawal of brand investment	45
Price premium over nearest competitor	33

Figure 7.1.   Most Influential Measures in Determining Brand Performance.

Source: Prophet's 2002 Best Practices Study

and R. R. Donnelley are among the forward-thinking companies that have truly heightened the importance of brand within their organizations. These companies have made it a reality within their respective companies that brand ultimately has a direct impact on the company's profitability and overall success.

Brand and the Balanced Scorecard

As discussed in Kaplan and Norton's book, *The Balanced Scorecard: Translating Strategy into Action*, a company's balanced scorecard generally covers four areas:[1]

- Financial performance (traditional financial performance metrics)
- Operations and internal business processes (manufacturing processes and order fulfillment)
- Customer satisfaction (degree to which the product or service met expectations)
- Learning and internal growth (degree to which a company is bettering itself for the future)

As the concept has grown and taken hold, many companies have realized that they need to rewrite their balanced scorecards in terms of what is important to their particular company's success. For many, this has meant introducing the brand into their scorecard for the first time. The key to successfully incorporating brand into a company's balanced scorecard is to determine which metrics make up the brand score within the overall scorecard.

A few Fortune 500 companies we have worked with use only three simple metrics to understand how well their brand is performing:

- Customer's overall satisfaction with the brand
- Customer's intent to purchase the brand again
- Customer's willingness to recommend the brand to others

By introducing such measures into its balanced scorecard, a company gives brand the attention it needs, the consistent focus it deserves, and the seat at the board of directors' table it has earned.

Brand Metrics Beyond the Scorecard

Whereas most companies have yet to include brand in their balanced scorecard, a few have formally adopted brand metrics into their daily operating environments and their overall culture—for example:

- 3M measures familiarity, relevance, differentiation, trust, leadership, and quality, which work together to drive the success of each of its brands.
- Teradata, a division of NCR, conducts a multicountry study measuring awareness, familiarity, favorability, customer satisfaction, and willingness to purchase.
- Accenture measures awareness, critical brand attributes, brand awareness, brand personality, and the degree to which employees can communicate and support the brand positioning through their daily lives. The company also measures whether its brand positioning inspires clients.
- Visa measures several critical brand attributes, including brand awareness, positioning, and persona.

• CIGNA measures brand awareness, understanding, and desirability and will soon also measure loyalty, passion, satisfaction, retention, and employees' understanding of the brand.

Brand metrics are becoming the norm for companies that are serious about leveraging, managing, and building their brand to drive future growth. But the diversity of metrics used by the companies mentioned above clearly demonstrates that there is no universal set of brand metrics applicable for every company. So how do you know which metrics are right for your company?

CHOOSING THE RIGHT METRICS

Most companies face three quandaries when launching their brand metric system:

1. What are the different brand metrics to consider to monitor our brand's performance?
2. How do we determine which brand metrics are the right ones to use, given our company's particular situation?
3. What is the most effective way to keep a brand metric system alive and well?

The rest of this chapter focuses on addressing these three critical questions. But first, there are two general observations about how to choose the right metrics.

Good Metrics Are SMART Metrics

How do you know if a metric is good? The simplest answer to that question is whether you can make a business decision based on the information provided by that metric. If not, then all that metric has provided you with is nice-to-know information. Need-to-know information is required to drive critical brand-driven business decisions.

In general, there are five basic screens to use in determining whether you have chosen the right metric for your company and your situation. The best way to remember them is through the acronym SMART, which stands for *simple, meaningful, actionable, repeatable,* and *touchpoint-oriented.*

Simple to use. If the data that have to be collected, analyzed, and leveraged are not fairly straightforward, then you will find yourself spending more time on the process of measuring the brand than actually using the information provided by the metric.

Meaningful. If it is not tied directly to either your corporate goals or objectives or to the brand touchpoint wheel, then it probably is not going to be able to help you ultimately improve your brand and company's performance.

Actionable. If you cannot make a business decision as a result of the metric, then you should probably use another metric. This is generally the difference between a nice-to-have and a need-to-have metric.

Repeatable in terms of how you gather the data. If you deviate from the methodology used last time something was measured, you might as well start over. Brand metrics become useful only if you can compare apples to apples. In addition, you should consider using only metrics that will be measured at least once or twice a year, focusing exclusively on the SMART metrics instead of spreading your investments too thin over too many metrics and getting minimal return on your investment.

Touchpoint-oriented to a specific group of stakeholders. Brand metrics should be set up for each stakeholder group; however, not all of the brand metrics will be applicable to all stakeholders. You will need to decide which of the brand metrics best measures the brand touchpoint you are interested in understanding better, relative to the specific stakeholder group you are measuring against.

All Brand Metrics Are Directly Linked to Either Business Strategy or Brand Touchpoints

Metrics have to be established to measure the brand's role in helping to achieve companywide strategic goals and objectives, the effectiveness of the brand across the entire brand-customer relationship, and all the brand touchpoints that relationship includes. In other words, there are two types of metrics that should be considered for your company's brand metrics system.

Brand touchpoint metrics provide a diagnosis of the brand's performance. These metrics help assess the various activities you are pursuing, related to current or potential customers, within one of the three touchpoint quadrants we discussed in Chapters Three through Six (prepurchase, purchase, and post-purchase).

Strategic metrics provide a diagnosis of the brand's impact on the business's performance. These metrics help assess the impact of your various brand-building activities on the overall performance of the brand, and thus the company.

Obviously, there is quite a bit of interdependency between strategic metrics and touchpoint metrics. For instance, if one of your strategic brand goals is to increase preference of your brand over competitive brands, then a few strategic and touchpoint questions immediately come to mind to help determine the level of your brand's preference—for example:

Strategic Brand Questions

- What are the key preference drivers in our category?
- How does our brand currently rank on these preference drivers versus competitor brands?
- Are we increasing preference of our brand over competitor brands over time?
- Are we converting preference into purchase of our brand?

Brand Touchpoint Questions

- How effective are our sales representatives at selling the benefits of our brand versus the competition's brand?
- How effective are our collateral materials in selling the benefits of our brand versus the competition's brand?
- How effective is our Web site in selling the benefits of our brand versus the competition's brand?
- How effective is our advertising in selling the benefits of our brand versus the competition's brand?
- How effective is the advocacy of current customers at selling the benefits of our brand versus the competition to potential customers' brand?

The interdependency of metrics between strategy and touchpoints is just as important as the variety of questions that can be asked per metric to be measured. It is the richness of the answers to these questions and your ability to link interdependent variables (strategy and touchpoint metrics) together that is the difference between a successful brand metric system and one that is not very useful.

WHAT BRAND METRICS SHOULD YOU CONSIDER ADOPTING?

A company cannot use every possible metric and get any value out of the exercise; that would yield too much information and leave too little time to digest it and even less time to do something about it. We recommend that six to eight metrics be adopted at any time because that probably represents the maximum amount of information that can be digested and useful. The seventeen metrics that we recommend you consider can each be linked to the particular brand touchpoint category (pre-purchase, purchase, and post-purchase) that they help measure. Figure 7.2 can help determine which metrics will help you measure how well you are performing relative to your brand strategy goals.

Eleven Brand Touchpoint Metrics to Consider

We recommend that you choose a few of the following eleven metrics to diagnose your brand's performance:

1. *Brand awareness and brand recognition*—provides direction on whether the entire marketing mix is effectively getting your brand out to its target audience. Brand awareness helps answer this critically important question:

- Are potential customers aware that our brand exists? Why or why not?

Brand recognition answers these questions:

- Do potential customers recognize what our brand offers? Why or why not?

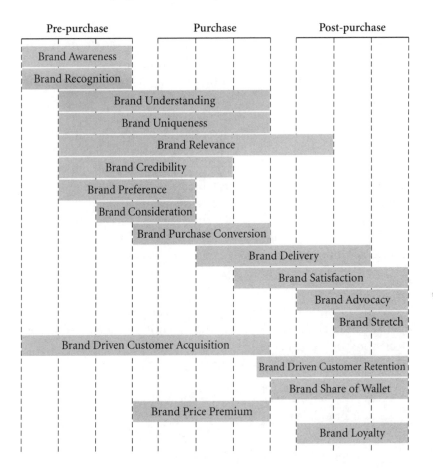

Figure 7.2. Brand Touchpoint Metrics.

- Can potential customers place our brand in the right industry, product category, and competitive set? Why or why not?

When brand awareness and recognition levels slip below benchmarks, it is necessary to increase communication activities to maximize the chances for current and potential customers to place your brand into their consideration set. Conversely, when these levels are high, this is a pretty good indicator that investment levels in other brand-building areas should be increased, while awareness and recognition efforts can be reduced to maintenance levels.

This metric is increasingly important today as many companies are either renaming themselves or spinning off new divisions with new names; examples are Verizon, Accenture, Cingular, Avaya, and Oncor. Every one of these newer brands represents a multibillion dollar company.

2. *Brand understanding*—determines whether potential customers have knowledge about what your brand stands for, the value it provides, and the benefits they can accrue from experiences with your brand. This metric takes you beyond the simple recall of information discussed in Chapter Four and establishes how potential customers think of you and how your brand fits into their world.

At a high level, brand understanding answers this question:

• Do potential customers have a deep understanding of what our brand stands for? Why or why not?

Brand identity understanding addresses how well current and potential customers can restate the brand's identity, including its core associations and personality.

The question that brand identity understanding addresses is this:

• Can potential customers describe the associations and benefits of our brand? Why or why not?

Brand understanding is the telltale sign of whether the identity and positioning you have adopted and brought to life in the marketplace are getting the desired traction or if there is a disconnect between what you believe you are bringing to life and the reality (stakeholder perceptions).

Although this concern is important for all companies, it becomes critical for those that are either repositioning themselves in the marketplace or positioning themselves for the first time altogether.

3. *Brand uniqueness*—measures the degree of uniqueness that current and potential customers ascribe to your brand, especially as it relates to your adopted point of difference. This metric is particularly useful for companies in highly competitive, commoditylike industries (such as utilities and telecommunications) where true differentiation and uniqueness in products and services are limited. In industries

where parity rules, brand uniqueness shows how effective you have been in building a point of difference for your brand that is perceived to be truly differentiating from the competition.

Brand uniqueness also answers these questions:

- Do potential customers believe that our brand promise, positioning, and benefit are unique? Why or why not?
- Can potential customers describe the differentiated benefit that our brand provides in relation to the competition?
- Do potential customers believe their overall experience with our brand to be unique? Why or why not?

For brand uniqueness to be effective, it has to be measured in relation to the competition, or else it will be a one-dimensional assessment of your brand.

Actions that relate to brand uniqueness should focus on ensuring that your brand's point of difference and other strategic points of uniqueness are communicated and demonstrated across all brand touchpoints. Often the actions required to increase uniqueness will be similar to those used to increase understanding since uniqueness is all about making sure customers and stakeholders understand your brand intimately and, you hope, in a unique and relevant way.

4. *Brand relevance*—takes a look at how meaningful and relevant the value of your brand is to the various stakeholders it serves, based on marketplace needs, wants, and unmet desires. This metric can also give you a firm understanding and grasp of what will be important to your various stakeholder groups in the future. Importantly, if you are serving multiple constituencies, the value that is relevant to each constituency may be different.

The questions that generally arise when measuring brand relevance include these:

- How relevant is our brand to you? Explain its level of relevance.
- How well does our brand meet problems, issues, and unmet needs and wants you may have? Why or why not?

This metric is important for all brands, although those that find it particularly useful are those that are looking to introduce their brands into new markets or brands that are facing tough competitive challenges when perhaps they previously had no true competition. For example, Evian owned the bottled water market ten years ago and resided at the top of the Brand Value Pyramid. Now it must reestablish itself as a leader in a category that is crowded with dozens of lower-priced competitors like Aquafina, Poland Spring, Dasani, and Sparkling Springs. In contrast, HBO has done a terrific job of increasing its relevance over the past three years with new programming (*The Sopranos, Sex and the City, Six Feet Under,* and other shows) that differentiates it from its close-in competitors. Brand-relevance metrics give each of them critical brand-building data.

5. *Brand credibility*—measures whether current and prospective customers find your brand's promise to be accurate and believable. It addresses this question:

- Do customers believe that our brand promise is credible?
  Why or why not?

Credibility can be lost if you are not able to deliver on a promise you have widely communicated through advertising and mass media (remember United's "Rising" campaign). Brands can lose credibility due to fiascoes (Firestone) or public backlash (*Exxon Valdez*). Regardless of the reason, loss of credibility is by far one of the most damaging things that can happen to a brand and is analogous to lying to someone and trying to regain trust.

Often the ultimate question to help determine whether your brand has credibility is this:

- Would you recommend our brand to someone else?

Putting one's reputation on the line is often the greatest sign of belief and trust that the brand is credible.

6. *Brand preference*—measures to what extent customers prefer your brand to others within their potential consideration set and category. This metric informs a company's ability to understand why its brand is preferred, or not, over competitor and near-proximity brands. The best way to obtain this information, generally, is to ask customers what their purchase process is within your category and how your brand satisfies what is most important to them.

The brand preference metric helps you determine why one brand is preferred over another within your category and what the key drivers of preference are. The questions to address include these:

• Why is our brand preferred over competitor brands?
• What are all the factors that are driving that preference?

Once you better understand the degree to which your brand is preferred over the competition's and key purchase criteria, you will be able to see both opportunity areas and potential threats.

7. *Brand consideration*—helps you make the link between brand preference and the degree to which customers are putting your brand into their final consideration set. For instance, travelers may prefer the service and overall experience that Southwest Airlines provides, but because it lacks a national route structure, travelers may not be able to include it in their purchase consideration set.

The question tied to brand consideration is this:

• When choosing among brands in this particular segment, are you considering our brand in your purchase decision? Why or why not?

It is the brand's role to move a prospective customer from awareness to consideration.

8. *Brand purchase conversion*—measures the degree to which your brand is put into a final purchase consideration set and your ability to convert that consideration into a sale. The former chairman of JCPenney once said something to the effect of "You can have the best advertising and communications plan in the world and the strongest brand, but if you cannot get that customer to go 'the last eighteen inches' in the store to make the purchase, then you have ultimately failed."

Brand purchase conversion means that your brand has made it into the final consideration set, and the customer not only intends to purchase your brand but actually does. If you are not converting preference and consideration into an actual purchase, then something is breaking down in your overall brand-building efforts. This metric is critical; it starts to point to specific areas in either the pre-purchase or purchase experience that may or may not persuade customers to choose your brand over a competitor brand.

The questions tied to brand purchase conversion are the following:

- Did you intend to purchase our brand when thinking about making a purchase? Why or why not?
- Why did you actually end up buying our brand over competitor choices?
- Why didn't you buy our brand even though you intended to buy it?
- What would make you walk away from our brand once you are ready to make a final purchase decision?

You must probe the reasons behind the answers. Was it the persuasion of the sales representative at the point of purchase? Was it a deal one of your competitors was offering that clearly allowed that offer to stand head and shoulders above the rest? Was it a colleague or friend who advocated a competitive brand? The idea here is to find out why or why not the customer ultimately chose your brand or a competitor brand. It helps to dig deep, especially if that same customer gave you a high score on brand preference and brand consideration.

9. *Brand delivery*—measures whether current and potential customers believe you are delivering on and fulfilling your brand promise. Your brand has a contract with its stakeholders; whether you are delivering on that brand contract is a different story.

The brand delivery metric is based on answers to this question:

- Is your brand performing against the expectations and promises it is making to its customers?

This metric should give you a fairly straightforward report on how you are performing against the promises you are making to customers and stakeholders, directly linking back to your brand strategy, identity, and positioning.

Of note, brand delivery seems to have a lot of resonance with senior executives because a strong brand implies a strong level of trust. Delivering on what you promise helps to drive trust, which drives loyalty.

10. *Brand satisfaction*—determines whether the brand lived up to expectations. This metric is analogous to product or service satisfaction and is a key question to address after the sale has been made and the customer is still fairly close to the point where the product or ser-

vice was used or consumed. Were the value, benefits, and delivery promises all real? Or were they just a great selling tactic used to persuade customers to choose your brand over competitors' brands?

The questions to address here are straightforward:

- How satisfied are you with the performance of our brand?
- Did it meet the expectations you had for it prior to purchasing it?
- What improvements would you suggest for our brand?
- Will you consider purchasing our brand again in the future?

11. *Brand advocacy*—measures and assesses those customers who are considered loyal to your brand and their willingness to put their reputation on the line by recommending your brand. This is by far one of the most powerful areas for any organization to focus on and one metric in which there is a direct correlation to profitability and brand success.

The questions to address here are straightforward:

- Would you recommend this brand to another person? Why or why not?
- How would you describe the brand to another person within your recommendations?

Six Strategic Brand Metrics to Consider

The eleven metrics we have just explained are the ones we believe should be considered for measuring the effectiveness of your brand touchpoint efforts. Exploring those questions will help determine where you are strong and weak and which brand touchpoints need more or less focus.

The next six strategic brand metrics start to indicate the impact of your brand-building and brand touchpoint efforts on your overall business performance. Some of these metrics offer overt ways of making a connection to the bottom line, while others offer a more indirect way.

12. *Brand stretch*—gets customers and other stakeholders to articulate where they believe the brand can or cannot stretch relative

to new categories, opportunities, and geographies. The theory with brand stretch is that the greater the value and emotional attachment a brand has with its customer base, the greater is its ability to go into new categories. Brands that ascend to the top of the Brand Value Pyramid have a much higher likelihood of being able to stretch into other categories or use occasions.

The key questions to consider tied to brand stretch include these:

- What other categories, products, or services can you see our brand credibly offering?
- What would our brand have to do to prove ourselves to you in a new category?
- Would you be willing to purchase that product or service? Why or why not?

For instance, because Marriott has such a strong and powerful brand that stands for a high-quality overnight stay, travelers are willing to give it the elasticity to stretch from the highest end in terms of price point and perceived value (time share or the Marquis) and to the lowest end in price point and perceived value (Fairfield and Residence Inn).

13. *Brand-driven customer acquisitions*—depicts actual new customers you are attracting or acquiring as a result of your brand asset management efforts. This metric may resemble typical sales measures, but the intent is very different. The brand customer acquisitions metric is aimed specifically at identifying and acquiring customers:

- Who are the new customers buying your product or service today who have not bought it in the past?
- Who are win-back customers who have come back to your brand or were not in the database within the time frame of your last measurement?
- How many customers have bought your brand as a direct result of your brand-building efforts?

The challenges here are to understand why a customer bought your branded product or service in the first place and then to link that reason for purchase specifically back to your brand-building efforts. Giving respondents a number of reasons to choose from will help you gain more specific responses to questions on the purchase.

14. *Brand-driven customer retention*—measures the number of customers you would have lost had you not activated a sound brand asset management strategy, providing understanding of the degree of loyalty that customers have to your brand. This is another difficult metric to measure because it entails asking your customers if they have considered leaving your brand since the last measurement period. A good approach is to ask customers these questions:

- What other brands have you considered purchasing since your last purchase?
- Why did you ultimately choose our brand again?

Specifically, you want to see which brands have entered your current customer's decision set, why the customer did not choose any of those other brands, and why the customer decided to stick with your brand.

15. *Brand share of wallet*—measures the number of existing customers who are buying more products or services from you as a result of your brand building efforts; they are giving you more money. This measurement is determined by looking at current customers who have reached into their wallet to purchase additional products or services beyond the ones they initially bought from you.

The best example of how this works is your local telephone service provider, which does not make much profit on basic service. It is the call waiting, Caller ID, DSL, and second-line services, on top of the basic offering, which really start to increase revenue per customer and profits per customer.

This measure is designed to answer two critical questions:

- What additional products or services related to our brand have you considered purchasing? Why?
- Which new products or services related to our brand did you actually purchase? Why?

In addition, you need to be able to capture new revenues associated with these branded extensions to understand fully the level of success and resulting implications from your extended brand. This measure can also help you place a more accurate lifetime dollar value on your customers.

16. *Brand price premium*—determines the premium your brand is able to command over other competing brands within your category.

We suggest you try to understand the premium you are able to receive relative to a private label or commodity version of your branded product or service and two or three of your closest competitors.

A question to address in determining brand price premium is this:

- What dollar or percentage premium would you be willing to pay for your brand of choice before you walked away and went to a competitor brand? Why?

Research has shown that of customers who state they are loyal to a brand, 72 percent state they would be willing to pay up to a 20 percent price premium for the brand they are most loyal to.[2]

17. *Brand loyalty*—measures if customers are coming back to your brand time and time again. This is the final strategic metric to consider and obviously the most important. Brand loyalty starts to tell you if all of your brand-building efforts are paying off. It ultimately tells you how well you are delivering on your brand promise, how you are performing against the competition, and, to a large degree, how profitable you are. As noted in Chapter One, an increase in brand loyalty can result in a direct corollary increase in profitability.

The simple but powerful question tied to brand loyalty is the following:

- Would you buy our brand again? Why or why not?

These final six brand performance metrics, examined qualitatively here, can all be translated into quantitative metrics fairly simply, allowing you to satisfy the needs of those who must see the numbers and the data. We believe that some combination of quantitative and qualitative metrics is the most powerful way to assess your progress because you can compare and benchmark numbers and at the same time have the depth you need to make smart business decisions.

The Seventeen Brand Metrics in Action

Each of these seventeen metrics has the ability to tell a story on its own; however, the real power comes when you are able to see the cause and effect of one tied to another, as well as tied to individual activities within a particular brand touchpoint. Two hypothetical situations will help illustrate this point.

BRAND CHALLENGE

Your brand stretch is low.

Potential Rationale

- Your brand competes on functional benefits and has not connected with customers on an emotional level.
- Your brand's credibility or relevance is low, which impedes your ability to stretch into other categories.
- You are having a hard time convincing current and potential customers to put your brand into a new category's purchase consideration or preference set.

Potential Brand Touchpoint Solutions

- Train sales representatives on how to cross-sell better.
- Increase expertise and credibility testimonials.
- Offer promotions to get initial trial.
- Have the call center prepared to sell new offerings whenever a customer calls with a question.

BRAND CHALLENGE

Your brand delivery is low.

Potential Rationale

- You do not really know what is important to customers in making a purchase decision in your category.
- You have not done a good job at understanding what your brand should and should not promise.
- You have not operationalized your brand promises.

Potential Solutions—Some Touchpoint, Some Not

- Conduct a study to understand better the ideal brand contract in your category and how you stack up against that ideal.
- Understand better which functional areas and employees are needed to bring the promises to life.
- Train and provide incentives to employees regarding their role in bringing each of the promises to life.

Once you have the answers to questions related to your metrics, then, and only then, can you prescribe an approach to fix whatever challenges you are facing. Equally as important, you now have a database of information that allows you to benchmark your performance against the competition, as well as the ability to see what future investments are required for a specific brand touchpoint.

WHICH METRICS ARE THE BEST ONES FOR YOU TO USE?

Critical to success in building a brand-driven business is your ability to define which metrics are right for your situation. We gave you a few general guidelines earlier in this chapter, which included using the SMART screen and our advice that a company should never try to adopt more than eight of the seventeen metrics outlined. We also believe that the right mix of touchpoint and strategic metrics is somewhere around four or five touchpoint metrics (spanning the pre-purchase, purchase, and post-purchase phases) and two or three strategic metrics, which are directly linked to the strategic goals you have established for the brand.

Without clarity on the specific goals and role of the brand, you will be consistently challenged as to which metrics make sense for you. Figure 7.3 gives you an idea of what metrics may be most relevant for the goals you are trying to achieve.

As your goals shift, so should the metrics on which you focus your time and efforts. For instance, a very well-known national shoe retailer has incredible brand awareness but obtains very little consideration because it is known as a national discounter. Perhaps less of its brand-building effort should be tied to building awareness and recognition, and instead be aimed at increasing preference, consideration, and conversion. Over time, once the manufacturer gets more customers to consider its brand, its focus will turn to ensuring the product and service delivery experience are aligned with the brand. This will then eventually allow it to focus directly on building brand loyalty and garnering customer advocacy from those customers.

METRICS AS A WAY OF LIFE: ENSURING THAT THE SYSTEM LIVES ON

Companies are wonderful at starting new initiatives, whether it is Total Quality Management or customer intimacy or training. But when

Brand Goals	A	B	C	D	E	F	G	H	I	J	K	L	M	N	O	P	Q
Getting more customers to know your brand	X	X	X	X		X									X		
Expanding into new geographic areas and customer segments	X	X	X	X		X									X	X	
Leveraging your brand's equity into new areas			X	X					X	X		X				X	
Increasing the loyalty of the brand			X		X		X	X			X	X	X	X			X

A, Brand Awareness
B, Brand Understanding
C, Brand Relevance
D, Brand Credibility
E, Brand Delivery

F, Brand Preference
G, Brand Purchase Conversion
H, Brand Advocacy
I, Brand Stretch
J, Brand-Driven Customer Acquisition

K, Brand-Driven Customer Retention
L, Brand Share of Wallet
M, Brand Price Premium
N, Brand Loyalty
O, Brand Uniqueness

P, Brand Consideration
Q, Brand Satisfaction

Figure 7.3. Bringing Together Brand Goals and Metrics.

times are tough or there are shifts in management or lost focus, the effort is often stopped, and the value is lost.

The trick to employing a successful brand metric system is to be able to show its impact on business performance and ultimately have it be a tool that management relies on to maximize brand and business performance success. We are firm believers that if this system is implemented well and consistently leveraged, you will continue to push your brand efforts forward and ultimately achieve great success.

Five important elements are required to successfully implement a brand metric system.

Continue to Focus on the Big Picture: Building the Business

As much of this book has emphasized, brand building is not an expense but an investment in the brand's and the company's future. If you cannot consistently show the impact of the brand on the bottom line, then you will most likely be spinning your wheels in trying to get senior management to buy into brand building as a system. You must demonstrate the added value of brand building that has a direct impact on the bottom line and performance of the business.

Understanding how money is spent to develop your brand and the brand's relationship with customers are the keys to unlocking the value of your brand. This understanding will allow you to reduce spending in some areas and increase it in others, therefore optimizing the experience customers have with your brand. This should result in more dollars dropping to the bottom line. Brand metrics help you identify the areas in which your dollars should be focused.

When measuring the value of your brand, it is important to remember that you want to be measuring the activities that help you reach the goals you have set. You are not measuring just to know; you are measuring for action, which will allow you to improve the value of the brand.

The brand touchpoint activities you are focusing on have to be tied directly to improving the value of the brand, which needs to be driven by the business and brand strategy. The strategy should highlight the area of the brand-customer relationship that needs to be fixed, reinforced, and built and the strengths that can best be leveraged. Based on those strategic decisions, you would choose the activities that can add the most value to the brand, and your selection of brand metrics will help demonstrate the impact on business performance.

Take Action as a Result of the Information

The absolutely worst thing you can do is gather all of this rich information, reach some meaningful conclusions, and then not take action. If no action is taken, this becomes a costly exercise in futility. Even if business results are currently terrible (arguably the best time to make some brand changes), there are always actions you can take along certain brand touchpoint activities, whether it is improving training, upgrading your sales force, or creating some type of loyalty device.

Measure Your Brand with Multiple Stakeholders

It is critical to assess the success of the brand with stakeholders other than customers. Several other important influencers and stakeholders have a relationship with the brand and can have a great impact on others' value perceptions of your brand or even directly drive significant value to the company.

Recently, a global utility company was deciding which brand metrics to use for its brand goals and objectives. It had traditionally tracked the effectiveness of its advertising with residential and commercial customers and varied its marketing and advertising mix based on the results. This was more than adequate in a regulated market, but with increasing deregulation around the United States and across the globe, this utility realized that there were many other stakeholders with a vested interest in its brand who could directly or indirectly hinder its value and the company's success: regulators who set rates, senators who sat on the Committee on Energy and Natural Resources, and analysts who closely tracked the performance of this utility, for example.

Not all metrics have to be leveraged with each stakeholder group, but they need to be considered, and some action needs to be taken against them.

Set Up a Metric Rhythm

There will be many questions from senior management that will require establishing a system for measuring the brand consistently. Here are some good metric rules of thumb to consider:

• Measure consistently throughout the year. At a minimum, measure your brand two or three times a year, but strive toward measuring it once a quarter. This way, you will have a constant pulse on the touchpoints you are activating, the impact of each, and the ability to make course corrections as needed. The only danger in measuring this frequently is that if results are not seen quickly enough, then a key brand touchpoint activity may be pulled prematurely. To mitigate these types of reactions, set expectations for how long to measure and what magnitude of changes to expect.

• Schedule a regular time and place to present the results to senior management. Without regular opportunities to show senior management the results of your brand-building efforts and help them understand the relationships between the different brand touchpoint activities and metrics, there will be little reason or way to demonstrate how brand has added value to the organization. In addition, regular presentations offer a dependable path to increasing funding or shifting focus of activities, which most often need senior management approval.

• Always show a mix of quantitative and qualitative metrics. Most metrics can have a quantitative flavor to them, so you should be able to see if you are improving. However, purely quantitative measures will never give you the richness and depth of information you need to make changes. Purely qualitative data will most likely not stand up in the boardroom. Your goal is to find the right mix for what you are trying to achieve.

• Make sure you are always showing measures in relation to your key competitors. All of the metrics you leverage have to be measured across your brand and at least two key competitor brands. Without this information, you will be operating in a vacuum and benchmarking your performance only against your own past performance.

• Measure against multiple customer groups. All of the metrics you leverage have to be measured across current, potential, and lost customers. Although it is always important to know what you did to win a customer's loyalty, it is equally important to understand why a customer left your brand to go to another, as well as how potential customers in the decision-making mode are assessing your brand in real time.

• Keep all reports simple. The process you used to measure the metric may be of great interest to you, as might all of the statistical data you gather, but it is just noise to many senior executives. Think about a summary metric report flowing as follows:

1. What is the metric?

2. How did we perform on the metric?

3. How does our performance compare to our past performance and competitor performance?

4. How does our performance compare to our stated goals and objectives?

5. What implications and actions should be taken as a result of the information provided by that metric?

6. What should our goal be the next time for that metric?

Set Up an External Metric Advisory Board

One of the best ways to keep a brand metric system flourishing is by having a set of valued and important customers acting as an external metric advisory board. This allows you to have a built-in mechanism for regular measurements, a group of customers who are intimately involved in your brand success and progress, and, most important, a commitment by senior management to make metrics a regular part of your business success and processes.

For some companies with limited resources, this is the only way they will be able to implement a brand metric system. For others, it is a way to endear valued and important customers to the brand long term. And for others, it is a way to show customers that you respect them so much that you want them to play a role in the future of the brand.

WITH A GREAT METRIC SYSTEM IN PLACE, YOU ARE DESTINED FOR BRAND SUCCESS

Setting up a brand metric system for your company's brand is not a luxury; it is a requirement. If you are serious about linking brand and business performance together, about managing all of your brand touchpoints, about spending your brand-building dollars wisely, and about tracking how your brand-building efforts are progressing, then there is no other choice than to adopt a brand metric system to help you accomplish those results.

With a solid brand metric system in place, you will now have, perhaps for the first time, the missing linkages needed between investments, touchpoint activities, brand success, and ultimately business success.

CHAPTER EIGHT

Building a Brand-Based Culture

A s we have suggested throughout this book, we believe that every company should strive to build a brand-based culture. The brand can guide critical business decisions, determine appropriate employee behaviors, and ultimately help drive companywide profitability. The reasons to build a brand-based culture are straightforward and fairly difficult to dispute—for example:

- It provides a tangible reason for employees to believe in a company, which keeps them motivated and energized.
- It allows each employee to see how he or she fits into the grand scheme of delivering the brand vision and promise to its customers and the effect of these efforts on the business goals.
- It develops a level of pride tied to fulfilling the brand's promise.
- It provides a great recruiting tactic as well as a powerful retention tool.
- It confirms that the customer and the brand are the things to focus on.

Most important, making the brand the central focus of the organization helps clarify for any employee what is on-brand and what is off-brand. In the field or in an executive suite, it then becomes easier to make the right strategic decision. The whole organization will now have a brand lens in place to make smart and strategic brand-based decisions, whether it is new product development (for example, at Nokia, the design has to be sleek and a point of differentiation) or pricing (John Deere charges a premium for its equipment because it is commensurate with its value and, more important, the brand's promise) or a strategic acquisition that helps to build the value of the brand (General Mills' recent acquisition of Pillsbury was clearly seen as a win-win for all).

Building a brand-based culture is not just about creating short-term buzz. It is also about developing a genuine and ongoing commitment to the organization's brands. To create a brand-centric environment, you have to ensure that employees are living the brand consistently on a daily basis, across functional areas, divisional boundaries, and geographical markets. This is not an easy task, but it can be done. How this gets done is the focus of the rest of this chapter. You will also need to ensure that the organization is structured to support, sustain, and develop a brand-based culture. This has to do with senior leadership attitudes as well as organizational design and will be dealt with in Chapter Nine.

HOW DO YOU GET EMPLOYEES TO EMBRACE YOUR BRAND?

Someone at a major health insurance company said to us, "We are in the business to enhance and extend life. I have been curious as to how Coca-Cola, which sells a product made of water and sugar, has employees who can be so excited about their brand and company, whereas our company helps people medically, and we don't have that sense of pride." These thoughts get right at the heart of a dilemma that many companies face: many employees do not have a sense of pride in, ownership of, or personal connection with their company, its brands, or its customers. There is no energy, no excitement, no empathy, no passion, no purpose, no conviction. To the Coca-Cola Company's credit, it has spent years adding energy and excitement to a category that basically makes products from sugar and water. But there is nothing magical about the carbonated beverages category that allowed the company to do this. That sense of purpose and excitement is within the reach of most companies as long as the right levels of leadership, focus, and commitment for the brand exist on a consistent basis.

Whether you are in retail, a high-touch service business, or a low-touch packaged goods or industrial component supply business, getting your employees to understand the brand promise and align their behaviors around that promise is an essential part of building a brand-driven business that delivers sustainable, profitable growth. Customer-facing employees may play the leading role in this drama, but every employee is part of the cast and has a role to play in effective brand building. In this chapter, we explore the relationship the employee has with the brand, or the brand-employee relationship, by introducing the concept of *brand assimilation*.

ENABLING EMPLOYEES TO LIVE THE BRAND: THE BIG PICTURE

Becky Saeger, Visa's executive vice president of brand marketing, said it best: "Our employees are our brand. Every single employee has a customer contact."

Brand assimilation involves developing a set of activities designed to increase the probability that employees will behave in a way that is consistent with the brand over time. Said another way, when people inside your firm deal with key customers, prospects, or other stakeholders, you want them to think, speak, and behave in ways that create the kind of customer experience and lasting impact that your brand aspires to deliver.

In an organization with a strong brand-based culture, the behaviors that consistently manifest themselves are driven by brand and are focused on the customer. These behaviors repeatedly lead to customers who are satisfied, pleasantly surprised, and emotionally connected to the company and its brands. Southwest Airlines and Wal-Mart are great examples of companies that have done this well with a value-driven positioning, and brands like Mercedes, Tiffany's, and Goldman Sachs are some that have done it with a more premium positioning. We have extolled the value of consistency and execution in the previous chapters, and nowhere is that more important than here.

From Superficial to Conceptual to Emotional and Personal

Figure 8.1 highlights the three primary stages your employees must pass on their journey toward becoming passionate advocates of the brand. For this to happen, employees have to understand what a brand is and how it is built, what your brand stands for, and what their role is in delivering on the brand promise. So your first job is to generate excitement around the brand and demonstrate the company's thoughtful commitment to it. You must then present a persuasive and convincing argument about the value of the brand and ensure that employees understand the impact of the brand and its positioning on their individual activities. If you do this well and reinforce it consistently, over time employees will begin to live the brand, instinctively, naturally, and with an ever-increasing fervor. The brand becomes an old friend to them, someone they want to do well by, be proud of, defend, and protect.

Companies with strong brand-based cultures have many employees operating out of a "living it" mind-set for long periods of time. These companies are good at maintaining those brand-driven behaviors, with careful monitoring and periodic refreshment and reinforcement. What is important to remember is that the brand-employee

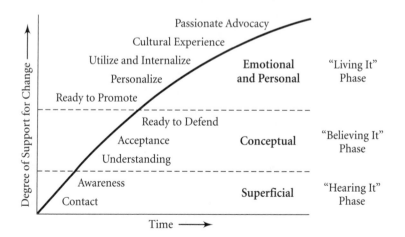

Figure 8.1. Driving the Brand-Employee Relationship.

relationship is just as fluid as the brand-customer relationship. No company can afford to rest on its laurels and assume that employees who have embraced the brand in the past will continue to do so forever without additional care and attention.

Employee Belief Systems, Not Corporate Mission Statements, Drive Behavior

If the objective of brand assimilation is ultimately to have employees manifest on-brand behavior, on-brand thinking, and on-brand interactions just as naturally and unconsciously as they might breathe or laugh, the important questions to consider are these:

- What do employees believe our company does?
- What do employees believe our brand stands for?
- What drives employees' behavior?
- What motivates them?
- Why do certain things happen and other things do not, no matter what senior management says it wants?

A number of factors, like people's individual capabilities and values and the organization's values and culture, are important determinants of whether brand-driven behavior exists. One of the most overlooked drivers of behavior is the spoken and unspoken beliefs that employees hold as truths about the organization—for example:

- What do employees believe is rewarded at the company?
- Who gets promoted and why?
- What do employees believe is really important?

All of these personal opinions over time take on the weight and power of fact, regardless of how far from reality they have actually moved.

It is absolutely critical to understand what employees believe about these kinds of issues and how they consciously and unconsciously make decisions that drive their behavior based on these operating beliefs. The development needs of employees can be done in-house or outsourced. What you will need to assess fairly quickly is whether these operating beliefs create some natural areas of tension or critical issues for the brand-customer relationship that you are trying to create. When the tension areas are numerous or intense, the ability to effectively train and educate employees about brand assimilation is diminished.

BRAND ASSIMILATION OVERVIEW: FROM EDUCATION AND INSPIRATION TO EXECUTION

To be effective at brand assimilation, an organization needs to master two main types of activities: one set emphasizes education and inspiration, and the other emphasizes driving business process improvements through a commitment to brand-driven operationalization. We provide a quick overview first and then go into more detail on how these processes look in action.

A Commitment to Education and Inspiration

At its core, brand assimilation involves educating employees about the brand and inspiring them to behave in a way that is consistent with it.

Brand-driven education and inspiration activities take many different shapes and forms, depending on a company's situation. But at its simplest, you are trying to point employees in the right direction so that ultimately, they realize a sense of pride in the company and its brands. By helping employees understand the brand's rationale and its emotional components and by giving them some tools and frameworks to facilitate day-to-day decision making, the hope is that employees will start to feel a deep and lasting connection to the brand and will be better motivated to do the right thing by the customer and their fellow employees.

STRUCTURED BRAND ASSIMILATION PROGRAMS. It is not always this straightforward. In some organizations, you cannot assume that every employee is intrinsically motivated to exhibit brand-driven behaviors just because they are pointed in the right direction. For example, you could have high turnover in your workforce (as at McDonald's) or a unionized workforce that often finds itself at odds with management (as at United Airlines). In these kinds of situations, explicit strategies may need to be put in place to fix, modify, or compensate for the different motivations of specific individuals or groups.

Alternatively, you could have just acquired a firm with different values and thus different operating beliefs (an example is AOL and Time Warner). Or you could have grown too quickly and now be facing a dramatic freefall in your core business, as most dot-coms are. Or perhaps you are experiencing rapid market shifts that are fundamentally changing your competitive context (as IBM and Target experienced in the early 1990s and many deregulating industries are experiencing today). Whatever your situation, it is no longer business as usual, and most companies need to help point all of their employees in the right direction quickly.

In situations such as these, when motivations are questionable or dramatic action is required, brand assimilation efforts should get executed in the context of a structured program, or they will not be effective. This type of process usually offers the right balance of rigor, urgency, focus, and speed, and it merits the extra financial and human resources required to execute it effectively. We present a structured brand assimilation approach later in this chapter.

MAINTAIN, REFRESH, AND MONITOR. At firms like 3M, BMW, and Amazon, attacking brand assimilation efforts with a formal, initiative-like program may not make any sense. In firms like these, educating and inspiring employees to live the brand is a natural part of their DNA.

Whether it is because there is a long-standing culture with low turnover based on brand values such as innovation and trustworthiness (3M), a higher-order connection to something universal like driving fast, well-made cars (BMW), or that sense of purpose that comes from believing you are going to change the world (Amazon), employees who are passionate advocates for the brands run wide and deep.

These companies generally rely on a few core capabilities, like having internal brand-building prowess and strong alignment between brand and employees, to bolster a strong brand-based culture. They use these capabilities to engage in activities and manage an ongoing dialogue with employees that reinforces the brand, keeps it top-of-mind for employees, and weaves it into the fabric of their daily operating procedures.

Even in these exemplary companies, however, the brand-employee relationship needs to be refreshed and maintained as consistently as it needs to in companies that have undergone a formal brand assimilation program. During these maintenance cycles, educational activities and other programs are designed to reinforce brand-driven behaviors already exhibited by the employees. Consequently, it is important for companies to simultaneously monitor and measure the health and relevance of the brand-employee relationship.

A Commitment to Brand-Driven Operationalization

Sometimes education and inspiration, even in the form of a structured assimilation program, cannot deliver the goods. Said another way, despite the fact that your employees understand what you are trying to accomplish with the brand, your company may still not be effectively operationalizing the brand. Why, you ask? Well, sometimes you need to drop down into the operating components of the business to fix what is broken. This may show that there are major operational impediments—in the field, in engineering, in manufacturing, or in operational delivery—that are preventing employees, through no fault of their own, from delivering on the brand promise (examples include convoluted DSL installation processes and United's unfulfilled "Rising" campaign).

Thus brand assimilation must also involve a commitment to systematically examine your processes, capabilities, and operating systems to make changes whenever these elements are working in ways that explicitly or implicitly prevent your employees from delivering against the brand promise. In other words, you must have a *commitment to operationalizing the brand.*

Sometimes only small tweaks of a process are needed, resulting in incremental or evolutionary changes designed to facilitate on-brand behavior. Other times what is required is completely revolutionary: a complete overhaul. Your company needs to be able to discern one from the other and effectively manage both kinds of brand-driven operationalization. Your objective with both is to equip and motivate employees to become authentic and credible ambassadors for the company and the brand while removing any procedural or structural impediments that would prevent them from doing so.

A COMMITMENT TO EDUCATION AND INSPIRATION THROUGH STRUCTURED BRAND ASSIMILATION PROGRAMS

At certain times, many companies need to attack brand-focused education and inspiration with a structured brand assimilation initiative, one that gets managed thoughtfully, with some sense of urgency, and explicit program dollars behind it. This is often required when a major realignment or strategic course correction is necessary. For example, you have a new brand positioning or a new brand architecture, which requires employees to operationalize or deliver on the brand in dramatically different ways. Or you are approaching brand strategically for the first time, so no structures or systems are in place for effectively managing your brand. Or you have a new CEO or chair with an explicit mandate for change.

These are all examples of occasions when a structured brand assimilation process is the most effective approach for producing the kinds of results that you need in the necessary time frame. Our approach to brand assimilation blends marketing concepts with traditional change management thinking to give you a powerful platform for planning and then implementing a successful brand assimilation effort. At a high level, there are two key process components:

- Thinking through the role for a brand assimilation employee segmentation model, including motivation and morale levels of your existing employee base, and identifying an explicit program for each employee segment
- Evaluating the business benefits and costs of involving customer-facing versus non-customer-facing employees in the brand assimilation process

A Role for Employee Segmentation?

The first major question that you need to answer is tied to segmentation: Is there a role for a strategic employee-based segmentation model that drives the scope, depth, pace, and timing of your brand assimilation activities? Figure 8.2 depicts one way that you can think about strategically segmenting your employee base, primarily driven by an individual's level and formal and informal influence base and the probability that they will directly touch either marketing communications or customers.

Because each segment will have a different set of expectations from the brand assimilation initiative and will be required to do different things if the initiative is to be successful, thinking through the initiative based on such a segmentation framework can be fruitful. The more specific and tailored the behavior change need is for each seg-

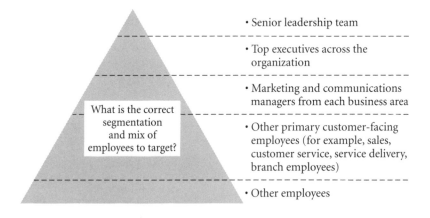

Figure 8.2. Intended Target Audience.

ment, the more beneficial it could be to call them out as a separate segment. Specific types of communications and experiences can then be targeted and tailored for relevance and impact for each segment. The timing and intensity of these efforts can then also vary.

It does not mean that the other employee segments are ignored, but it does mean that you are focusing your time and energy on the most relevant ones. While a decision to focus on customer-facing employees seems intuitive, especially if you are dealing with limited time and resources, a few companies that participated in Prophet's 2002 Best Practices study thought that it was just as important to focus on supply chain, procurement, and manufacturing employees because of their ultimate impact on the value chain of activities that support any brand-customer interaction. One way that some companies balanced this was to execute some broad-based brand education initiatives through existing communication vehicles or meeting schedules, thereby reaching these employees with little incremental cost.

Another helpful perspective on employee segmentation is depicted in Figure 8.3. It presents an attitudinal framework for understanding what motivates employees and their desire to embrace or resist new brand-driven initiatives. The spectrum moves from skeptics to evangelists, with several transitional states in between.

Figure 8.4 presents a way to think through an overall approach to brand assimilation in which evangelists are transformed into brand

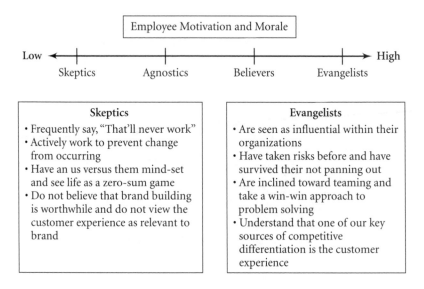

Figure 8.3.   Attitudinal Framework for Employees.

champions and brand skeptics are neutralized. By starting with customer-facing functional areas (such as customer service and sales representatives), you will end up prioritizing your efforts in a way that will drive the most immediate impact on the brand-customer relationship. This type of approach may be useful as a conceptual framework to think through overall resistance levels across the organization and particularly useful as specific line managers are brainstorming ways to handle brand assimilation inside smaller work groups.

A Structured Brand Assimilation Framework

We believe that leveraging a strategic employee-based segmentation model will best allow you to define and prioritize your brand assimilation program. Without this level of clarity, you run the risk of spreading the program too thin. With a strategic employee-based segmentation in place, though, you are ready to proceed with a three-phase structured assimilation approach:

Strategic Development Phase

1. Define the scope.

2. Define the company's internal audience segmentation.

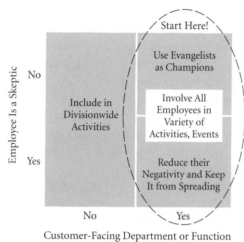

Steering committee to recommend:
- Content to share with employees and timing
  * Brand vision, brand promise, and brand positioning
  * Key elements of emerging brand strategy

Best combination of ways to engage them (for example, large group events, workshops, one-on-one sessions)
- Initially
- Continually

Figure 8.4.   A Framework for Brand Assimilation.

3. Develop an internal cultural identity.

4. Develop a detailed eighteen-month assimilation road map.

5. Create metrics for gauging success.

Foundation-Building Phase

1. Develop materials for workshops.

2. Conduct workshops with key managers and change agents, and train the trainers.

3. Identify key vehicles for implementation.

4. Prioritize and schedule the implementation.

5. Assess the need for comprehensive system overhauls.

Implementation Phase

1. Conduct training and workshops with all employees.

2. Use communications to educate, motivate, and internalize the brand.

3. Monitor and measure the effectiveness of the plan.

4. Modify for adjustment and improvement.

Within the strategic development phase, you are encouraged to develop a brand assimilation framework that ensures that key employee segments buy in to, support, and understand the new brand strategy and positioning. To do that, you need to articulate an internal cultural identity (if it does not already exist in a corporate or employee values document) and a detailed assimilation road map that identifies, by segment, your initial hypotheses around key objectives, messages, vehicles, and timing. Ideally, you will also start to identify key managers who could serve as potential change agents and help champion the initiative as it cascades throughout the organization.

During the foundation-building phase, much of the heavy lifting gets done in terms of developing the right brand messages and content within each segment. By holding a series of brand workshops with key managers and potential change agents, you are securing buy-in for the initiative and increasing the understanding of the new brand positioning. In addition, you are giving employees the ability to articulate what brand means for their respective areas and what touchpoints they need to start to own. This will allow you to begin to hypothesize how employees' behaviors, activities, and mind-sets may need to be modified to support the brand going forward.

In addition to holding these workshops, another team should begin to develop key communications, events, and other experiences that will be instrumental in supporting the implementation phase.

Figure 8.5 displays what a hypothetical brand assimilation framework might look like, outlining specific vehicles, events, and other activities by segment for each stage in the brand assimilation process. You will know that you have been successful at the end of this type of change management program if employees are aware of the new brand positioning and optimal customer experience, understand how it benefits them personally and the company, and know how to deliver on the brand promise.

If you are expecting or experiencing resistance to this type of initiative, visible senior management support and leadership will be critical to your overall brand assimilation success. Sometimes the senior leadership team may need to commit to highly visible symbolic activities to show the organization that they are serious about this new approach to building the brand and the business. Some truly strategic gestures cited in our 2002 Best Practices study included removing individuals from specific leadership positions, shedding businesses that were distracting from the new positioning, or otherwise tackling

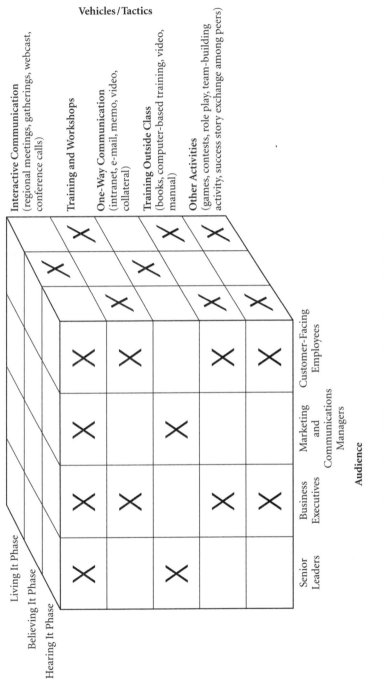

Figure 8.5. A Hypothetical Brand Assimilation Framework.

sacred cows that by their very existence contradicted everything a structured brand assimilation initiative was trying to achieve. These may seem extreme, but it may be exactly what is needed. As one executive noted, "Until the chairman replaced the head of [a specific division], where rumors of ethical infractions were rife, no one was listening to a word we were saying."

Special Circumstances, Special Needs

Although this type of structured brand assimilation program applies to most situations, you will need to stay flexible in the way you apply it. Your company may find itself confronting specific situations that require a different approach. Some types of situations, like a recessionary layoff-prone environment (as with the telecommunications and high-tech sectors in 2001), hypercompetition (JCPenney or Sears) or a company otherwise under siege (Microsoft during the antitrust trials), can severely dampen employees' motivations, causing people to operate from positions of fear and stress. Finding a way to defuse that and realign the organization around some core purpose will be critical. Other situations, like a high-growth or a postmerger environment, may require a more aggressive focus on aligning disparate operating beliefs or operational brand touchpoints or keeping core beliefs from being diffused too thinly. Figure 8.6 highlights different ways to modify the brand assimilation program to accommodate these special circumstances.

Nike's Maxims: A Case Study

After seven to ten years of "Just do it" and Michael Jordan–inspired aggressive growth, Nike had hit a wall. Between the 1997 Asian economic crisis, negative child-labor press, and slowing growth, Nike employees (a large percentage of whom had just been hired over the past three years) were getting a little disruptive and overly concerned about internal politics and direction. At the same time, two new divisional presidents were named, both of whom had been with the organization for over twenty-two years.

Nike was simultaneously wrestling with some perennial self-identity questions: Was it an athletic and performance brand, or was it a fashion brand? The new presidents and the CEO had some answers to those questions, but needed to reset the tone and anchor everyone around a

Postmerger Environment	Recessionary Environment	Hypercompetitive Environment	Global Environment
Establish guidelines for continued growth	Focus on achieving motivational impact on employees	Assess employee satisfaction through surveys	Seek opportunities to make best practices visible globally
Highlight commonality to bring company together and avoid conflicts	Anticipate and directly address insecurity, isolation, individualism, defensiveness	Highlight desired unique and differentiating behaviors and values	Emphasize inclusion, especially the offices with less visibility to senior management
Adopt incentives for employees to work together for shareholder value	Create visibility and open lines of communication to form tightly-knit community	Create mentorship opportunities to spread morale	Decentralize brand knowledge and idea generation
Set expectations that upfront investment will result in long-term benefit	Foster sense of ownership in strategic direction	Implement awards structure that further invests employees in company success	Leverage technology to provide virtual training

Figure 8.6. Customized Approaches to Different Company Situations.

bold new vision for the future. They also wanted to draw on Nike's rich cultural heritage.

CONNECTION TO A HIGHER PURPOSE. The team at Nike believes the company derives a huge benefit by being able to tap into everyone's ability to identify with the notion of sport. As they see it, sport is a universal activity that resonates with nearly everyone, regardless of age, culture, or socioeconomic situation: "All employees are connected with something bigger than the company. That is sport, and the love and passion for helping athletes improve their performance."

"Sport" evokes authentic, meaningful, emotional responses from people, drawn from experiences as both participants and observers. Nike's employees share that with Nike the company, but it also resonates with all of their other pursuits in life as parents, coaches, players, and fans. While this is an interesting premise and does give the Nike brand an unusually rich playing field from which to operate, being able to leverage this higher-order universal connectivity and put it to work on behalf of a company and a brand is not a forgone conclusion.

THE MAXIMS. With this understanding, Nike put together a small team of people to distill these ideas into a brief set of statements, which became known as Nike's Maxims, that incorporated this new sense of direction and reflected a core set of operating beliefs:

1. It Is Our Nature to Innovate.
2. Nike Is a Company.
3. Nike Is a Brand.
4. Simplify and Go.
5. The Consumer Decides.
6. Be a Sponge.
7. Evolve Immediately.
8. Do the Right Thing.
9. Master the Fundamentals.
10. We Are on the Offense. Always.
11. Remember the Man (Bill Bowerman [the company's founder]).

These eleven maxims sought to build direct connections between employees, the company, and the brand. They are anchored on the core belief that Nike's mission is "to bring inspiration and innovation to every athlete (if you have a body, you are an athlete) in the world." And they explicitly address the natural tensions that arise from the sport versus fashion debate. The maxim "Nike is a brand . . . the symbol of global leadership in sports products and attitude" coexists with the maxim "Nike is a company . . . Nike, Inc., exists to organize the pursuit and acquisition of opportunity as long as that opportunity brings with it innovation and the ability to serve human potential." The team understood the importance of explicitly addressing complex and potentially conflicting priorities. Other of Nike's maxims speak to very explicit types of behaviors, decision-making styles, and attitudes that people are expected to embrace, from "simplify and go" to "evolve immediately."

After the eleven maxims were decided on, a team began to develop the communication materials and rollout plan for the rest of the organization. In addition to printing up *Nike Maxims* books for distribution to all employees, a two-and-a-half-hour launch event was structured and produced for worldwide rollout. Drawing people from corporate communications, corporate training, the film and video production team, and senior management, the launch team encouraged many different individuals from all different regions to tell personal stories about one of the Nike maxims—what it meant to them and how it manifested itself in their life and jobs. These people told their individual stories during the launch events and then were filmed later on for inclusion on the Web site.

THE ROLLOUT. Employees were brought together in large groups (over a thousand per event) for the launch events. The two presidents hosted the multimedia, action-packed forums, infusing the events with energy, excitement, and fun. In each geographical region, Nike used local people talking live to their peers in their own words about how they brought the Nike brand to life in their job. This humanized the process in a culturally relevant way, which made it even more compelling. Everyone was given the book, and managers were directed to speak to all staff to make sure it made sense. It was also presented to field sales and incorporated into the new employee twelve-month orientation program (called Pre-Game) to become a part of the personality of that piece. Finally, a special site on the intranet was created with videos of stories for each maxim.

Since the initial rollout, Nike has been formulating plans to take the road show to Asia to help Asian workforces better understand "this

American company," using the maxims as a foundation. The company is also considering taking it out to key partners and suppliers. With the assimilation program in place, Nike is attempting to address the challenges of keeping this process alive over the long haul.

MAINTAINING, REFRESHING, AND MONITORING

Keeping a spread-out and diverse employee base actively in the Living It phase with the brand requires constant diligence and continuous support of the maxim program. After the formal brand assimilation programs are over and done with, as in the Nike example, there are still many things that a company can and should do to keep the brand-employee relationship alive and well. The objective should be to move the organization to a set of more natural, organic processes through which the brand-employee relationship stays relevant and fresh. Our 2002 Best Practices study identified a few core capabilities as critical to the maintenance of healthy brand-employee relationships. These included having an internal brand-building mind-set, making sure that marketing and other functions are aligned, and having human resources both train and bring in the right "on-brand" resources for the organization.

Internal Brand-Building Prowess

Whether you call it internal communications, internal marketing, or internal brand building, the key questions to address are these: How good are you at keeping the employees informed and engaged in the brand's evolving story and what it means for them? What kind of internal brand-building prowess do you have? Often the responsibility for this gets caught in a virtual no-man's-land between the human resource department's employee communications function and the marketing team, which, with its allies of external public relations, direct marketing, and advertising firms, focuses mostly on external stakeholders.

The primary objective of any internal marketing effort should be to increase employees' understanding of the brand, while eliminating any perceived barriers to embracing it. So whenever you are doing something meaningful that has an impact on the brand-customer relationship—new product or service launches, a new advertising campaign, a new store format, new strategic distribution alliances or

R&D relationships—communicate with employees too. Better yet, create experiences where they can feel the promise and the excitement of these activities at first hand.

BMW North America has very distinct ways of doing that, including making sure that every employee has a personal experience driving each new model that comes out or prelaunching any new advertising campaign with all of the employees three to five days before it hits the airwaves. Think about the emotional and experiential punch these kinds of efforts must pack, as opposed to reading a launch announcement by way of company e-mail. Every company would benefit from developing experiential approaches to promoting the brand and weaving them into the company as well-established brand-building practices.

Sometimes employees are unaware of the brand-customer stories or the collective brand power of the organization. Generally, a company that has developed strong internal brand-building instincts will leverage these stories consistently and promote them throughout the organization. During our 2002 Best Practices research, a Sony executive observed that "the Sony brand was already in the blood of most people; we just had to pull it out and distill its meaning." Panasonic's Bob Greenberg told a wonderful story about a game called "stone soup":

> Each brand manager throws a stone into the soup, so one brand manager told us about how the Honda Odyssey is now using Panasonic DVD, and another talked about the Vatican [using Panasonic systems], the other about the sound system in Pac Bell Park. Ultimately, through all of these realizations, we made a video called the "Panasonic Power" video and a booklet on the power of the brand.

Similar stories came out of companies like Amazon, Nike, 3M, Kodak, and even Itron.

Other companies, like IBM, Microsoft, Hewlett-Packard, United Technologies, and Accenture, have developed advertising aimed at changing the perceptions of their customers and their employees. All of these organizations were trying to orchestrate some significant change or were under siege and saw that they could leverage advertising spending effectively to change the brand perceptions of both sets of constituents. IBM's advertising around the Internet and e-business in the late 1990s was a good example of this, as was HP CEO Carly Fiorina's "Back to the Garage" campaign.

These types of internal brand-building activities, whether communications or experience oriented, need to be focused and credible. At a minimum, they should be educational in nature and resonate with values that are important to the employees. Just as with external communications, each brand-building activity needs to be supported by proof points that support and build on whatever the brand does or should promise. They should emphasize role models and stories that have the potential to become company folklore by spotlighting star performance and performers at all levels, thereby helping people understand what success looks like. Ideally, any internal brand-building activity also starts to provide the basis for the necessary emotional connections required to truly build a brand.

Getting Marketing and Other Communication Areas Aligned

Another aspect of maintaining healthy brand-employee relationships is getting alignment around brand's role within the organization's various marketing and communications functions. Although this seems obvious, for many companies like GE, UBS, Kodak, AT&T, and others that participated in our 2002 Best Practices study, it was a challenge that took some time to overcome. The challenges were mostly tied to the breadth and complexity of their business: diverse business lines, varied go-to-market structures, expanding global footprint, and others. Without the necessary alignment, you will face major roadblocks to effective and consistent internal brand assimilation efforts.

Each of the organizations mentioned from our study invests heavily in systems, processes, and brand-related training for the marketing and communications professionals inside the firm to ensure consistency of marketing execution, which has to include key brand messages, tone, and visual imagery. Both AT&T and GE leveraged intranet sites for their marketing and communications communities, which contained best practices for guidelines on trademarks and naming and communication elements, research, brand valuation, brand health metrics, and tool kits to help people talk about the brand effectively and apply it in business decision making. UBS has been working for two years with a global communications task force to begin aligning its brand efforts across functional areas, such as marketing communications, investor relations, and corporate communications.

Obviously, internal alignment plays a critical role in brand assimilation. Nothing kills the buzz for employees more than visible contradictions from company executives. Brand building that is taken in different directions or is openly contradictory can fuel cynicism toward internal brand assimilation efforts. Inconsistent communications may create even more consternation with employees than with customers. Customers see only communications targeted at them; employees see them all.

It is not easy to get everyone to align around common ideas, because each group serves a slightly different master. For example, one of the 2002 Best Practices research participants talked excitedly about the progress that she had made in getting higher billing for the brand in all of the CEO's speeches and external communications. But it took her eighteen months of "constant attention and frustration" to get the public relations group to include the brand positioning at the end of press releases.

Recruiting, Employee Orientation, and Ongoing Employee Training

Many of our 2002 Best Practices research participants emphasized how important they think it is to partner with the company's human resources and hiring managers to make sure that a brand lens is brought to bear on the new employee sourcing and recruiting process. The irony is that over 40 percent of the respondents said that "human resources and employee training" are "not at all" driven by brand strategy. This is a missed opportunity.

Brand issues should play an important role in defining core competencies, behavioral characteristics, and other key employee success factors. For example, personnel evaluation processes should provide feedback and coaching about brand-appropriate versus inappropriate behavior. Some employees will not want to change the way they behave and will prefer to leave the company. Others will embrace it and help champion it throughout. Over time, through these processes, your organization should increasingly be composed of employees who understand your brand and live it.

3M's Anne Greer believes that "more than half the battle is in selecting the right people. When you get the right people, they will be good for building the brand." Working effectively with those inside your company to help shape the brand dialogue could be the most important thing you can do over time to make your brand assimilation efforts succeed.

Another key point that was made repeatedly by our study participants was to "get 'em early." Said another way, make sure that the brand promise and its implications for employee behavior play a prominent role in all new employee orientation and training. Companies like Goldman Sachs, Merck, Accenture, and Visa place significant emphasis on this, and it pays off. Accenture, for example, produced a twelve-minute new-employee orientation video that features the chairman and CEO describing the brand and its desired relationship with clients. The purpose of any such effort should be to communicate the values of the brand in a straightforward and practical way. You want new employees to understand why and how their tasks and activities create value for customers and other constituents.

Finally, many in our 2002 Best Practices study felt that the brand should drive investments in continuing employee education and training. Some companies find creative ways to make sure that education and training are tied back to the value they are trying to create. The more the organization works on brand building, the more attractive the company will become and the easier it will become to recruit the best talent to help bring a brand-based culture to life. Over time, it will become a self-fulfilling prophecy; new employees will think of their purpose in whatever job role they have as one that focuses on building the brand and consistently fulfilling its promise.

Monitoring and Measurement

All of these practices—a focus on strategic brand–human resource alignment, marketing functional alignment, and internal brand-building prowess—are part of an ongoing brand assimilation maintenance program designed to keep employees connected to the brand. The effectiveness of these programs and the overall health of the employee-brand relationship deserve constant monitoring and periodic measurement. This would include

- Conducting regular assessments of internal brand perceptions against key brand objectives
- Tying increased brand alignment to business unit (or department) results
- Establishing success targets and measuring against these

For example, you could establish a minimum percentage of customer-facing employees who must be aware of the new brand positioning, understand why it is important to them personally and to the company, and know how to deliver on the brand promise. You could then implement a mystery-shopping program explicitly designed to test for that.

We suggest considering the following seven brand-employee metrics when assessing how well your assimilation efforts are progressing:

1. *Business understanding.* Understand who we are (including the company history), how we make money, who our customers are, and current year financial goals.

2. *Brand understanding.* Articulate key valued and differentiated elements of the brand.

3. *Brand influence.* Describe specific ways that employees have an impact on the customer experience.

4. *Brand trust.* Understand the level of trust that employees have of the ability of the company leadership to do the right thing relative to the values of the brand.

5. *Brand credibility.* Measure whether employees believe that the company is capable of delivering on its promises to customer and employees.

6. *Brand delivery.* Measure whether employees believe that the company fulfills its promises to customer and employees.

7. *Brand preference, advocacy, and satisfaction.* Understand the extent to which employees prefer to work at the company rather than its competitors and the degree to which employees are comfortable referring friends and family to their employer. It is also important to track employee retention and turnover and internal satisfaction relative to the brand assimilation process.

It is not a coincidence that some of these metrics are similar to those discussed in Chapter Seven because external metrics can also be relevant internally.

The Role of Brand-Building Incentives

Having the right combination of individual and firmwide bonus structures, tied to the success of the brand, is the best way to permanently shift behaviors of employees who have a direct impact on the success of the brand (we believe that this includes every employee). All employees should have part of their annual goals tied to their personal contribution to brand-related efforts. In addition, all employees should participate in a companywide bonus pool tied to the company's reaching its annual brand-building goals and objectives. In these ways, both the individual and the entire organization are responsible and rewarded for brand-building success.

In support of this, our 2002 Best Practices study showed that companies that have high senior management commitment to brand building tend to have long-term brand strategies in place, as well as both intangible rewards (such as internal recognition and senior management exposure) and tangible rewards (such as bonuses, salary increases, and stock options) given to those responsible for driving brand success.

A COMMITMENT TO OPERATIONALIZING THE BRAND: WHEN EDUCATION AND INSPIRATION INITIATIVES FALL SHORT

No matter how focused the communication or how memorable the educational experience, sometimes education and inspiration activities are not enough to get people to change their behavior. Employees can understand the positioning and strategic intent of the brand and even feel some emotional connection to it, but still may not feel as if they can or should do anything different because of this new understanding.

Existing information systems or the business processes may be holding them back. The functional area in which they work may seem too dysfunctional to them or perpetually underresourced to get the job done right. Many employees may not have the critical skills to do what is necessary to support the new positioning or may be financially motivated to pursue a different set of behaviors. Or just as demoralizing, the organization may not have the core operational capabilities to deliver against the stated brand promise.

Regardless of the reason, if you do not have a brand assimilation mind-set that is flexible and empowered enough to dive deep occasionally and tackle the root causes of employee inaction or brand-customer relationship breakdowns, your company will always be handicapped in its attempts to build a brand-driven business.

Sometimes internal processes are broken. The store experience is frustrating. Customers are perplexed by the complexity of your sales structure. Orders are being lost. The usage experience and product and service quality fall short of expectations. Key aspects of your operational delivery are just not happening. Sometimes the breakdowns can be isolated at specific brand touchpoints, tackled as discrete initiatives and as a result be focused on incremental process improvements. Other times, whole systems may need redesign before you can get to the root cause of the problem. If you do not build cross-functional alliances and tackle these issues head on, your organization could lose its brand as the critical weapon it is.

As a brand asset manager, once there is a commitment to tackling an issue, you should be part of the cross-functional team that diagnoses and analyzes the challenges, begins to design the new solution, and brings a brand lens to the approach to drive to the right answer.

There are countless examples of companies that realized that in order to assimilate the brand effectively, they were going to have to go beyond education and inspiration and tackle more difficult brand touchpoint–related human resource, operational, or organizational issues. Xerox, for example, in trying to reposition a core part of its offering away from hardware and more toward software, solutions, and services, realized that the national sales structure was going to struggle with the transition. Rather than introduce potentially disruptive changes to the overall structure, it focused on using a core team of specialists designed to augment the sales force, bring deeper knowledge of the new offering, and drive adoption of the new offerings through win-win relationships with the existing sales team.

The Starbucks leadership team also faced an interesting dilemma: trying to build a warm, rich, inviting, and friendly European café experience in an economy where that type of workforce often turns over at over 100 to 200 percent per year. The Starbucks leadership team took a different approach with employees, whom they call *baristas*, investing in comprehensive work policies, compensation, and benefits programs that would allow them to attract and retain better talent and continue to overinvest in the types of training that allow employees to deliver the "magic of coffee."

Sometimes tackling issues at the individual brand touchpoint level is not enough. It takes broader systemic change, from processes and measurements to organizational structure, to optimizing the brand-driven business for success. Brand-driven businesses let no barriers stand in the way of creating an environment where employees can become and remain passionate advocates for the brand. Creating and maintaining the structural support for that environment is the subject of Chapter Nine.

Establishing a Brand-Based Organization

Focusing on the Structure and Roles to Support Brand-Driven Change

Assimilating your brand-building efforts into the organization is critical if you want to change behaviors permanently and dramatically affect the way in which customers and stakeholders perceive you. Although education, inspiration, and other brand assimilation activities may often have the immediate effect you desire, if the structure is not there to support those efforts for the longer term, your brand-building efforts will ultimately be for naught.

Lasting brand change can take place only if the right structure is organized to support it and the right assimilation efforts are in place to drive a brand-based culture. Without this level of real change, your brand-building efforts can be viewed as superficial internally and as an empty promise externally. With this level of change, your ability to live the mantra of managing every one of your brand touchpoints consistently, over time, can become a reality.

We believe that the transformation to a brand-driven organization requires fundamental changes in how the company is organized, where the brand reports, how all the functional areas participate, and ultimately what type of spirit exists within the company. This has to start with the CEO and how his or her passion is translated into real and meaningful change. This chapter shows what this brand-driven organization and culture looks and feels like.

THE SHIFT FROM TRADITIONAL BRAND-BASED ORGANIZATIONS TO A BRAND-DRIVEN CULTURE

Figure 9.1 illustrates how traditional brand management has consistently pushed responsibility for the brand down to the most junior members of the marketing team. Today's brand-based organization is described best as a hierarchy:

The president or CEO, who often has a vested interest in the brand, generally delegates it down one to three levels.

↓

The senior vice president of marketing or chief marketing officer sees the whole picture, is responsible for the one- and three-year brand plans, has to make the tough budget trade-offs, and reports directly to the president or CEO along with five to ten other senior vice presidents.

↓

The vice president of marketing generally has a high-level perspective of what the company is trying to accomplish with its brands.

↓

The category or division manager is responsible for making sure the annual plan is being executed and that coordination is taking place between other brands in the category. This manager has decision-making authority and is ultimately accountable for reaching goals and objectives, which naturally produces some tension in balancing the short-term financial goals with the long-term brand goals.

↓

The brand manager is in charge of day-to-day operations and coordination of the brand. Brand managers generally work very closely with sales, distribution, and the advertising agency to make sure promotions and advertising are being implemented appropriately and deliveries are on time.

↓

The assistant brand manager is in charge of collecting all the data and statistics in place necessary to make decisions at a higher level.

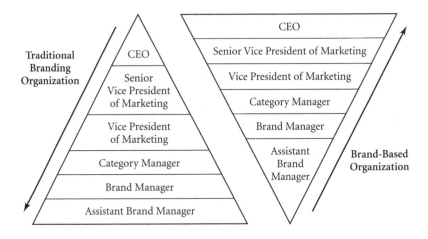

Figure 9.1.   Traditional Brand-Based Organizational Structures.

This organizational construct pushes down brand responsibilities so that the person who should have the most accountability for the brand actually has the least.

So where do you start to look for examples and role models in building your brand-driven organization? We continue to see the increasing numbers of CEOs and senior executives climbing on the brand bandwagon and starting to live the brand. We look to companies like IKEA, Wal-Mart, UPS, Itron, and CIGNA as role models, not to mention inspiring companies like Amazon and Starbucks.

This newer breed of company is embracing brand in new and exciting ways that starts to set the tone for how others can get their foot in the door and start their own cultural revolution. The key is to determine the change agents within your company who will champion this cause and help make it a reality. If you do not do this, you are destined for brand mediocrity. With a brand-driven organization, you can take control of your company's brand-based destiny.

THE CRITICAL ROLES THAT ENABLE A BRAND-DRIVEN CULTURE TO BECOME A REALITY

There are five specific roles required to operationalize the brand and shift the culture for good. Not all of these titles may currently exist within your organization, and it may require identifying people to fill certain roles that do not currently exist. But we believe with these five in the fold, a brand-based culture is certain to develop.

- CEO
- C-level executives reporting to the CEO
- Executive branding council, composed of cross-functional brand ambassadors
- Companywide brand change agents or individuals known to have successfully helped shift or change part of the organization in the past
- Employees

Understanding the role each of these players and the required behavioral shifts each person needs to make to bring the brand to life within an organization is the first step to making brand-driven change take hold within your company.

Brand-Based Culture and the CEO

While the preference in building a brand-based organization would be to start at the top and have the CEO push brand out to the rest of the organization, in reality, very few companies today completely revolve around the brand and have their CEO as the ultimate ambassador. It is still the norm when talking about the CEO and brand building to hear comments like these:

"He just doesn't get it. His background is in operations and finance."

"She thinks that all of that brand stuff belongs in marketing and should stay that way. She often asks me, 'Isn't that why I hired you?'"

"He says the company has been successful for seventy-five years without worrying about the brand, so why worry now."

"She says it will just cost too much."

Nevertheless, many CEOs are recognizing that they are the linchpin in building a brand-based culture and reaching brand-driven success. At Panasonic, for example, "it all starts with our chairman and CEO," says Bob Greenberg, senior vice president of marketing.

Customer-first and brand-first are his mission and mentality, and he has made it part of the company, every single day. He manifests it by talking about it in his speeches, sending out memos, consistently investing in the brand, and fully understanding its importance. His long-term vision is to put Panasonic into other businesses where we currently don't participate and he knows that we need brand to allow for this extendibility.

At 3M, where brand involvement is extremely high throughout the organization, brand strategy manager Anne Greer states:

Our CEO leads our branding efforts and is supported by the brand management committee, chaired by the vice president of corporate marketing. The committee, representing all 3M businesses, is focused primarily on strategy and consists of high-level, cross-functional representatives, including the senior vice president of R&D, senior lawyers, and brand experts. It all starts with the CEO.

BRAND IGNITERS FOR THE CEO. When you talk to executives at Panasonic, 3M, and other companies about why and how their CEOs saw the light, a few general themes stick out. Here are some that you can suggest to elevate your CEO's commitment to building a brand-driven business:

- Show the positive financial impact that brands have had on other companies to demonstrate more explicitly the tight linkage between building the brand and helping the company achieve its longer-term strategic and financial growth goals.
- Have your CEO meet with CEOs of brand-centric companies to help convince him or her that it is critical for future success.
- Register your CEO for daylong brand seminars (such as those run by the Conference Board) that will help reiterate the importance of brand.
- Keep track of your organization's brand successes, and when you have accumulated a few, try to have a recognized business journal feature a story on you.

CEOs of the future will not need these igniters because they will naturally embrace the brand as an asset and drive it through the organization on a daily basis. In addition, we believe CEOs of the future will more easily see that the brand is their responsibility; they have ultimate fiduciary responsibility for their organization, and building the brand is one of their greatest tools for reaching their longer-term financial and strategic goals and objectives (that is, shareholder value).

THE CEO'S DAY-TO-DAY BRAND REMINDERS. The most effective way for the CEO to elevate the importance of brand within his or her organization is to be the most vocal proponent of brand. That is, he or she must regularly acknowledge that the brand is a reason to believe in the future success of the company. Richard Branson at Virgin, Fred Smith at FedEx, Herb Kelleher at Southwest, Ralph Lauren at Polo Ralph Lauren, and Howard Schultz at Starbucks do this as often as possible. Sam Walton at Wal-Mart and Roberto Goizueta at Coca-Cola were probably the ultimate brand champions.

There are many ways for CEOs to show that brand is on their mind every day:

- Spreading the word. In every interview conducted, every press release sent out, and every presentation made, the CEO not only mentions the brand but talks emphatically and emotionally about it in a way that conveys his or her overall commitment to brand building.

- Asking for customer feedback. Many CEOs rarely go out to see their customers or listen to what they have to say about their company and their brand. An easy way for CEOs to show they are brand- and customer-centric is to make a habit of talking to customers and asking what they do or do not think about the brand.

- Blending brand and business strategy. Within the strategic planning process, the CEO needs to make sure that a significant portion of time is spent discussing ways to build and leverage the brand over the next three to five years and that a specific financial goal is placed against the brand.

- Having some of the CEO's compensation tied to brand. There is no surer way of showing how serious a CEO is about brand building than to tie a portion of total compensation to the overall performance of the brand.

- Adding brand to the balanced scorecard. Adding brand to the company's balanced scorecard guarantees that the level of brand importance is not only high but also fairly permanent.

• Sharing the brand with shareholders. Within the letter to share-holders in the annual report, make sure that brand is mentioned as one of the keys for organizational success.

Interestingly, many of the great CEO brand builders over the past ten years, who survived the dot-com frenzy, can provide valuable lessons to CEOs from old-line companies now trying to create a brand-centric or-ganization. Whether it is ex-CEO Tim Koogle of Yahoo! or Meg Whit-man at eBay, many Internet superstars founded or ran their companies with fairly simple premises and an always easy-to-understand promise and benefit to their stakeholders. Technology stars Michael Dell, Scott McNealy, and Larry Ellison built their companies on a brand-driven promise and worked tirelessly to fulfill it.

Today, because they fulfilled their respective promises and built a company to support those promises, they are considered to be leg-endary brand builders. Each of their companies has survived and for the most part thrived, while a majority of their direct competitors have gone by the wayside.

A public commitment to a brand-based culture by a CEO is the ul-timate sign of his or her belief in the brand and that brand building will be taken seriously. Even when the business doesn't allow for major investment, such as during an economic downturn, the CEO should show support for the brand. Ruth Fornell, the CMO of Teradata, a di-vision of NCR that offers analytical solutions that help businesses drive growth, gives a few examples of how this is done at her company: "Even though our business isn't yet large enough to afford a big advertising budget, senior management [CEO/COO] invests what they can. They also support the brand building by making it a key part of their inter-nal messaging as well as speaking at public forums, attending net-working events, participating in media interviews, etc."

If the CEO is not willing to support the brand during hard times and focuses only on cutting brand-building initiatives, it is a sure sign that the CEO was not serious about brand building from the start.

Brand-Based Culture and the C-Level Executives

Each of the direct reports to the CEO (that is, the C-levels) has to help the transition to a brand-driven organization. The CEO cannot take on this monumental task alone. Without having brand accountabil-ity across the very top of an organization, decisions will most likely be undersupported. Senior management has to believe in the power of the brand and the need to manage it across the organization. In addition, if all senior executives believe that the brand is one of the primary mechanisms to fill the growth gap, then it should make sense that all senior executives have to be involved in building the brand.

Each of the CEO's major reports has a role to play in helping to make this transformation.

CHIEF OPERATING OFFICER. The COO has a singular focus of operating a company as effectively and efficiently as possible, from the plants and machinery to the people. This executive also often owns the profit and loss statement for the company, which dictates what investments will or will not be made.

As we move into this future state of companies revolving around the brand, the COO is as likely a candidate as anyone else to become the brand czar within the company. He or she has the opportunity to control all of the resources that ultimately affect the brand. So when we talk about controlling every brand touchpoint, this is the one executive who can do just that.

It is now the CEO's responsibility to empower the COO to control the most important asset the company owns: the brand. In other words, "Does this decision positively or negatively affect the brand?" should be the COO's constant mantra.

In effect, all investment decisions, personnel shifts, operating changes, and ultimately brand enhancements now rest with the COO. Since many COOs do not have true brand management or marketing experience in their backgrounds, there is an opportunity to educate and enlighten these individuals. Working with the rest of the executive team, you can help the COO take a fresh look at the brand and determine ultimately how best to manage it, invest in it, leverage it, and nurture it over time. Ruth Fornell, CMO of Teradata, describes how it might be done:

> We showed the value of the brand to our COO by giving context around the benefits of branding and how it would affect the business, in language he understood. I recognized that he had never thought about business in this way before and would need to be educated on branding. I also knew that the COO needed to fully understand the value of branding before he would authorize specific spending on branding in the future.

Her insight on putting branding into his terms greatly benefited both of their brand-building efforts going forward.

CHIEF FINANCIAL OFFICER. The CFO manages the purse strings for a company. While others can come up with brilliant R&D plans that should be approved, geographical expansions that should be implemented, or marketing campaigns that are totally buttoned up, it is the CFO who will ultimately make the recommendation of whether this investment is a good one or a bad one. The CFO's responsibility is quite simple. The question all CFOs should have stamped on their heads is, "Why should I fund your initiative?"

The CFO wants to know what the return on investment will be on your initiative and how quickly that return will be realized. If the answers to those questions are not in line with the CFO's investment posture, then the investment decision generally gets bumped back up to the CEO to decide whether the company should make an exception for this particular investment. Our hope is that the CFO will not only see the value that brand has in driving profitability, but also will support funding that enables its longer-term growth.

There are many approaches to dealing with CFOs:

- Be prepared. When building the business case for making an investment in brand, leverage the benefits of building the brand discussed in Chapter One.

- Get them involved. When possible, have someone in the CFO's group be part of the brand-building team. Cross-functional representation is a requirement for successful, companywide brand-building initiatives. Why not have the CFO be the representative from the financial function?

- Garner small wins, and document them. Make sure you are able to bring examples of your own brand investment success (possibly from metrics you have been employing) or from other companies in building your case.

- Show different scenarios when pitching for funding. Because CFOs are very analytical, provide options showing three or four alternative brand-building investment scenarios and commensurate returns.

- Line up your allies. Presell as many of the C-level executives as possible before you meet with the CFO.

- Review your plans in advance. Before going into any major meeting where you are seeking brand-building funds, be sure you have worked out your plans with the CFO ahead of time.

• Seek ownership. Have the CFO own many of the metrics discussed in Chapter Seven so that he or she is knowledgeable about the brand-building efforts and results. The CFO should help drive the brand as part of a company's overall balanced scorecard, assuming that you have heard the CFO's concerns and issues and everyone has bought into the need for delivering against these metrics.

CHIEF INNOVATION OFFICER. This is a new position that does not exist in many companies today, so you may need to think instead about the vice president of new product development or the vice president of research and development.

New product failures generally result from either a poor understanding of what the marketplace really needs and wants or poor internal management and coordination in managing the new product process (both of which are under the control of the company). Many times, going deeper into the internal reasons for failure reveals a poor connection between the brand and the new products launched. The CIO has to be the one who guarantees that every new product or service launched at a minimum helps the brand's position stay neutral. Of course, the goal is for every new product or service to help drive the value of the brand higher over the longer term.

The reason that brand-based extensions are so powerful is that the newly introduced product or service comes with instant credibility and a built-in endorsement because the brand has already been accepted and proven in the marketplace by another existing product or service. In considering new brand-based innovations, the CIO always has to ask the following important questions:

• Is the extension consistent with the brand promise?
• Does the extension help uphold and strengthen the value of our brand?
• Is the extension consistent with our overall brand positioning?
• If this extension fails, will it be a major or minor setback for our brand?

Successful brand-based extensions can have a direct impact on brand loyalty and brand value. In the words of Bob Passikoff, president of Brand Keys, "Since an increase in customer loyalty results in a lifetime increase in profitability, strategically leveraging your brand into smart brand extensions is one of the surest approaches to growing the overall value of your brand."

For more information on this topic, refer to Chapter Nine in *Brand Asset Management.*

CHIEF PEOPLE OFFICER. Next to the COO, the chief people officer, who generally reports directly to the CEO, may play the most critical role in bringing a brand-based culture to life. Because this title does not yet exist in many companies, you might think of the senior vice president of human resources when you consider filling this important role.

The CPO's brand-related responsibilities include recruiting for brand success, establishing incentives and rewards, and developing long-term brand career tracks. As we explained in Chapter Eight, recruiting and creating motivators and rewards should occur with the brand vision and positioning in mind. The CPO should use the brand to help define core competencies, behavioral characteristics, and other key employee success factors to select individuals who will effectively deliver the brand. The CPO should also help define motivators and rewards to help shift behaviors of those employees that have a direct impact on the success of the brand.

While most companies do not have brand-oriented career tracks in place, the CPO is the one individual within the company that can make this both a priority and a reality. By setting up longer-term brand career tracks that focus on the consistency and longevity of the manager's relationship with the brand, companies can realize the brand's long-term success potential.

CHIEF INFORMATION OFFICER. If it is true that information is the key to longer-term company success, then this familiar CIO (as opposed to the chief innovation officer) is an important enabler in helping a company maximize its brand potential. For example, in thinking of customer relationship management as a path to understanding better how customers want to be treated and what their needs and wants are, the CIO provides not only the technology to obtain this information but often also the information itself. For many companies, integrating the CIO role with that of the head of market research allows them to address critical brand-related questions and will most likely help increase their power base as the one that has or has access to the answers needed to drive the brand. They can help address questions such as these:

- Who are my most valuable customers?

- What is the lifetime value of my most valuable customers?

- What is my retention rate (or loyalty rate) to date, and what will it take to increase that over time?

- How well am I addressing the overall needs and wants of my key customers?

- How well do I understand how to service my key customers?

- Why do customers choose other brands besides ours when making a purchase decision?

- What are the key criteria driving purchases in my category, and how do I rate against each?

The CIO often can fill in the gaps that help turn a decently run branded organization into a top-tier brand-driven organization. However, like the other C-level executives, CIOs have to understand clearly their role in bringing the brand to life within the organization and how best to leverage technology to get there.

CHIEF MARKETING OFFICER. The CMO can be the greatest enabler or deterrent to building a truly great brand-driven organization. What separates the best CMOs from the rest?

The CMOs who achieve greatness in their role are those who realize they not only have to come up with a great brand-driven plan to help guide the company to increased awareness, trial, and penetration but also recognize that they have to lead the charge in getting the rest of the organization to understand and buy into their role in the brand's success. In contrast, CMOs who are territorial, believe that they are bigger than the brand itself, or believe that building the brand is really marketing's function are the CMOs who will fail.

Traditionally, CMOs have been charged with developing the right segmentation, targeting, and positioning strategy. With this, they are armed with the knowledge to spark great creative advertising, implement strong marketing programs, and assess the health of the brand regularly.

The great CMOs realize that they need every single person in the organization to work with them to fulfill the promise that the brand is making. To get the type of cooperation the role requires and deserves, the CMO must understand how to make other brand participants feel important and part of the brand-building process and success. This involves not only talking to others throughout the organization in a language that is relevant to them when discussing brand, but also including them in any rewards and recognition that the CMO receives for brand-building success. The surest ways of getting others committed to companywide brand building are to acknowledge their role in that brand-building process publicly and provide them with appropriate rewards and incentives.

Brand-Based Culture and the Executive Brand Council

One of the most effective tools we have seen CMOs use to drive internal brand-building efforts is what we call an executive brand council (EBC). An EBC brings together the heads of business units and functional areas to tackle as a team the tough brand issues that will arise. Typical issues for an EBC to deal with include the following:

- Changes to the name of the company
- Acquisitions and divestitures of any brands
- New aesthetic treatment of the brand
- Naming guidelines tied to brand extensions, as well as co-brands (Citibank Advantage), subbrands (Sony Walkman), and endorsed brands (Courtyard Inn by Marriott)
- Licensing agreements in which the brand will be handed over to another organization to manage
- New creative advertising to support the brand

When TXU established its EBC a few years ago, it had several goals and objectives in mind. For the first time, brand building was starting to catch on as a necessary strategy for going beyond the great creative work executed in prior years. TXU was making several acquisitions overseas where brand-related issues were starting to cause some internal strife. Many of these new entities wanted to retain their preacquisition identities, while corporate wanted to move to one global TXU brand. While European TXU had already gone through deregulation, TXU Dallas had to prepare for deregulation in 2002. Most important, service was going to become a point of differentiation in the brave new world of competing utilities. Thus building a brand was not a luxury but a requirement for TXU to survive and thrive.

Susan Atteridge's challenge as TXU's chief communications officer was to pull together all of the functional and business unit entities around the globe to develop a brand strategy that everyone agreed on. In Susan's words:

> The executive brand council was established about a year and a half ago at my request, with the CEO's blessing. He set it up through a formal memo distributed to the top executives within TXU. We purposefully had the lead person in each geography become part of the executive brand council. He put it in place. This was critical at the stage we were in, with no history or definition of a brand. As a group, we had to wrestle with some thorny issues. We did not have an agreement on the company strategy and thus could not completely agree on the brand strategy. Over the past fifteen months, I believe we have made significant progress and have hit some big milestones. We have declared victory on our strategy, positioning, and persona. Our charter as a council was to guide and direct the brand, and we have done that. We will continue to meet, although less frequently, and we will remain solely focused on brand and seize every opportunity possible to continue down the brand path we started back in the summer of 2000.

Scores of companies have successfully implemented their own versions of an EBC. At Kodak, for example, where "brand stewardship is shared by everybody within the company," according to Paula Dumas, director and vice president of brand marketing,

> we manage brand impact through our brand management council, which is chaired by the CEO. The CFO, COO, business unit presidents, external consultants, and the CMO all participate. It basically serves as a board of directors for our CMO. The annual operating plan reflects specific strategies that have gained approval of the brand council. So if we are interested in changing policies tied to the brand or if we want to request new investments behind the brand, these requests would be presented to our brand management council for approval.

Another example is H&R Block, where, according to Karl Ploeger, vice president for creative service and brand management, "Management and leadership of the brand clearly starts at the top. We have an executive committee, comprising our senior managers, who all need to agree on corporate objectives. Elevating brand was identified as a corporate objective. We are now all brand stewards."

Other Key Change Agents to Drive a Brand-Based Culture

As would be the case with any new initiative, certain individuals or entities will lead others in making a brand-driven organization a reality. Beyond the CEO, the C-level reports, and the EBCs, there are other leaders who may help in building a brand-based organization (see Figure 9.2). Each has the power and position to promote the mindset that the brand is an asset, critical to the long-term success of the organization, and that every employee is ultimately a brand ambassador. They are the ones to help the employees move through the Hearing It, Believing It, and Living It phases of commitment presented in Chapter Eight (see Figure 8.1).

Following are a few examples of what we collectively call *brand change agents*. Some of these roles we have seen formally set up at companies. Some have been observed operating informally, and others are those we would like to see set up in the future.

CHIEF BRANDING OFFICER. Our belief is that there is a critical need to have someone at the top focused on the short-term objectives (the next twelve months) and someone focused on the long-term objectives (the next three years) for building the brand and brand portfolio. We also believe that the chief marketing officer should take on these responsibilities but be renamed the chief branding officer to show the breadth and importance of brand building to the organization.

The chief branding officer should have accountability and empowerment over all the brand-driven decisions needing to be made. He or she needs to own the strategy, the budget, and the teams that will help to drive the brand forward. Most important, this should be the one person in the organization who is overseeing all of the company's brands, the individual performance of each, the interrelationships among them, and the care and maintenance of the portfolio as a whole.

BRAND ASSET MANAGEMENT OPERATION COMMITTEES. In the brand-driven organization, cross-functional brand asset management (BAM) operating committees would exist a few layers below the EBC and would consist of middle-level managers on a fast track for success. The

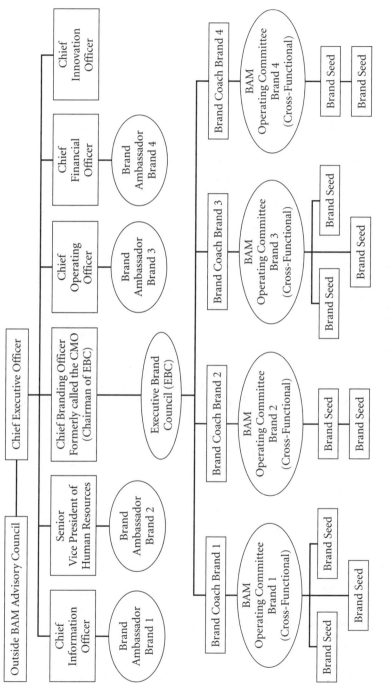

Figure 9.2. A Brand-Based Organizational Chart.

individuals on this committee would focus on a single brand and handle all of the day-to-day brand-related issues, from new product development to advertising to internal and external communications to strategically laying out the operating plan for the brand. Wyeth has these teams already in place, according to Andreas Eggert, director of global strategic marketing:

> We are like a spider weaving a web . . . [with] lots of interdependencies. We went through organizational restructuring in early 2000 to facilitate a common approach and be divided into cross-functional business units called therapeutic area teams. We also have R&D and marketing people together to form global brand teams. Supply chain, medical and regulatory affairs, and the affiliates are all crucial to brand-building efforts. Representatives from these areas sit on the therapeutic area teams and the brand teams. For example, if we have delays in supply chain, this affects the relationship that we have with our customers. We need for supply chain to understand their role in the overall experience, so that we collaborate in communicating issues to customers. For that we don't talk to them in brand language but about the end value and benefit that supply chain adds to the customer experience.

The success of the BAM operating committee would be directly tied to the relationship that the individuals on the committee have with senior management (or the EBC) and how strategic and committed they remain to the brand. In particular, the BAM operating committees should be charged with the following responsibilities:

- Providing tremendous day-to-day insight into the brand from their functional area's perspective
- Gathering input from key players in their functional area as needed on the project
- Serving as strong communication links back to their functional areas
- Leading the communications and education efforts that need to take place to get full company buy-in, participation, and ownership

BRAND COACH. The brand coach would run the BAM operating committee and have ultimate responsibility for making sure the brand is operationalized. Similar to the traditional definition of a brand manager, this role would run both the offense and the defense for the brand. The brand coach would have ultimate responsibility for the bottom-line performance of the brand. The coach would invoke the BAM operating committees as an advisory board and work with the brand ambassador in making strategic brand decisions, but in the end would be held accountable and responsible for achieving the brand's goals and objectives.

BRAND AMBASSADOR OR CHAMPION. Regardless of the exact title used, whether brand ambassador or brand champion, every brand in the organization should have a C-level executive assigned to it, with the following primary responsibilities:

- Providing advice to the brand coach or brand manager and brand vice president
- Providing the brand coach or brand manager an enabler at the top of the organization when he or she runs into a bottleneck or has an issue that needs immediate resolution
- Showing everyone in the organization that the C-levels believe in and own their brands

Not only will the CMO and the CEO own a brand, but the head of information systems, human resources, finance, operations, and so forth, across the board, will also each own a brand and be responsible for championing the efforts of that particular brand's coach or manager.

In theory, the brand ambassador will be constantly thinking about the brand, along with his or her regular day-to-day job. The obvious benefit of instituting the brand ambassador role is that it forces every senior executive to be involved in brand building in some capacity.

BRAND SEEDS A brand seed is someone who has experienced success in one branded entity within an organization and is "seeded" into another, with the goal of bringing that same degree of success to the new brand-building efforts. We have also seen this work when a company must stagger its brand-building efforts and can focus on only one brand at a time. Thus an individual from the next brand in line is staffed on the current brand-building team to learn the ropes and transfer lessons learned when it is his or her brand's turn to start the brand-building journey.

OUTSIDE BAM ADVISORY COUNCIL. It makes a lot of sense that outside practitioners or experts that do not directly compete against your brand can help bring informed and unbiased perspectives to your brand-building efforts. Although advertising agencies and consultancies are supposed to play this role, it is often hard for them to criticize the efforts of the client who, in effect, is paying their salary.

To make the most of a BAM advisory council, you would have to bring together a group of outside experts who all have something different to contribute and will give you direct and honest feedback tied to your brand-building efforts. We are currently implementing a brand advisory council with one of our food-manufacturing clients, who requires that direct store distributors (DSDs) be on board with brand-building efforts to maximize brand success. In this case, we have brought together five DSDs who are well respected throughout the country to serve two purposes:

• To make sure we are getting great outside advice from those who arguably have the strongest relationships with retailers

• To build a group of brand believers who can take our brand-building message to other DSDs who need to be bought into this process too

We would call the second benefit for this client a hidden but equally important benefit of having a BAM Advisory council. If managed properly, those serving on the council can also be external brand ambassadors.

Brand-Based Culture and the Employee Base

A company can have the best support structures in place and consistent senior management support, but without total organizational alignment and the recognition that every employee has to be motivated to deliver the brand's promises, brand building within the organization will not work.

In the brand assimilation chapter (Chapter Eight), we discussed moving the brand into the day-to-day lives of employees by making sure they understand the strategy for the brand, their individual roles in fulfilling that brand strategy, and the fact that brand building is ongoing.

Organizations that have succeeded in building a brand-based culture have a few common traits. They have demonstrated senior management commitment to brand building. They have strong incentive and reward systems in place to keep managers motivated to make the best possible brand-building decisions. And they generally have career tracks in place that motivate employees to want to stick with the brand long term.

ADDITIONAL TIPS FOR BUILDING A BRAND-BASED CULTURE

The following case studies show how several companies have built and maintained their brand-based cultures through their own brand assimilation and brand-based organizational efforts. The tips distilled from their experience can be applied to all types of organizations that are serious about using brand to drive profitability.

3M's Eight Brand-Building Steps

Anne Greer at 3M is justifiably proud of the formula used for building 3M's brand-based culture and for getting employees to think about the critical importance of brand building relative to eight important brand-building steps. Each step provides an opportunity for all employees to see brand building in action and gives clear signals that brand building is a serious undertaking:

1. Secure active and consistent senior management involvement. You want their leadership and their commitment to and sponsorship of the brand. Make sure senior executives are walking the talk.

2. Make sure the brand and its promise are consistent over time. Innovation and upgrading the products and services supporting the brand certainly are critical for brand relevance, but do not change the meaning of the brand every three to five years.

3. Have a relevant and differentiated promise for each of your brands. If employees know what each brand stands for and why it is special and unique, then they are better able to understand what each brand (or business unit) is trying to accomplish and what role they play in bringing that promise to life.

4. Always focus on customers and their needs. This will naturally keep you focused on the brand. Also, involve as many employees as possible in brand research.

5. Consistently conduct needs-based segmentation. This ensures a strong link to customer focus so that employees always know where they are directing their brand-building efforts.

6. Maintain consistent and frequent brand-driven communications. When 3M talks communications, it is really talking about every audience, internal and external, that can either be influenced by or influence the brand.

7. Align the organization around all brand-building efforts. This is tied to many of the principles shared in Chapter Eight and for 3M includes facilitating ongoing learning and education across the company, such as 3M's Earning Customer Loyalty program, involving a cross-functional team in strategy development aimed at improving the likelihood the strategy will succeed, and being specific about functional area members' roles and expectations relative to achieving brand success.

8. Measure consistently. Set up a few metrics, and consistently measure them. Make improvements based on the results.

Anne also says, "Our goal is tied to getting everyone involved in delivering the brand promise. We encourage all employees to have their say and input and then decide on a plan and turn that plan into action, with responsibilities assigned. This is how 3M establishes, builds and maintains a brand-based culture over time."

Seven Key Principles at Medtronic

Medtronic, the world's leading medical technology company, has identified seven key principles to ensure that the organization and all its employees are on board with the brand and understand the implications for their jobs:

1. Obtain endorsement and involvement of senior management. When acquiring a new company, the CEO of Medtronic goes out to the newly acquired company and talks about the Medtronic's brand to all the employees. Medtronic also has an acquisition screen about culture.

2. Seek help from experts. Medtronic hired an outside consulting firm to help relaunch its brand because it felt it had more credibility in telling the brand story.

3. Link the brand to the company's culture. The mission written by the founder of Medtronic in 1960 has never been edited. Every employee must go through a "mission and medallion" ceremony that explains the purpose, value, and meaning of the company. Every new CEO has also adopted this mission.

4. Provide emotional benefits. Medtronic's mission first and foremost is to return people to full health. It is not centered around making a profit.

5. Make it simple. Medtronic recognizes that there is little time to communicate; therefore, the brand message should be easy so the employees remember it.

6. Be firm and consistent but flexible in implementation. Medtronic has established corporate identity standards and guides for all product advertising.

7. Give employees the tools they need to be brand ambassadors. Medtronic provides training to every employee (including assistants) on the benefits of brand management, the brand strategy and personality, corporate identity standards, and the brand Web site, and offers a four-hour brand seminar for employees every quarter. It also has an intranet site focused on brand that all employees are encouraged to use.

Medtronic understands the depth of a brand-based culture. The director of global brand management of Medtronic, Bill Stoessel, has taken Medtronic's brand story on the road and educates other industries on the success of becoming a brand-driven organization, furthering the Medtronic story and brand.

Lessons from Itron

Randi Neilson, vice president of marketing for Itron, the leading global solutions provider and source of analytical knowledge for electric, gas, and water usage and delivery data, followed several distinct steps when her CEO and executive management team committed to transform the company into a brand-driven organization through a new business and brand strategy.

HAVE CEO AND TOTAL C-LEVEL BUY-IN. Randi has an executive management team that completely buys into the brand strategy, in large part because it was involved in designing the strategy and endorsing it. All executives had individual brand objectives that they had to deliver on in their functional area. Because of this leadership buy-in, motivation, and passion, it has been easy to have employees rally around this strategy and understand exactly what it will take for them to succeed.

HAVE EMPLOYEES EMBRACE THE BRAND STRATEGY. Because of the depth of C-level buy-in and support, employees embraced the new brand strategy and were energized to do their part in bringing the brand to life. Itron got employees to reach this level of commitment in a variety of ways:

- Conducting an all-employee communications meeting. The purpose of the companywide meeting was to discuss the new brand strategy, the action steps, and specific employee requirements.

- Having fun. Itron threw brand launch parties that involved every employee at all of its different locations, including lots of give-aways, gift bags, and brochures on the "new Itron," and generated an overall feeling of excitement and fun.

- Giving "living the brand" presentations to all employees. This helped to explain the brand's importance and included discussions around how employees could contribute to the brand. "Our employees came up with a number of creative ways that they, and we, could proliferate and live our brand internally and externally. We listened to the employees and demonstrated that we'd internalized their suggestions and either enacted them or explained why we were not able to act on them," Randi says.

- Continuing to reinforce the brand through ongoing meetings and company communications. This was a way to reinforce the importance of the brand and make sure that no one thought that delivering the brand was a one-time event or novelty. The results of the branding efforts to date have been communicated to employees in follow-up living-the-brand sessions. Additionally, the employees continue to be educated on new trends in branding and what needs to occur to take the brand to the next level.

- Challenging employees to continuously identify ways in which they could better live the brand on a day-to-day basis. In Randi's words, "Not only have we communicated the results and impact of our branding efforts, but we continue to brainstorm with our employees on new ways to raise the bar. Again, we've made sure that we either actually changed the ways we approached managing the brand or told the employee with the suggestion why it would not be enacted."

SET UP INTERNAL BRAND METRICS AND REWARDS SYSTEM. For this to work and have the level of internal credibility it required, Itron knew that it had to determine what the right internal metrics should be to measure progress. Without these metrics, Itron management believed that there was no way for employees and management to see how they were progressing on their brand-building activities. Two of the metrics were particularly important.

First was tying brand-building efforts to profit sharing. Management had a strong desire to put together a reward system that was meaningful and directly tied to all brand-building activities. Randi states:

> One critical measure for actually getting employees to live the brand is tied to linking their brand-driven performance to varying levels of profit sharing. In order to get a certain level of profit sharing, employees have to create a plan for how they will live the brand. This, in effect, sets up a contract with senior management for achieving the same. At the end of the year, then, employees are evaluated against this contract to determine what level of profit sharing they will receive.

The other important metric was regularly measuring employee morale. Itron management believed that brand building's effect on employee morale would provide a good gauge on whether there was a positive shift in employees' attitudes about and belief in the company and the Itron brand. Randi says that "employee morale and belief in the company is higher than it has been in eleven years."

INSTITUTE EXTERNAL METRICS TO MEASURE EXTERNAL BRAND PROGRESS. Similar to the internal metrics, Itron management felt they had to set up a number of external gauges to see how their brand building efforts were perceived externally—for example:

- Conducting year-end customer satisfaction evaluations. "We felt that the only way to see if we were making real progress against our brand-building efforts was to hear it directly from our customers. This provided us with a great yardstick to measure our progress, as well as a jump-start to the following year's brand goals."

- Gathering ongoing feedback. Similar to the year-end customer satisfaction surveys, Itron makes sure it consistently receives real-time feedback.

- Tying stock price appreciation to brand-building efforts. Although it is generally hard to isolate the role of brand in achieving stock price and profitability gains, one cannot argue that there was a cause-and-effect relationship between Itron's brand-building efforts and its stock price. Randi states, "Our stock price, since we launched the brand, has increased from $3.70 a share to $32.40 a share. Tied to this increase, Itron's market capitalization went from $200 million to $500 million." It is hard to imagine a stronger message or endorsement on the payoffs of brand building.

- Seeking coverage of financial advisers and investors. "We are getting more coverage from financial investors than we have in the past," Randi says.

BUILDING A BRAND-DRIVEN BUSINESS: THE CHOICE IS YOURS

This book has focused on achieving success through operationalizing your brand. In Chapter Two, we explained how crucial it is to link brand and business strategy as one. Once a company is able to link the two together successfully, there is a higher likelihood that brand building will be consistent, taken seriously, and considered to be the powerful tool that it is in helping a company reach its longer-term growth objectives.

In Chapter Three, we explored the topic of taking control of all your customer touchpoints, acknowledging that most companies today do not recognize or manage all of their brand-related touchpoints. Significant internal and external brand confusion can result from inconsistencies across touchpoints.

In Chapters Four through Six, we noted that most brand touchpoints can be divided into three major brand life cycle stages: pre-purchase experience, purchase experience, and post-purchase experience. This allowed us to reach the conclusion that every functional area within an organization is involved in managing and maintaining the brand and thus is responsible for bringing the brand and its promise to life.

In Chapter Seven, we reviewed the latest and greatest thinking on brand metrics relative to both touchpoints and strategy and the idea that with effective and actionable brand metrics, we can garner a better understanding of how we are benchmarking against our past brand-building efforts and those of key competitors.

In Chapter Eight, we mentioned that if indeed every functional area is involved in bringing the brand promise to life, we must determine how to reach all employees in a way in which they not only start to understand their role in executing the brand but also actually start to internalize it and live it.

For any of these operational concepts and organizational constructs to take hold within the organization, a major shift has to take place in how the company is run, what values are embraced, and what culture should be adopted, with brand being the obvious lens to use for each.

In the end, the most important element of building a brand-driven business is your employees. Without their belief, guidance, ownership, and participation, you might as well put your investment in Treasury bills. However, with employee buy-in, involvement, and support from the top down, there is no telling what the true limits of brand-building success for your company can be.

⟿ Notes and Sources

Quotations, examples, and cases throughout the text are from Prophet's 2002 Best Practices study, additional surveys, and personal interviews conducted by the authors or Prophet staff, and client cases, unless noted below. All are used with permission.

NOTES

Introduction

1. Levering and M. Moskowitz, with L. Munoz and P. Hielt, "The 100 Best Companies to Work For: In a Tough Year These Companies Tried to Do Right by Their Employees," *Fortune*, Feb. 4, 2002, p. 72.
2. J. Sung and C. Tkaczyk, "America's Most Admired Companies," *Fortune*, Mar. 4, 2002, pp. 75–80.
3. Association of National Advertisers, *2002 Best Practices for Operationalizing Your Brand* (San Francisco: Prophet, Feb. 2002).

Chapter 1

1. S. M. Davis, *Brand Asset Management for the 21st Century Study* (Chicago: Kuczmarski & Associates, 1995).
2. S. M. Davis, *Brand Asset Management: Driving Profitable Growth Through Your Brand* (San Francisco: Jossey-Bass, 2000).
3. N. Gross, "Tallying Up Those Invisible Assets," *Business Week,* July 2, 2001, p. 4a2.
4. Davis, *Brand Asset Management.*
5. R. Passikoff, "My Brand Is Here to Stay," *Channelseven.com, Ad/Insight,* Aug. 6, 2001.
6. Passikoff, "My Brand Is Here to Stay."
7. Davis, *Brand Asset Management for the 21st Century Study.*

8. Davis, *Brand Asset Management for the 21st Century Study.*

9. Passikoff, "My Brand Is Here to Stay."

10. S. M. Cristol and P. Sealey, *Simplicity Marketing: End Brand Complexity, Clutter, and Confusion* (New York: Free Press, 2000).

Chapter 2

1. J. Champy, "Form Follows Customers," *Forbes,* Mar. 8, 1999, p. 130.

2. W. M. Bulkeley, "As PC Industry Slumps, IBM Hands Off Manufacturing of Desktops," *Wall Street Journal,* Jan. 9, 2002, p. B1.

3. J. C. Collins and J. I. Porras, *Built to Last: Successful Habits of Visionary Companies* (New York: HarperCollins, 1994), p. 216.

Chapter 4

1. Davis, *Brand Asset Management.*

2. Passikoff, "My Brand Is Here to Stay."

Chapter 5

1. R. Alsop, "Reputations Rest on Good Service," *Wall Street Journal,* Jan. 16, 2002, p. B1.

2. F. Vogelstein, "Sun on the Ropes," *Fortune,* Jan. 7, 2001, p. 82.

3. "The Dell Vision: The Dell Direct Model," Dell.com, Mar. 2002 [http://www.dell.com/us/en/gen/corporate/vision_directmodel.htm].

4. S. Hansell, "Web Sales of Airline Tickets Are Making Hefty Advances," *New York Times,* July 4, 2001, p. A1.

Chapter 6

1. S. A. Hatlestad, "A Step Above Service," *Chain Leader,* Oct. 2001, p. 47.

Chapter 7

1. R. S. Kaplan and D. P. Norton, *The Balanced Scorecard: Translating Strategy into Action* (Boston: Harvard Business School Press, 1996).

2. Davis, *Brand Asset Management for the 21st Century Study.*

SOURCES

"2002 Best Practices for Operationalizing Your Brand"

Participants in Prophet's 2002 Best Practices study, sponsored by the Association of National Advertisers

⟶ The Authors

Scott M. Davis is managing partner of and opened Prophet's Chicago office. He provides leadership on all brand strategy–related engagements, bringing his expertise to bear through his proprietary brand asset management model with clients such as TXU, Universal Studios, the *Chicago Tribune,* SaraLee, Standard & Poor's, Whirlpool, Allstate, Textron, and Teradata. He is the author of *Brand Asset Management: Driving Profitable Growth Through Your Brands* (Jossey-Bass, 2000), which was named one of the top thirty books of 2000 by Executive Book Summaries. He has been a featured speaker and chaired numerous branding conferences and seminars, is frequently cited in the business press, and is an editorial writer for *Brandweek.* He is an adjunct professor at the Kellogg Graduate School of Management at Northwestern University, where he received his M.B.A.

Michael Dunn is president and CEO of Prophet and is responsible for the firm's tremendous growth over the past several years. He oversees the development of the firm's people, practices, and thought leadership and also serves as a strategic adviser on client engagements. Most recently, he has provided key insights for clients including AT&T, Williams-Sonoma, UBS, and BP. He has authored numerous white papers and articles and serves frequently as a source for professional and mainstream media for insights on companies facing business and brand challenges. He received an M.B.A./M.A. in Asian studies from the University of California at Berkeley.

⟶ Index